IDENTIFYING

Sarah Coventry

JEWELRY
1949-2009

Sandra Sturdivant
Shirley Crabtree

Schiffer Publishing Ltd

4880 Lower Valley Road • Atglen, PA 19310

Other Schiffer Books by the Author:

Other Schiffer Books on Related Subjects:

Copyright © 2012 by Sandra Sturdivant & Shirley Crabtree

Library of Congress Control Number: 2012947058

Designed by Justin Watkinson
Type set in Swenson/Zurich BT

ISBN: 978-0-7643-4214-1
Printed in China

Published by Schiffer Publishing, Ltd.
4880 Lower Valley Road
Atglen, PA 19310
Phone: (610) 593-1777; Fax: (610) 593-2002
E-mail: Info@schifferbooks.com

For the largest selection of fine reference books on this and related subjects, please visit our website at www.schifferbooks.com.
You may also write for a free catalog.

This book may be purchased from the publisher.
Please try your bookstore first.

We are always looking for people to write books on new and related subjects. If you have an idea for a book, please contact us at proposals@schifferbooks.com

Schiffer Books are available at special discounts for bulk purchases for sales promotions or premiums. Special editions, including personalized covers, corporate imprints, and excerpts can be created in large quantities for special needs. For more information contact the publisher.

In Europe, Schiffer books are distributed by
Bushwood Books
6 Marksbury Ave.
Kew Gardens
Surrey TW9 4JF England
Phone: 44 (0) 20 8392 8585; Fax: 44 (0) 20 8392 9876
E-mail: info@bushwoodbooks.co.uk
Website: www.bushwoodbooks.co.uk

Dedication and Acknowledgments

To our mothers, Jackie Paul
    and Elizabeth Williams
To Jim Sturdivant
To Yvonne Marrou, best friend

Photography by Sandra Sturdivant
Jewelry is from the authors' collections,
    except where indicated
Proof readers, Yvonne Marrou, Pam Eade

Our special thanks goes to Gene Jackson, who graciously opened her home to Shirley. It turned out to be a Sarah Coventry museum filled with glittering treasures and awards from the more than 30-years that Gene worked for the company. She gave us a wealth of personal recollections about the company and how it operated. She fell and broke her hip, passing away quietly in her sleep one week after surgery. We greatly miss her.

The following contributors provided us with all manner of help, including, but not limited to, personal experiences from working for the company, copies of missing paperwork we needed for provenance, loaning jewelry from their own valuable collections, and anything else that we needed. We are grateful to everyone. In alphabetical order, they are:

Sue Beaver   Louise Blood
Louise Chargo   Jan Coody
Pam Eade   Karen Walck Haley
Lisa Helms   Connie Hoffman
Anne Marrero   Joy Robson
Colleen Van Kempen   June Wellisley
Fay Williquette

Contents

Preface

It began with a chance meeting in 2001. Shirley makes jewelry and exhibits in central Texas. At the time, Sandy was writing Western legend and lore for a literary group that publishes American history magazines. On one of Sandy's research trips through the small town of Gonzales, she entered Shirley's world of jewelry at a craft fair. Sandy had a massive amount of Sarah Coventry with some unsigned pieces that needed identification, and Shirley had the knowledge to help identify it. Shirley's mother was a Fashion Show Director for 30 years, and Shirley went to all the shows, modeling the jewelry for the customers. Her collection was even larger than Sandy's. Although both women are recognized Sarah Coventry experts, they still needed each other to identify every single piece in their combined collections. They have been fast friends ever since.

The plans for this book surfaced around the holidays in 2002. We were each contacting collectors and sellers, scouring flea markets and craft fairs, searching for missing pieces and any provenance for what we had, and it astonished us to discover that people did not know much of anything about Sarah Coventry. We found non-Sarah items being sold in legitimate Sarah Coventry packaging, along with the corresponding sellers telling us that we were nuts for suggesting the item was not Sarah. We found extremely rare Sarah pieces selling for peanuts, along with many unsigned beauties being sold simply as "vintage." All of it was a mass of confusion for the buyer, the seller, and the collector. Unfortunately, none of the books already in print adequately solved any of the problems.

Deciding we needed to put our collections together into a book, we set out to prove every single piece we had was a legitimate Sarah Coventry item. We already had the catalogs and cardex cards, and Shirley had most of the shopping guides, but what we needed was the paperwork documenting the very early years of 1949-1953. Most people do not believe it is Sarah Coventry unless the piece is signed, but Sarah was in business long before signing jewelry became a standard. The simple truth is that there are hundreds of Sarah Coventry pieces that are not signed, and without a book showcasing these items, how is anyone to know if the piece is legitimate Sarah Coventry or not? We needed the early paperwork to document and prove that our items were the genuine article.

Since there were already books in print with nice photos of known Sarah Coventry pieces, and since Sandy learned that two other books were already works-in-progress on the same topic, we decided that Sandy should do her Avon book first, while Shirley continued acquiring the provenance needed for verifying our collections. In 2008, Schiffer published Sandy's book, *Identifying Avon Jewelry*, and that same year Shirley located the badly needed *Inspiration Pages* of 1950-1953 from Lisa Helms. She also found Karen Walck Haley with the jewelry and paperwork from 1949.

This book is about Sarah Coventry from 1949 to 2009, something that is not in print anywhere. It begins with the unsigned years of 1949-1963, covers the cardex years of 1954-1965, includes the catalog years of 1966-1984, and has a smattering of beauties from the years that Lifestyle Brands acquired the rights to the trademark for other concerns. All of it has been carefully researched and documented. There is no guesswork in this book.

Not every piece from 1949 could be found, but 99 percent of the jewelry from 1949-1984 is represented in this book. We do not include any International pieces, and we have very few pieces made by other companies licensed to sell jewelry under the Sarah Coventry trademark. Our goal was to concentrate on the American jewelry from the years that Sarah Coventry was part of the C.H. Stuart Company, since we had all the paperwork for this company. We also do not represent any of the watches, since watches are too easy to alter with band changes.

This book has more than 1,270 items from 1949-1965, more than 3,500 items from 1966-1984, and many pieces from 1985-2009. We also include the award jewelry and some of the other items that managers were able to obtain. Everything is in glorious color. It has all been carefully researched. We trust everyone will find this book useful.

—Sandy and Shirley

Introduction

Created in November 1949, Sarah Coventry Jewelry was the brainchild of Charles William "Bill" Stuart, although the family business did not begin with costume jewelry. Great-great-grandfather William Harvey Stuart was a farmer. When he died, his son, the first Charles William Stuart, grew up to begin the family dynasty. Through succeeding generations, it would incorporate a direct-sales marketing technique that would employ thousands of people over the course of thirteen different companies, selling all manner of wares directly to the consumer. By the time it came to a close, Sarah Coventry would be the largest direct-selling jewelry company in the world.

The Stuart Family Genealogy

There seems to be some confusion about the origins of the Stuart family, which gave birth to the costume jewelry legend of Sarah Coventry. Most references accurately trace the family business from pioneering Newark, New York, businessman Charles W. Stuart, but the claims that he arrived in America in 1852, and that the name "Coventry" was taken from his homeland in the Coventry area of England are wrong. We even found these exact same claims attributed to his son, Charles Henry Stuart, and Charles Henry was not born until 1869.

The simple truth is that Sarah Coventry is an American success story. It began with the birth of William Harvey Stuart in 1809 in the tiny hamlet of Westerlo, New York. His parents are listed as John Stuart and Sarah Dutton, both born in New York, but this could be incorrect information because there were two William Harvey Stuarts born in 1809 in Albany, New York, and without delving further into the archives of Albany, we could have the wrong parents. We know only that William Harvey Stuart was a farmer, and this information comes from the census.

William Stuart married Adeline Boardman in 1836 in Westerlo, New York. She was born in 1813 in Westerlo, and her parents are known to be Silas Boardman and Keziah Hallock. Father Silas was born in Massachusetts in 1768, and he died in Westerlo in 1823. Mother Keziah was born in New York in 1775, and she died in Albany in 1851.

In the 1840 Federal Census, William and Adeline Stuart are shown with two children: Charles William Stuart, born in 1837, and Silas Boardman Stuart, born in 1840. It is clear from the census that Charles W. Stuart was born in New York, so the claims that he was born in England and immigrated to the United States in 1852 are false. The Stuart family's roots are documented and established in New York.

Since William Harvey Stuart disappears from the 1850 census, and suspecting he had died, we resorted to the New York State census to locate him. In looking at the census for 1844, we found the family had one more son, John Electus Stuart, born in 1843. To make sure we had all the children, we examined additional genealogy files and discovered that son George E. Stuart was born and died in 1842, living only 6 months. The cause of death was listed as illness. We also learned that William Harvey Stuart died in October 1844, and his widow never remarried.

Jumping ahead to son Charles W. Stuart, born in 1837, we discovered that he married Caroline Emmons in 1866 in Newark, New York. In the 1880 census, she gave her age as 39 and her place of birth as Connecticut, but there were two Caroline Emmons born in 1841 in Connecticut, one in Colchester, New London, Connecticut, and one in New Milford, Litchfield, Connecticut, and without further information, we do not know which one Charles Stuart married, nor do we know her parents. The couple made their home in Newark, and they had five children: May A., born in 1867, Charles H., born in 1869, Carrie M., born in 1871, Sarah R., born in 1873, and Kenneth E., born in 1876. On the 1880 census, mother Adeline Stuart was living with the family, and there was also a governess and a handyman. Charles W. Stuart listed his occupation as nurseryman, and Caroline listed hers as housekeeper.

In January 1895, son Charles Henry Stuart married Jane Rebecca Reed Knight in Manhattan, New York. She was born in 1871 in Englewood, New Jersey, the oldest of three daughters born to Catherine Palen and Azariah Lyman Knight, a New York pioneer wholesale oil dealer, leather merchant, and family friend. The *Rochester Democrat and Chronicle* printed on January 19, 1895, that the "marriage of C. Harry Stuart, of Newark, and Miss Jane Knight, of New York City, was solemnized last night at the bride's home in New York City. They will reside in Newark."

The 1900 census enumerated the following Stuart family group living in the family home in Newark: C.W., age 62, Caroline, age 59, Harry, age 30, Jane, age 28, Sarah R, age 27, Kenneth, age 25, Adeline, age 86, and Silas B, age 60.

Charles Henry Stuart went by the name of Harry. He and his wife Jane had a son, Lyman Knight Stuart, born in 1898 in Newark, New York. When Lyman was 6-years-old, he suffered a tragic accident. Printed in the November 3, 1904, *Rochester Democrat and Chronicle* is an article: "**Little Son of Newark Man Had Foot Crushed.** On November 2, Lyman Knight Stuart, the 6-year-old son of C. Harry Stuart, a well-known businessman, sustained a serious accident at the Willow Avenue crossing of the West Shore at 5 o'clock this afternoon. The family lives just north of the crossing on Willow Avenue and was returning home with his mother from over town. A freight train was passing slowly and the gates were down. The little lad ran ahead and went inside of the gates and kept striking at the cars with his hand. It is thought he made a misstep and was thrown under the wheels. His right foot was crushed and it was necessary to amputate above the ankle."

Lyman Stuart married in Christ Church in Glen Ridge, New Jersey, in 1921 to Harriet Burt Sanford, born in 1898 in Warwick, New York. She was the younger of two daughters born to Julia Dent Burt and William Moore Sanford. Her older sister was Margaret Coventry Sanford. Both of the Sanford sisters, Harriet and Margaret, were named after their maternal grandmother and great-aunt, Harriet and Margaret Coventry. Both of the Coventry sisters were the only children of Newark's last horse and buggy doctor, John Coventry. Thus, John Coventry was the great-grandfather of Lyman Stuart's wife, Harriet, on her mother's side of the family.

Lyman and Harriet Stuart had two children, daughter Margaret and son Charles William "Bill" Stuart. Margaret Stuart married James Beale, and their daughter Sarah Coventry Beale was born in 1949. It was the birth of this child that would prompt her Uncle Bill Stuart to give her name to what would ultimately become the most famous costume jewelry company in the world.

From the family genealogy, we can definitely say that the claims we found printed in several sources that the name "Coventry" came from the region in England "where Charles William Stuart," and in some printed documents, "where Charles Henry Stuart was born" is false information for both men. Charles William Stuart was a second generation American, making his son Charles Henry a third generation American. We also discovered that Dr. John Coventry was a first generation American, born in New York in 1805, and although his parents were born in Scotland, we could find no evidence that his surname originated from some obscure connection to the Coventry region of England. The simple truth is that "Coventry" is a Stuart family name and has always been a Stuart family name.

The Sarah Coventry Jewelry Genealogy

It seems strange to claim that Sarah Coventry Jewelry has a genealogy, but it does; however, trying to find information about a company that has been out of business for more than thirty years is almost impossible. The paper trail has all but disappeared, and what remains is a convoluted maze of various companies competing against each other, even

merging on occasion to form new companies, and that makes it difficult to document.

It starts with the death of William Harvey Stuart in 1844. He was very young when he died, leaving a young wife to raise three young sons. The oldest of the boys was 7-year-old Charles W. Stuart. We do not know how Adeline managed, but we are told that in 1852, Charles W. Stuart was already in the jewelry business in Syracuse, New York. We also learned that his brother John Electus was a "maaaanufacturing jeweler," and we suspect that brother Silas was also.

We do not know exactly when Charles W. Stuart arrived in Newark. It is printed in *Jewelry from Sarah Coventry and Emmons*, Schiffer 2005, that "he once had a jewelry company in Syracuse, New York, called Commercial Enterprises, which he left to pursue his first love of farming," and we found the first mention of a date and the town of Newark in the book, *Emmons Fashion Magic Jewelry*, Schiffer 2005. On page 7, it states, "In 1864, Charles W. Stuart, a 'manufacturing jeweler' in Syracuse, New York, decided to move west for health reasons." On the same page is a photo of a business card: "C. W. Stuart & Co., Nurserymen, Newark, New York," and it states that it was "Established 1852, 600 acres, Growers of Nursery Stock."

Since the date printed on the business card is 1852, and since the date given in *Emmons Fashion Magic Jewelry* is 1864, a difference of 12 years, we decided to check the date of Newark to see if we could determine exactly when Charles Stuart arrived in town. It was a small village originally called Miller's Basin, situated on the Erie Canal about halfway between Rochester and Syracuse. In 1853, Miller's Basin incorporated to include the small village of Arcadia, previously known as Lockville, and it then changed its name to The Village of Newark. It was already being called Newark by the time that Stuart settled there, and his house was located in the Arcadia area of town. Exactly when he arrived, though, we were not able to learn. All we know for certain that Sarah Coventry began with his orchards.

Charles W. Stuart bought a fruit tree orchard of 600 acres on Willow Avenue on the north end of the town of Newark. He began growing fruit trees and berry bushes, and his farming business bore the name of C. W. Stuart & Company. His employees went door-to-door selling trees, fruit, seeds, and juices directly to customers throughout New England. As his company expanded, he acquired other nurseries and farms, resulting in the need for a central facility and warehouse, which he built in Newark. Sold under his umbrella were all manner of orchard and nursery products. By 1872, Newark was known as the "Nation's Nursery City," and it can be directly attributed to C. W. Stuart and his many acres of fruit trees and berry bushes.

In November 1895, Stuart formed a second nursery company to compete with his C. W. Stuart & Company nursery. He called this new company Knight and Bostwick. Since Stuart formed yet a third nursery company in 1897, called Emmons and Company, and since it now appeared he was using family names in the formation of his nurseries, we presume his company of Knight and Bostwick was named after family members; however, we were unable to find a family link to the name Bostwick, and it is entirely possible that Bostwick was either a financial backer, a business partner, or both.

In an excerpt from the *Party Manual for Jewels by Sarah Coventry* from 1950, parts of which were furnished to us by Karen Walck Haley, it states on page 7 that "the company is over 97 years old and that Mr. Stuart designed and manufactured the first scatter pin in 1852." It goes on to say that the pin was in the "possession of his great-granddaughter, the mother of Sarah Coventry." This "Mr. Stuart" clearly refers to Charles W. Stuart, who was 15 years old in 1852, and the mother of Sarah Coventry is Margaret Stuart Beale.

Charles Henry "Harry" Stuart was already in control of the company by the time his father died in 1923, and he decided to implement some of his own ideas for expanding the family's fortunes even further. The idea of selling door-to-door greatly appealed to him, and he set out to develop other products that could be sold by the nursery salesmen when they called on their clientele. He was a trained chemist, having graduated from Cornell University, and his passion for chemistry gave him the necessary knowledge to experiment with extracts and tube flavoring. In 1908, he incorporated a company to manufacture and sell extracts, flavors, perfumes, and other chemical products using the direct-selling method established by the nurseries. His entrepreneurial skills soon blossomed the family-owned nursery into several other enterprises with the addition of tea, coffee, aspirin, cough syrup, spices, hand cream, bath crystals, and puddings. These different product lines all thrived with one common thread — door-to-door salesmanship.

With his business bursting at the seams, Harry Stuart needed a central location for managing it. He constructed a new office building in downtown Newark, called the Commercial Building, and it became home to his direct selling companies under the name of Commercial Enterprises. Sold were the original fruits, nuts, trees, seeds, and berries of his father's nursery empire, and added were the new companies formed to sell cosmetics, household goods, foodstuffs, boats, china, and furniture. It was all sold directly to customers via commissioned

sales people, who went door-to-door with direct-marketing techniques learned under his supervision and leadership. At one time, it boasted 13 different companies and about 18,000 employees!

It is during Harry Stuart's management that we get our first positive proof that Commercial Enterprises was a Stuart company, and whether or not it is the same Commercial Enterprises that was listed as the jewelry company his father left in Syracuse when he was 15-years-old to start his orchards in Newark…well, we do not know, and we could not find anyone who did.

Lyman K. Stuart was also a graduate of Cornell University, and in 1924, he became president of C.H. Stuart & Company. The stock market crash of 1929 that triggered the Great Depression made it necessary for him to consolidate the many individual companies down to a handful, but the success of selling door-to-door never failed. The Depression also brought out-of-work people to the company, and the continued success of direct selling during such hard times had a great impact on him. As the economy stabilized, he expanded into silverware, since these items had been popular as prizes and premiums, especially in laundry soap powders, and this led to newly created, converted, or merged companies, adding new product lines as he felt the situation demanded.

The harsh winter of 1948 caused Lyman Stuart to consider adding a totally different product line, since finding good nursery stock was declining. His idea was to convert the Emmons and Company nursery business to costume jewelry and sell it in the home on a party plan. The party plan system was not new, as Avon had been using a version of it since the turn of the century to sell cosmetics, but it had never been tried with jewelry. Most women bought their jewelry in department stores where they were seldom allowed to try on the pieces. The idea of the party plan called for the party hostess to gather her friends and family to her house, and the sales consultant would then show the actual jewelry. Stuart wanted to call the new company Emmons Jewelry, and in February 1949, he set out to see if it could be the beginning of the party plan of jewelry salesmanship.

There was one giant hurdle to overcome. Nobody had any real clue about the jewelry business. At the time, costume jewelry was most widely used in the entertainment industry, making any attempt to market to the housewife and career woman an untried and skeptical proposition. Also, most women already had what they wanted in a few favorite pieces and family heirlooms. Would they be willing to attend a party to purchase additional items? Company executives resorted to hiring a consultant who had worked for Trifari, and this consultant gathered together a collection of pieces, about 75 of which were selected to be sold by Emmons Jewelry. Not knowing exactly how a party plan would operate with jewelry, company executives also studied the business method of Stanley Home Products, which had been using the party plan successfully since 1931. The first show was a test case to see if the jewelry could actually sell, and the first attempt was an unscripted, ad lib fashion show with a handful of local jewelry bought specifically for the occasion. It worked much better than expected, and the papers for Emmons Jewelers, Inc., were filed on April 21, 1949.

Bill Stuart, Lyman Stuart's son, became President of C.H. Stuart & Company in 1949, and with Emmons Jewelry doing well, he decided to launch yet a second jewelry company, using the same party plan, as a competing company to Emmons. Competition: it was a tried and true formula in the nursery business, and he believed it would work with the jewelry. His sister and brother-in-law, Margaret and James Beale, had just become parents to a baby daughter whom they named Sarah Coventry Beale, and Uncle Bill Stuart thought the novelty of two names for his jewelry company would be catchy enough to be successful. He named his new company Sarah Coventry Jewelry, and in November 1949, a legend was born.

All That Glitters

From a social and economic standpoint, the timing of Sarah Coventry could not have been more perfect. During World War II, women by the thousands took to the work force, while the men were away on the battlefields, and these ladies became used to earning their own money. When the women were then forced from their jobs to make way for the returning veterans, many of them were eager to find new ways of supplementing their household income. With free jewelry kits that required no up-front cash, but included cleverly crafted sales techniques and generous incentives for performance, thousands of women flocked to Sarah Coventry to sell jewelry at home parties.

Specially trained sales consultants, called Fashion Show Directors (FSD), showed the jewelry in the party plan. The party hostess called together her guests, the FSD arrived with a suitcase of jewelry samples, and following cue card techniques the FSD had learned, the guests were asked to remove their own jewelry and allowed to try on Sarah Coventry, modeling it for each other. By trying it on in a home atmosphere, with their friends around to confirm their judgment as to what looked appealing, the party method worked for everyone.

As the sales orders added up, the FSD was careful to explain the free jewelry the party hostess earned from her sales. She earned $1.50 worth of jewelry for each guest who attended and purchased, and she earned 50 cents worth of jewelry for each guest who attended but did not purchase, up to a maximum of $12.00 retail. This greatly encouraged guests to sign up for their own parties. If two or more of the guests agreed that night to host a party, the party hostess earned an extra $2.00, swelling her gifts to a total of $14.00 retail. Women went nuts. Part of the satisfaction was that women could be their own bosses. Sarah Coventry's success capitalized on the fact that "hardly a housewife breathes who isn't interested in swelling the family's financial coffers."

Originally, Emmons and Sarah Coventry sold several of the same exact pieces under both

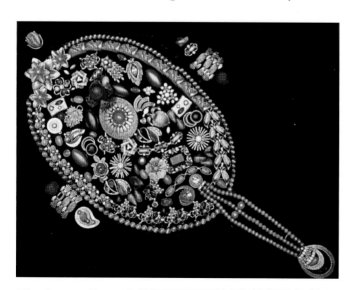

Miscellaneous Picture. This pre-1965 framed picture of the Sarah Coventry hand mirror logo is a treasured memento from years past when women saved broken pieces of jewelry to turn into works of art.

Wedgewood Cameo and *Azure Snowflake* pins sold by both Emmons and Sarah Coventry simultaneously in 1949.

company names, which had the added brilliance of drawing Emmons customers into the new Sarah Coventry line, but, at the beginning, these two companies did not sell in the same geographical location, so selling the same item was not a problem in competition. If Emmons already had a sales consultant in a specific area, a Sarah Coventry sales consultant had to take a different area, and it kept both companies viable and in operation. The *Wedgewood Cameo* and the *Azure Snowflake* pins are examples of jewelry sold by both companies at the same time.

Packaging was never a problem, either. In 1949, each company used individual paper sales tags attached to the item, but in 1950, they graduated to the same clear plastic jewelry cases, and all that was needed were printed card inserts for each company. Names of the specific jewelry items

Fantasia, 1956, showing the clear plastic cases used by both Sarah Coventry and Emmons in the early years.

were not printed on the cards, so it was easy for both companies to sell the same items. It also kept printing costs down. As each company's sales grew, packaging did become an issue, and after 1955 both companies began to abandon the clear plastic jewelry cases in favor of individual cardboard boxes, some with clear cellophane windows. For Sarah Coventry these cardboard boxes were gold, and for Emmons they were blue. They also bore the name of each company, and in many cases, had the jewelry name printed on the insert.

The plan for both companies was to phase out, or retire, the jewelry as newer ideas and pieces arrived in inventory. This makes finding the very early years extremely difficult, since none of the pieces are signed. Also, the early paperwork of 1949 did not include a description or drawing of the piece, and the only clue is a sheet of paper with a name and item number. The *Lucky Leaf* scatter pin from the 1949 Sarah Coventry literature does exist, but knowing what to seek from the paperwork was impossible.

Lucky Leaf, 1949, emerald and aqua stones, listed by name only in the 1949 literature and fully described in the *Descriptive Phrases for Jewels* in 1950.

In January 1950, this changed with the addition of the *Descriptive Phrases for Jewels by Sarah Coventry*, a pamphlet that did provide some attempt at identifying the jewelry. The description for the *Lucky Leaf* scatter pin reads, "Here is a four leaf clover to wear that will bring you luck always. Dainty pearl leaves cluster around a bright center either aqua or green."

The *Descriptive Phrases* also provided suggestions for selling the jewelry. In describing all clip-on earrings, the FSD was instructed to say something like this: "Clip-on fasteners afford you the opportunity to wear these pieces as scatter-pins on the square-cut neckline of your evening dress or the lapel of your smartly-tailored business suit or, perhaps, you would prefer to wear them on your belt. They can also be used as unusually attractive

Examples of some of the black and white and color cardex cards. They all came with a photo of the item on one side and had a printed description and item number on the back.

Carnival dancer pins and a set of turquoise pins with rhinestone insets that we were never able to identify. Several former FSD's have them, as do some collectors, so we know they are legitimate pieces.

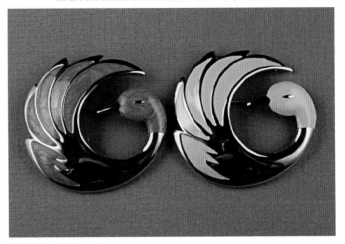

Morning Dove on left and the White Dove commercial version on the right. These are identical pins except for the epoxy inlay.

buckles for your shoes or worn decoratively on your hat brim. For an added touch of glamour, fashion-wise girls, today, clip these beautiful earrings on their gloves."

In the *Inspiration Pages*, a small, unbound pamphlet of item descriptions used between 1951-1953, there was an attempt to include the actual drawings to go along with the printed descriptions. Some of the drawings are difficult to interpret, and we were not able to locate a few of the items because of this. With the black-and-white cardex cards in 1954, actual pictures of the pieces were part of the sales techniques. The picture was on one side of the card, and the description was on the back. The color cardex cards arrived in 1957, and the actual color catalogs came in 1966. Even with all this help, we still had three items we were never able to identify, two carnival dancer pins and a set of three turquoise pins with rhinestone insets.

In 1953, Sarah Coventry began an aggressive magazine advertising campaign. They started with *Vogue* in March, and the company then placed ads in June, September, and November of that year. For all the years right up through 1980, advertisements can be found in all the top women's fashion magazines, including *Glamour*, *Seventeen*, *Cosmopolitan*, and *Woman's Day*, to mention a few. Many advertisements used celebrities to model the jewelry, and all suggested the reader should contact the company to schedule a party. The company even ran commercials on the three major television networks. By the end of 1968, Sarah Coventry was the acknowledged big sister to Emmons, with a

predicted $50 million in net sales in comparison to Emmons $2 million.

Both Sarah Coventry and Emmons never made their own jewelry. It was outsourced to the various artisans and companies in the area, and usually the only difference was a change in color between a commercial piece and one sold by either of the Stuart companies. The *Morning Dove* pin for Sarah Coventry is mauve, whereas the one sold commercially is cream.

There were often only subtle differences in a design between the two companies. The *Golden Bell* for Sarah Coventry is identical to the corresponding design for Emmons, except in the dangles. Likewise, the Sarah Coventry *Reflections* is identical to the Emmons *Blue Fire*, except for the color of the stone and the orientation of the tie bar. When Lyman Stuart won a $5,000 First Prize photo contest sponsored by *Life* magazine, beating out

Golden Bell lariat and bracelet from Sarah Coventry have different dangles from the Emmons version on the right. Both are from 1950.

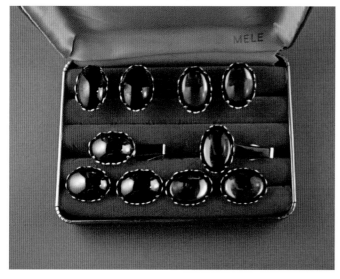

Reflections clip earrings, tie bar, and cuff links from Sarah Coventry are identical to *Blue Fire* clip earrings, tie bar, and cuff links from Emmons, except for the color of the stone and the orientation of the tie bar. Both sets are dated 1957 and have a matching ring.

Romanesque from 1969 is generally found as a pendant without the additional chains, which were originally sold as part of the necklace. *Romanesque* from 1975 is generally referred to as the "Romanesque Cross." Both have the exact same item number of 8270.

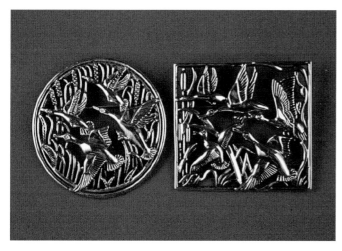

Birds in Flight from Sarah Coventry and *Ducks in Flight* from Emmons are both from 1967. Lyman Stuart was an avid bird photographer, and his "Birds in Flight" photographs won First Prize in a photo contest sponsored by *Life* magazine. Sarah Coventry and Emmons honored his achievement with similar sets. The Sarah Coventry set was a pin and clip earrings; the Emmons set was a pin, clip earrings, and bracelet.

35,000 photos submitted from 49 countries, both Sarah Coventry and Emmons honored the occasion with similar pins. Stuart's "Wild Birds in Flight" became translated into the Sarah Coventry large silver circle pin *Birds in Flight* and the Emmons large silver rectangle pin *Ducks in Flight*.

The jewelry was always well-made, versatile, inexpensive, and used a concept drawn first on paper by a jewelry designer. Since matching completer pieces were often made in different years, we learned that it was the responsibility of one person at the corporate headquarters to keep the name and all item numbers for the same design together until the completer pieces were finished.

Imagine the chaos of *Celestial Fire*, which had the necklace, bracelet, and dainty screw back earrings made in 1955, only to add daring screw back earrings in 1956 and clip earrings in 1960! Still, we found names used more than once, and in at least one occasion, both the name and item number associated with the name are exactly the same: *Romanesque* necklace from 1969 and *Romanesque* necklace from 1975 have the exact same name and item number, 8270.

There were rewards for the sales consultants, as well as rewards for other employees. Not only did they earn free jewelry for top sales through a series of friendly competitions involving incentives for recruiting and parties, they could earn gift certificates for all manner of merchandise. There were bonus cruises, jewelry ensembles not offered for general sale, and the coveted opportunity to be part of Sarah's Jewelry Selection Committee, among other things. The entire system was based on incentives. There were even pieces that could only be earned during special programs running only a week or two.

Sarah Coventry also had many pieces that could only be purchased by the FSD to give as gifts to the party hostess, thus further increasing recruiting and interests of the customer. Everyone was special, and Sarah Coventry never let anyone forget it. Still, turnover was high, and for every recruitment, there were just as many leaving the company, but for those who stayed, working for Sarah Coventry was fun.

Sarah Coventry Jewelry went international around 1964, and the name was changed to Sarah Coventry, Inc. The first international location was in Toronto,

Canada. In 1975, the company then expanded into Great Britain, France, and Belgium before going to Australia. There was talk of taking it to Japan, but that country's small homes and customs were not conducive of the party plan system of salesmanship, and the company never entered the Asian market. Many of the international pieces were identical to the American versions, except for metal color or choice of stone. In this book, we only have the American versions, since we did not have provenance for any of the international pieces.

Since Emmons and Sarah Coventry are considered "sister" companies, the name "Caroline" was added to the Emmons Jewelers in 1970, mostly because Sarah Coventry was already doing well as a two-name company, but also because Bill Stuart thought a two-name title would make Emmons jewelry sound more sophisticated. By this time, both companies were selling in overlapping geographical locations, with some of the pieces often resembling each other with only slight variances. Although "Caroline" was not stamped on the jewelry, it became part of the official company name and was put on all documents. Both companies also merged into the C.H. Stuart & Company, Inc., which changed in 1974 to simply C.H. Stuart, Inc. Emmons merged in 1969, and Sarah Coventry merged in 1977.

The jewelry catalogs came out three times a year in January, April, and August. The Shopping and Quick Reference Guides were more frequent. We found items listed in the December Shopping Guides that did not show up in the catalogs until January of the following year. Originally, the January catalog was called the Spring/Summer Collection, with the April catalog being simply the April Collection. The August catalog was the Fall/Winter Collection, or even the Fall/Holiday Collection. In 1975, this changed. January now became the Spring Collection, April became the Summer Collection, and August became the Autumn/Winter catalog. The exception is 1977 with only a January and an August catalog, but that year, there was an 8-page leaflet called the 1977 Summer Jewelry Collection, which listed 27 new items that would be in the August catalog. The idea was to cut costs by just listing the new items, only no one liked it, and in 1978, Sarah reverted to the three-times-a-year catalog schedule, where it stayed until 1981, when it dropped back to two catalogs per year.

Many times, the jewelry never made it to the next catalog. The *Maharani* ensemble was issued in the 1969 Fall/Winter catalog, marking the 20th anniversary of the company. It was possible to purchase just one piece of the set or all the pieces, but if a person wanted a bold look to the earrings, then she needed two pendants, which came with a hook on the back to dangle from the bottom of

Maharani was in honor of the 20th birthday of Sarah Coventry and premiered in August 1969. It sold out before the January 1970 catalog could be distributed, forcing a revised catalog to be quickly printed with "Stop Sale" stamped across its photo.

the earrings. This meant that if a person wanted the "total" look, she needed one pin, three pendants, and the earrings. By the time the January 1970 catalog could be printed and distributed, *Maharani* was completely sold out. Another January 1970 catalog had to be quickly printed and distributed with "Revised" stamped on the cover, and "Stop Sale" across the photos for the *Maharani* set.

Sarah Coventry also chose to honor America's bicentennial birthday on July 4, 1976. The company selected 16 rings, all from 1976, most of which were

SC Bicentennial Collection. America celebrated her 200th birthday on July 4, 1976, and Sarah Coventry selected 16 rings to celebrate the event. All rings were from 1976, and many were not yet listed in the catalogs. All would later be sold individually. They came in a special commemorative presentation box striped red, white, and blue on the bottom with "SC Bicentennial Collection" on the cream top. Shown left to right, top to bottom, are: Ambrosia, Fire Lite, Misty, Heritage, Moonmist, Directions, Three Cheers, LaBelle, Hidden Rose, Jet Set, Marie, Deep Purple, Starbright, Blue Feather, Ingrid, Blue Night.

not yet available for sale, to be sold together in a special presentation ring box striped red, white, and blue on the bottom with a cream top stamped "SC Bicentennial Collection" in gold. The satin lining said, "Sarah Coventry Bicentennial Collection." It immediately sold out. The rings would be sold individually later in the catalogs, but for one glorious moment in the history of the company, beautiful rings grouped into one presentation box were an instant best seller.

To our knowledge, there were only two holiday gift leaflets, each one four pages long. One was in 1977, which featured two pieces of shiny gold jewelry, perfect for the holiday season, and three pieces of the Limited Edition items, which would have the molds destroyed in December. The 1978 leaflet featured glittering rhinestones pieces and a beautiful cameo in the regular line, along with several items of Lady Coventry, four Limited Edition holiday pieces, and two Hostess Bonus rings. All of these items were handpicked for the holiday season.

In April 1979, Sarah Coventry launched the Coffee Break Shows. The idea was to turn daytime hours into profit by holding morning and afternoon shows, since coffee klatches were known to be

Coffee Cup, 1979, pierced earrings to be given at the Coffee Break Shows.

everyday occurrences in many neighborhoods. To ensure success, the company created the *Coffee Cup* pierced earrings especially for these shows and suggested the sales consultant use them as a special gift to the party hostess. Many women only had free time during the day, and the idea was to reach them with a jewelry show within walking distance of their homes. The brochure promised the Coffee Break Shows would open a whole new market by providing shows to women whose husbands wanted them home during the evening. "Instill desire on the part of others to own these lovely Coffee Cup Pierced Earrings, which *cannot be sold*. Book a Coffee Break Show the Sarah Coventry Way!"

Throughout the years, Sarah Coventry sales depended on the party plan for success, but as trends changed, Sarah Coventry had to find other ways to keep the market share. They began in 1959 by putting the jewelry into special presentation packaging and giving it as consolation prizes on the

The Coffee Break Shows of 1979 were an attempt to increase sales by suggesting morning and afternoon shows. As encouragement, dainty *Coffee Cup* pierced earrings were provided to all FSD's to instill a desire on the part of others to be the first in their neighborhood to own them. The earrings could not be sold.

Shindig shown in the 1965 *Queen for a Day* television show consolation prize box.

television show, *Queen for a Day*. Actors wore it on *Days of Our Lives* and *Barnaby Jones*. Other shows such as *To Tell the Truth*, *Hollywood Squares*, *Wheel of Fortune*, *Family Feud*, and *The Price Is Right* all proved to be successful television campaigns. On the cover of the Fall/Winter 1976 sales catalog is a photo of Anne Marie Pohtamo of Finland, Miss Universe 1975, wearing the official crown created by Sarah Coventry. Other crowns were used in the various Miss America pageants. Special charms and pieces were designed for the various conventions and as sales incentives. Always, the jewelry was fashionable and versatile, "created for the many sides of your life – the fashionable, the casual, the practical." Sarah Coventry meant for the jewelry to be worn in multiples, mixed and matched, and layered, and the company took every advantage to market it.

Organization of the Numbering System

From the beginning, the jewelry was easy to itemize. In 1949, all item numbers began with 1xxx, which was the same numbering system used by Emmons. When Sarah Coventry revised their list in January 1950, they changed all item numbers in inventory to a 5xxx sequence. Emmons retained the 1xxx numbering system.

Sarah Coventry used the 5xxx numbering system through 1953, and all pieces in the same ensemble carried the same sequence. *Mystery* became 5272, 5372, and 5472 for the earrings, necklace, and bracelet. If there had been a pin in the ensemble, it would have been 5172. *Bursting Charm* was 5180 for the pin and 5280 for the earrings.

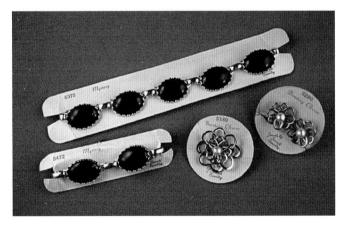

Mystery necklace and bracelet, and *Bursting Charm* pin and screw back earrings, both from 1951, demonstrate the early numbering system.

With the advent of the black and white cardex, Sarah Coventry moved to a better numbering system. The pins were changed to a 6xxx series, earrings to 7xxx, necklaces to 8xxx, and bracelets to 9xxx. Rings remained in the 5xxx series. The

new numbering system worked well for organizing the warehouse inventory. There were always exceptions, yet they were logical exceptions. Since charms were wrist accessories, they carried a 9xxx item number. Pendant drops took the 8xxx numbering system of the necklaces. The only true exceptions we could find were the cuff links and tie clips with the 5xxx series numbering system.

With the exception of the Hostess Bonus items, which had several variations in the numbering system over the years, the warehouse inventory numbering system remained consistent after 1954. It changed in 1981, after the company was sold, to include the 2xxx and 3xxx series when The New Sarah Coventry emerged with real diamonds and karat gold, and it changed again during future acquisitions by other companies to include other variants, even to adding a letter of the alphabet preceding all item numbers.

Sarah Teen Collection

From the beginning, Sarah Coventry planned to pioneer teen jewelry. The company was already supporting teen beauty pageants, and since department stores were not selling jewelry sized to teen necks and wrists, Sarah jumped at the opportunity to sell it with the party plan. Adult jewelry looked awkward on young girls, which prompted Sarah to ask in the 1951 *Inspiration*

Ballerina, inside, and *Chatter*, two teen bracelets from 1953.

Pages, "How many times does a little girl imagine herself as a fairy princess? How many times does a little girl dream of pretty, pretty things? How many times does a little girl watch a lovely dance and long for wings on her feet so that she can weave and sway and glide lightly?" That year, Sarah Coventry presented the *Ballerina* necklace and bracelet to satisfy and thrill all children. The popularity of the

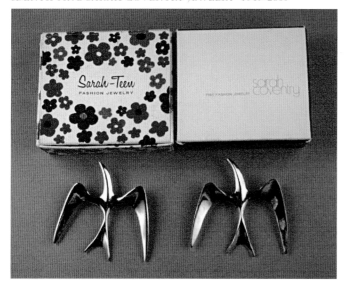

Swedish Modern from 1967 with its Sarah Teen box, and *Mr. Sea Gull* from 1974 with its black and white box. These are identical pins with two different names, and it is not possible to tell them apart without the original packaging.

book chain style prompted Sarah Coventry to create the *Chatter* necklace and bracelet, stating, "Have you ever listened to two little girls talking to each other and heard the constant, steady flow of words? *Chatter* is tailored jewelry specifically for youth."

Originally, the teen jewelry had the same sequence of item numbers as the rest of the Sarah Coventry jewelry, but in 1967, a whole new catalog of teen jewelry was introduced with the preface of "T" in the item number. One large, silver flying bird, named *Swedish Modern*, was so popular that Sarah Coventry released it again in 1974 to the adult audience as *Mr. Sea Gull*.

The jewelry was not limited to young girls. Most of the young men's jewelry in the early years consisted of tie clips and cuff links with wonderful,

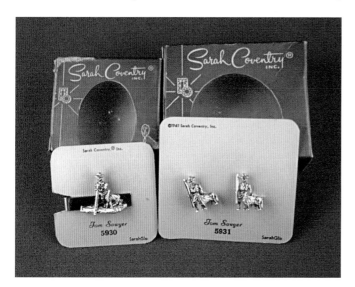

Tom Sawyer, tie bar and cuff links popular for young men, originally sold in 1959 in the clear plastic cases, a packaging system that was discontinued in favor of the yellow cardboard boxes with clear cellophane windows.

whimsical appeal. The *Woofer* set of 1956 was so popular that Sarah quickly followed with *Tom Sawyer* in 1960, the *Royal Mountie* in 1963, and *The Santa Fe* in 1964, all specifically designed with the pre-teen in mind. As young men began sporting long hair and gold chains, the line was expanded in 1970 to include necklaces, bracelets, and rings, all designed for the teenager.

Limited Edition

In the Fall/Winter catalog of 1972, Sarah expanded again with another promotional line for the customer. It was called the Limited Edition and was so popular that Sarah Coventry carried it through to the end of the company. It began with

Cathedral Charm Box, 1972, the first Limited Edition Charm came in this elaborate special presentation box. The lid was carved to mimic the actual charm.

the *Christmas Cathedral* charm, and it came in an elaborately ornate, ornamental special presentation charm box with the design of the charm carved into the lid. It immediately sold out, and it was the only Limited Edition charm to have such an elaborate presentation box.

In the Fall/Winter catalog of 1973, Sarah introduced the first of the Limited Edition commemorative crosses with the *Victorian* cross. It came in a special square red presentation box lined in red velveteen, and it had an accompanying identification paper explaining the design. The presentation box was red again the next year for the *Florentine* cross, and then the boxes began to change colors. It was blue in 1975 with blue velveteen lining, and then gold in 1976 and 1977 with black velveteen lining. In 1978, the box changed from square to oblong with a black bottom and gold top lined in black velveteen, and it continued in this manner until the end of the Limited Edition series with the *Celebration* cross of 1981.

Limited Edition Cross: *Peace*, on the left from 1975, was inspired and copied from a family heirloom cross over 150 years old. *Florentine*, on the right from 1974, was adapted from a traditional cross motif, the "Cross Cotised," a heraldic cross going back to the time of the Crusades. All Limited Edition crosses came with a romance card explaining the origins of the designs.

These are examples of the various Limited Edition Charm and Drop special presentation boxes used from 1973-1980.

The Limited Edition charm returned in 1974 (there was not one in 1973) with the *Partridge in a Pear Tree*. The elaborately carved charm box used in 1972 was replaced with a small special presentation charm box, and this continued through to the end of the series with the *Cherub* in 1980. The color of the charm boxes ranged from silver to blue to gold foil, and some were stamped with the Sarah Coventry logo.

The Limited Edition Drop appeared in the 1976 holiday flyer with the *Christmas Heritage* drop. All of the drops were large enough to be used as ornaments on the Christmas tree, but they could also be worn as pendants. None of them came with a chain, but you could order any chain from Sarah's chain collection. They came in different colors of special presentation gift boxes, some imprinted with the Sarah Coventry logo on the top of the box. The drops continued through 1980 at which time they were discontinued.

All Limited Edition items were holiday pieces. All are signed with the year on the back of the piece, and all the molds were destroyed on December 31 of the year of release. The two exceptions to being signed on the back are the *Crystal Snowflake* drop and the *Crystal Nativity* drop, and both of them have the date cut into the crystal design. All Limited Edition pieces are extremely rare, valuable, and highly collectible.

Lord and Lady Coventry

In April 1965, Sarah Coventry launched the Lord and Lady Coventry line with ten new pieces of expensive jewelry shown in a flyer. It was in answer to requests for karat gold, sterling silver, semi-

precious stones, and a more expensive look. The line did not qualify for the company's special pricing offers, making it a selective line for a selective clientele. The *Theatre Set*, a pin and earrings set described as "Austrian Navette cut Crystals in Silvertone" promptly sold out, as did *Oxford*, a tie tac and cuff links set described as "Genuine Onyx in Silvertone." They were brought back the next year, along with two additional sets in the Lady Coventry line and one additional set in the Lord Coventry line, with more being added each year as the popularity of the line increased. It included items made with genuine jade, cultured pearls, onyx, ivory, coral angel skin, opal, mother-of-pearl, tiger's eye, and simulated diamonds using sterling silver and 14kt gold. By the summer of 1979, the line had included a collection of semi-precious birthstone charms and pendants, and a variety of earrings, bracelets, rings, and men's items. Even the packaging was special, with black or green leatherette cases and velour linings. The line continued to be called Lord and Lady Coventry until the Fall/Winter catalog of 1979, when the name changed to Sarah Coventry Treasures.

The Hostess Plan

There were several versions of the Hostess program, and they are all called "Hostess," but they refer to different aspects in the party plan, which makes it confusing for people to understand. The first hostess gifts were presented only to the employees for loyalty and salesmanship. Many of these items were distributed each year at Christmas, and none of these unique items were ever repeated. Two examples are the red and green carved plastic necklaces given out in 1956, and the wonderful *Ye Old Calendar of Cookery* in 1973. The Christmas items were always non-Sarah jewelry items or some kind of unique merchandise intended only for the employees.

Theatre Set and *Oxford*, 1965, two sets in the black leatherette presentation boxes that began the Lord and Lady Coventry line. Later items came in both black and green leatherette.

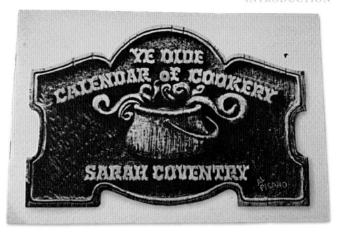

Ye Olde Calendar of Cookery, 1973. This was given to company employees during the holiday season of 1973 in celebration of Christmas and Sarah's 25th Anniversary. It has twelve recipes, one for each month, submitted by executives from across the country. Each recipe was chosen for the season and included a short statement about the executive who submitted it. From January to December, the recipes are: Hoppin' John, Fruit Cocktail Cake, Irish Beef Stew, Early Rising Easter Rolls, Steak Diane, Meatball Stroganoff, On the Wing Appetizers, Columbus Cheese Pudding, Deviled Crab, Goblin Carrot Cake, Holiday Marinade, and Oyster Stuffing.

Red and Green necklaces. These are thought to be the earliest Christmas hostess gifts presented to active employees during the holiday season of 1956. There was no choice of color. We were unable to locate other items for other years, but they do exist.

you wanted one, you had to book your own party or buy enough jewelry to be the top sales volume at someone else's party.

In 1968, the official Hostess Plan originated for the party hostess, changing only slightly in 1969 to define large parties of 10 or more guests. The FSD could still purchase jewelry to reward the party hostess, but the jewelry was now all Sarah Coventry pieces, not special items purchased outside the regular inventory. The pieces were usually former best sellers and discontinued items, and not only did the party hostess receive the gift, anyone signing up to become a consultant could also. Sarah Coventry jewelry sold itself, the company did not, and the company needed sales consultants. By starting this type of Hostess Plan, the company could realize additional sales and recruiting at the same time. The Plan stated that you could earn an unlimited amount of jewelry at no cost, and you could select your own jewelry.

The company also started the Preferred Hostess Plan. A Preferred Hostess held three shows of $50 or more within one year, at which time an additional 10 percent in jewelry could be selected. Customers could save money because for every two items of Sarah Coventry jewelry purchased at regular price, they could purchase another item at half price. By this time, the FSD was able to purchase Sarah jewelry pieces at discount prices, and these items were then the special gifts given to the party hostess. The exceptions were special presentations, such as the Lady Coventry line, which never became part of the hostess jewelry. This plan remained standard all through the catalog years.

Sarah Coventry also had special ways of rewarding the party hostess. The FSD could purchase special jewelry pieces not offered for sale to the general public and give them as gifts for hosting the party. In this case, it was always non-Sarah jewelry items bought in bulk quantity from an external source and made available to the FSD at inexpensive prices. As a reward system, it served as incentive for guests to book their own party to receive something special that nobody else had, and it offered the added incentive of increasing sales, since the FSD had the discretion of presenting it to a guest for top sales volume. The *Silver Poodle* is an example of this type hostess plan, which became modified to include signed pieces such as the *Winking Rabbit*. Always, the items were not offered for sale to the public, and if

An offshoot of the Hostess Plan for the party hostess was the Hostess Credit Plan for the FSD. Under this plan, the FSD earned bonus credits for sales volume. The following items were then made available and could only be acquired by credits, not purchased with cash. All of these items were previous top sellers from the cardex years and not available otherwise:

5010 – Starburst Pin and Earrings
5011 – Black Diamond Pin and Earrings
5012 – Blue Lagoon Pin and Earrings
5013 – Sultana Necklace and Earrings
8000 – Cool Surrender Necklace
5014 – Cool Surrender Bracelet and Earrings
5015 – Galaxy Pin and Earrings
5016 – Dancing Magic Necklace and Earrings
5017 – Kathleen Pin and Earrings
5018 – Golden Avocado Necklace and Earrings

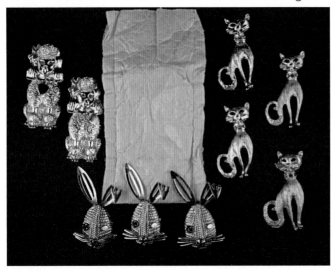

Poodle, Winking Rabbit, Cats, 1960-1963, all pins could be purchased by the FSD for 50 cents each and given to the party hostess for booking the party. They came wrapped in white paper sacks with several layers of soft cotton lining, and we do not know if they had item numbers. The Poodle has a blue bow, blue rhinestone eyes, pink collar with silver dangle heart, and pink toenails. The Cats have pink rhinestone collars. The Winking Rabbit has one red eye and a red nose. The Winking Rabbit is signed Sarah Cov. The Poodle and the Cats are not signed.

In 1971, the following items were added to the Hostess Credit Plan:

5064 – Antique Garden Bracelet and Earrings
5065 – Midnight Magic Earrings
5066 – Midnight Magic Necklace
5067 – Radiance Pin and Earrings
5068 – Nature's Choice Pin and Earrings
5069 – Silvery Nile Necklace and Earrings
5070 – Fashion Flower Pin and Earrings
5071 – Bird of Paradise Pin and Earrings
5072 – Saucy Pin and Earrings
5073 – Bittersweet Pin and Earrings
5074 – Silvery Splendor Pin and Earrings

In 1972, the Plan was still in place, but there were no more specialty items available only to the FSD. Under the new plan, the FSD could earn an unlimited amount of jewelry at no cost through sales volume, and the jewelry would be selected from any in the product catalog. It changed in 1978, when the Plan once again featured special jewelry selections available only to the FSD. This time, many items that were originally available to the customers in silver, now became available to the FSD in gold. This continued until the company ended.

There were also pieces available to the Preferred FSD Hostess. This special jewelry was in lieu of the 10 percent bonus jewelry she would ordinarily receive from the regular Sarah Coventry Jewelry. It could not be purchased, and she only had that year to redeem as much of the collection as she could earn. The first collection was in 1969, called the Ultra-Fashion Collection. It was created by one of the top designers of high fashion jewelry in the country, and each piece was finished in Sarah's special golden satin finish. All the rhinestones were hand-set and polished and were of fine imported Austrian crystals. The enameling was hand-applied, and a baking process followed the application of each color to insure longer wear. It all came individually boxed in a cornflower blue leatherette case, lined in velveteen and satin and bearing a golden Sarah Coventry crest. There were 18 pieces in the collection: 8 items in the Golden Ice Collection, 5 items in the Peacock Collection, and 5 items in the Bahama Blue Collection. It took an extremely active FSD to be able to earn all the pieces in the year allowed.

Another special presentation occurred in 1981. In a program that ran from July 2 to July 16, there were a total of 29 items designed as a salute to the entire corporation during Sarah Coventry's 32nd birthday celebration. It was available only to the active FSD's, and all of the pieces are so rare as to be non-existent. The pieces we have are not signed. With the company in bankruptcy at the time, these pieces are collector items. .

Signature Marks

Since Sarah Coventry never made any of their own jewelry, the signature marks used had to reflect the various artisans who did make it. Sarah Coventry offered a 100 percent satisfaction guarantee stating any piece could be returned for repair or replacement. By the various signatures used, the company had a record of where the piece was originally made and how well it performed. Also, contrary to what has been printed in nearly every source we consulted, Sarah Coventry did not begin to sign their jewelry until 1956. Unfortunately,

Golden Ice Sunburst pin with the matching *Golden Ice Earrings* in the blue leatherette presentation boxes from the Ultra Fashion Collection of 1969. It took an extremely busy FSD who could earn enough bonus points to acquire all of this collection.

someone claimed the first signature was "Coventry" in 1950, and others then copied it, even attempting to refine it to include the various other signatures according to their own guesswork, and this has now been bandied about as gospel. They are incorrect. The first signature is SAC on the *Golden Maple* earrings of 1956, and our research shows that the first time "Coventry" occurred was in 1971 with the *Blue Sun* ring.

Signing jewelry goes back to a lawsuit in 1955 when Trifari filed against Charel for copyright infringement. Charel contended that costume jewelry was "junk jewelry" and not subject to the Copyright Protection Act of 1909, but the Federal District Court for the Southern District of New York disagreed. The Copyright Act protected works of art, and models or designs for works of art, but about the only jewelry being filed for copyright protection were those from Trifari and Coro. From 1858-1955, only 7,731 jewelry patents were granted, with Philippe for Trifari and Katz for Coro being responsible for most of them. After the lawsuit was settled in November 1955, jewelry design patents all but disappeared, since all a designer had to do was to stamp their pieces to prove ownership of the design. The stamp could be something so inconspicuous as a tiny dot on the screw of an earring.

Since using "Pat Pend" did nothing to identify the piece to a specific company, Sarah Coventry rarely used it. The first piece we found with that mark is the *American Beauty* earrings in 1961, and without further research, we do not know if it applied solely to the clip itself, or if it applied to the entire design of the earrings.

Our research shows first signed piece of Sarah Coventry was the *Golden Maple* earrings released during the holiday season in 1956. They are signed SAC on the clips. The pin, released at the same

time, is not signed, and neither is anything else. There were a few sporadic items signed between 1957 and 1962, but signing of all pieces did not begin in earnest until 1963. Even into the 1980s, it is possible to find pieces not signed, most of them pierced earrings and charms.

We feel it important to point out that the stamp of "SAC" introduced in 1956 on the *Golden Maple* earrings, does not stand for the initials of the namesake of the company, as has been reported by several sources. Bill Stuart's niece, and the namesake of Sarah Coventry Jewelry, is Sarah Coventry Beale, not Sarah Ann Coventry. "SAC" stands for "*SA*rah *C*oventry."

This book is the only definitive timeline for the signature marks used by Sarah Coventry Jewelry, and it really can be used as gospel, since we have all the jewelry and all the company paperwork for provenance. There is no guesswork.

1949-1955 – all items are not signed.
1956 – SAC is first used on the *Golden Maple* earrings. All other items are not signed.
1957 – SC is first used on *Chic*, *Beau Catcher*, *Cameo Lace*, and *VIP Tie Tac*.
1958 – some new items released this year are signed SARAHCOV, SAC, and SC, but most new items are still not signed
1959 – SAC is used on all new items
1960 – heavy use of SARAHCOV, plus some use of SAC and SC on new items
1961 – SARAH is first used on *Alaskan Summer*
1962 – mix of SARAHCOV, SC, and SARAH. SAC is fading out of use.
1963 onward – all new items are signed. The exceptions are mostly pierced earrings.
1971 – COVENTRY is used for the first time on the *Blue Sun* ring.

It is important to remember that signing pieces refers to the *new* items released for that year. Sarah Coventry did carry pieces over, sometimes for several years, and if the design needed to be reordered, it might come with a signature that was not there when it was first released.

The End of a Dynasty

The decline of Sarah Coventry was slow. In the mid-1970s, demographics began to change. Women, Sarah's target consumer, as well as its chief employees, became increasingly more independent, seeking other avenues in the work place. With women no longer staying home to raise their families, the party plan was no longer as successful. Sales dropped when fashion jewelry became increasingly more plentiful in department stores, and Sarah's huge inventory made it increasingly difficult for the company to remain viable. In 1979, Sarah Coventry of Australia and Sarah Coventry in Europe closed.

In March 1981, Bill Stuart filed for Chapter 11 reorganization in the U.S. Bankruptcy Court in Rochester. The parent company of C.H. Stuart, Inc., had 12 product divisions, had lost $24 million over the previous three years, and had 1,700 creditors. The reorganization called for consolidating everything, except one division, under the Sarah Coventry name, and this included the Caroline Emmons division. According to the *Emmons Fashion Magic Jewelry* book, "The company was to be run by executives of Catamore Company of Rhode Island, which had supplied much of Sarah Coventry's jewelry and was therefore a major creditor." Sarah Coventry of Canada was sold.

In January 1982, C.H. Stuart, Inc., officially changed name to become Sarah Coventry, Inc. No further pieces were made, and the family's jewelry dynasty came to a close.

A New Beginning

When C.H. Stuart, Inc. ceased Sarah Coventry jewelry, Lifestyle Brands Ltd acquired the patent for the trademark name, and a brief attempt was made to continue keeping the party plan alive with a new butterfly logo, new color catalogs, new packaging colors, a few new pieces, and a new name of "The New Sarah Coventry," but the decline continued. In 1984, R.N. Koch, Inc, acquired use of the trademark from Lifestyle Brands and initiated a revival of the name in department stores.

Robert Newman Koch, Jr, had been the president of Coro, the nation's largest costume jewelry maker, before he founded his own costume jewelry corporation with a factory in Providence, Rhode Island. He designed, distributed, and sold low-cost costume jewelry, many pieces under the Sarah Coventry trademark until 1985, when Peter and John Harvey, brothers who specialized in buying troubled companies for their tax losses and then merged them with profitable ventures, bought R.N. Koch for about $29 million dollars. The brothers also bought three more costume jewelry businesses during 1985-86, and the combined sales ultimately reached a peak of $128 million by 1987. The Sarah Coventry jewelry still carried the promise of a lifetime guarantee and could be sent back for repair or replacement to Sarah Coventry Jewelry in Providence, Rhode Island, but it was not the same company that Bill Stuart started. It was a new company using the original Sarah Coventry trademark with new designers, lighter metals with different alloys, and a better selection of stones and

pearls. All the pieces were well-made, versatile, in keeping with the latest trends in fashion and design, and were sold at affordable prices, but it was anyone's guess if it would manage to keep the loyalty of the Sarah Coventry customers.

In 1988, the R.N. Koch division officially became New Dimensions Accessories, Ltd, and non-jewelry accessories were then added to the line, but it lost more than $7 million on only $92 million in sales. While it continued to lead the field in costume jewelry and was being sold in 6,500 drug, discount, and supermarket stores nationwide under the Sarah Coventry trademark, the losses continued to mount while sales volume dropped. The company fell into Chapter 11 bankruptcy in 1992. The department store sales ended, and the last magazine ad was the April 1992 *Woman's Day.* Although the company emerged from bankruptcy in 1993, it ceased operations altogether in 1994.

Outward indications were that Sarah Coventry was gone, but in 2002, it revived on the Home Shopping Network. It continued to use the butterfly logo of The New Sarah Coventry, and the pieces now came packaged in black boxes. Most items used familiar designs from the original Stuart years with stone and color differences to draw in the clientele, and it worked for about two years. With low sales and high prices, HSN dropped the line.

After HSN came Sarah Coventry HPP, Inc, who acquired use of the license from Lifestyle Brands and once again attempted the home party plan of salesmanship. They stated that they would use "some of those same designers and manufacturers as partners again" to create a design team that constantly tracked trends in fashion, color, textiles, and materials, and translate them into jewelry and accessories utilizing the quality standards, skills, and craftsmanship that customers had come to know and associate with the Sarah Coventry name, but the idea did not work. Some of the designs were reminiscent of years past, using newer colors, metals, and stones, but it never really acquired the appeal it once had. In addition, it was far more expensive than customers expected to pay, and this kept sales and recruitment low. In an attempt to keep the company viable, the new owners invested in a new facility in 2006. They located it in Oldsmar, Florida, with more than a million dollars put into a 7,000-square-foot office, distribution, and warehouse space. They moved everyone and everything to Florida, and new exciting designs were added, but the high cost of the jewelry continued to be more than women expected from their beloved company. By 2009, the Sarah Coventry name was once again out of business.

Gone But Not Forgotten

Sarah Coventry always sold what women wanted. Margie Beale said in an interview for the *Finger Lakes Magazine* in 2009, "After World War II, women were eager to buy things — they had gone without for four years — but it also had to do with being social. In those days, women were home most of the time taking care of their families, and going to a jewelry party was a way to see friends and meet people. And of course, the jewelry was pretty. It was well-made, but the cost was low so women who wanted to look good, but didn't have a lot of money, could still afford it."

A mere 15 years after inception, Sarah Coventry was selling at the astonishing rate of 35,000 pieces each workday. It had been founded on the principles of small-town, small-business America, and, despite its size, it retained these ideals. By 1980, right before Stuart filed for Chapter 11 Bankruptcy protection, and 30 years after it was born, it enjoyed a name-brand recognition rivaling that of Kodak. The company brochures boasted that over 90 percent of the American public recognized the Sarah Coventry name.

Today, Sarah Coventry is a fond memory, yet the jewelry remains highly collectible. The early years are extremely rare and difficult to find, as are the pieces from 1980 through 2009, but all pieces have withstood the effects of time, attesting to the quality and craftsmanship used to make them. If the collector is diligent and patient, chances are that these hard-to-find pieces will eventually turn up. It is also possible to find items in their original packaging, having never been worn. With few exceptions, we have not found anything badly damaged with patina, plating-wear, missing stones, or broken parts, and the pieces we did find in that condition all appeared to be from improper storage and/or cleaning. Sarah Coventry was the Stuart family's legacy to everyone. It became the world's largest direct seller of costume jewelry and the acknowledged leader of costume jewelry fashion. It has never been rivaled.

Original Jewelry Prices in Today's Dollars

Every jewelry collector wants to know the value of her collection. Unfortunately, there is no industry-wide formula that can be applied equally across the board. Value is extremely subjective, and it depends on a wide range of variables, including scarcity of the item, size of the stones, type of metals and stones used, original pricing of the piece, condition of the piece, and whether or not it is a well-known designer or even if it is designer-signed. Originally, we decided we would value the pieces according to what we would be willing to pay for the item, but then we discovered the Federal government has a Consumer Price Index Calculator that adjusts for inflation at today's prices, applying a formula based on the original price of yesteryear. This calculator goes all the way back to 1913.

We decided to use it without any caveats or qualifiers, since we have the original prices for everything shown in the book. This does not mean you should expect to pay today's price for the item; it only means the Calculator has adjusted the original price for today's inflation. We rounded our value for presentation purposes. You might be able to acquire the item for much less.

Since Sarah Coventry used a full price and a half price on all the pieces, applying the half price only after two items had been purchased at full price, we used the full price in the Calculator. It means that the Lady Coventry *Jade Oval* bracelet, which sold for $27.00 in 1972, would sell for $144.34 at 2011 prices. Would you spend that much money today for a bracelet if someone invited you to attend a jewelry party? Collectors are urged to use their own judgment when valuing their collections.

Examples of Prices for Sarah Coventry Jewelry for the Selected Years

	1949	1959	1969	1979	1982	2011
Azure Snowflake Pin	1.71	2.09	2.64	5.22	6.93	16.06
Fiesta Clip Earrings		3.48	4.39	8.68	11.54	26.72
Instant Fashion Necklace			7.00	13.85	18.41	42.62
Gentle Trio Bracelet				10.50	13.96	32.32
Prairie Princess Ring					24.00	55.58

A Photo Is Worth a Thousand Words

We decided not to categorize the jewelry in this book; there is no section devoted solely to pins or bracelets, for example. We also decided not to approach it by date, since many items were held over for many years; the *Young & Gay* silver bracelet was originally sold in 1959, and since the design was wonderful for charms, it stayed in inventory through 1980, becoming no longer listed in the 1981 catalogs. Instead, we split the book into the cardex years and the catalog years. We did find two items released in the cardex that had matching completer pieces released in the catalog side. One was the *Fashion Parade* necklace, earrings, and ring from 1964, with the stick pin being released in August 1968, and the other was the *Golden Bangle*

Golden Maple, 1956, although both the pin and earrings appeared for the first time in the Fall/Holiday shopping guide, only the earrings are signed, making them the first piece of jewelry in Sarah Coventry history to be signed. The signature is SAC for *SA*rah Coventry.

Dogwood, *Tahitian Flower*, and *Flower Flattery* came in a variety of colors for the fashion wardrobe. There were other sets that also came in several colors with distinctive completer pieces to finish the look.

bracelet released in 1965, only to have the matching earrings in the first catalog of 1966. We kept these sets together in the cardex side of the book.

We have listed all the sets first, then listed all the non-set items for each classification. In this way, the collector can see all of a set at one time without having to flip pages to find the completers. Rings are the exception. We showed them first with their sets, but we also showed them as an individual classification.

We also did not group according to color or stones. Some books put all the rhinestones together and all the enamel together, but we opted for variety, since this is what Sarah Coventry did. Their aim was variety, offering a wide assortment of metals, colors, and stones to make the jewelry more

valuable as a fashion accessory for the customer. The idea was to mix and match. Any gold earring could be worn with anything gold in the line, and the same is true for the silver and rhinestones. There are specific ensembles like *Dogwood*, *Tahitian Flower*, and *Flower Flattery*, which did come with exotic completer pieces, but even they look great when paired with anything gold in the line.

We hope you use this book to identify your collection, as well as discover pieces to add to it. There are similar pieces in existence, and it is always "buyer beware," but by understanding that the jewelry was made by artisans in the area, and remembering that Sarah Coventry bought the rights to a specific design and color, it should be easy to understand why other pieces with slight variations do exist. Always count the number of petals in a flower and check the color of the rhinestones. If they disagree with what you see in this book, you may have a New Sarah piece, an International Sarah piece, or even a non-Sarah piece.

Notes

Much of this information comes from Sandra Sturdivant's research for her book Identifying Avon Jewelry, Schiffer 2008, and we present it here, with changes to reflect Sarah Coventry jewelry, because it is most useful for jewelry collectors.

According to legend, Prometheus is the father of jewelry. Hercules cut Prometheus loose from the chains that bound him to Mount Caucasus, and Prometheus then made a ring out of one of the links by carving a groove in the link to set a portion of the rock into the link, thus fashioning the first ring using the first gem with the first method of stone setting called a bezel-set. Many rings are designed with real or faux gems, making

Young & Gay silver bracelet first released in 1959 was sold continuously until the end of the 1980 season.

them versatile for dinner or daily wear, while others are so elaborately crafted they can substitute for museum pieces. Rings utilize all kinds of stones. The precious stones are diamond, ruby, sapphire, and emerald, which can be cut and faceted into any shape and size. A colorless-quartz is the crystal, not to be confused with man-made glass, which can also be cut and faceted to dazzling brilliance and is also called a crystal. Abalone, coral, and mother-of-pearl come from the ocean, while hematite, turquoise, lapis, quartz, and agates are dug from the earth. Rhinestones are faceted glass, which is set with a foil backing to give it brilliance. Marcasite is white iron pyrite, a form of fool's gold, which can be cut and faceted and set in silver. Most Sarah Coventry rings are stamped inside the band, but some are not signed.

In jewelry vernacular, a parure is three or more matching pieces to a set. A full parure is a necklace, bracelet, earrings, pin, and ring, and a demi-parure is a combination of any two of those items. Cameo and intalgio are two words meaning basically the same thing, but in reverse of each other. Cameos are molded or carved in shell, gems, coral, and other materials and generally depict a scene or portrait. They sit on top the shelf of the piece, whereas the intalgio cameo is carved or molded into the shelf itself. Some intalgio cameos are carved into the shell from the backside of the material, making it a reverse intalgio. Enameling is the firing of melted glass, which can be in any color, and cloisonné is a form of enameling. In cloisonné, the base metal forms cells (cloisons), which are then filled with enamel with each compartment being held separate from each other by the metal cloisons. The term faux literally means "false light," which is a way for gems and gemstones to reflect a false light where the brilliance is achieved by highly faceted glass and foil backing. It's possible to have faux turquoise, rubies, emeralds, and sapphires, as well as pearls, coral and other materials. Sarah Coventry used all these methods in their jewelry.

It has been theorized that the first piece of jewelry adornment was a brooch, since collars and cuffs were detachable, requiring something to hold them in place, and a nice-sized jeweled pin was considered the perfect choice. True or not, the popularity of the pin and brooch continues today. They range in size from a simple tack pin, having a tiny stud on the back to pierce the garment, which is then held in place with a simple clamping nut, to the exceptionally large and grandiose bar pins. Traditionally, pins are considered small and utilitarian, whereas brooches are large pieces of adornment laden with gemstones. Sarah Coventry used both styles, as well as the chatelaine, a fancy term for a pin "holding" another pin with a connecting chain.

Like the brooch, the necklace is a jewelry staple. Most important for the pendants were the chains. The links came in a great variety of styles, including square, oval, flat, twisted, cable, and rope, and varied in shape from oval, round, square, and octagon. Some were sterling silver and karat gold, but the vast majority were non-tarnishing goldtone or silvertone, generic terms meaning jewelry with the look and feel of real gold or silver but which have no gold or silver content. A single-strand necklace, which fit snuggly around the throat, was called a choker. The single strand could be made of pearls, gems, beads, or even incorporate material such as rope or velvet to which elaborate pendants could be added, many of them with the ability to be worn off-center. The dog collar choker could embrace the throat higher up than the simple choker and have row upon row of beads and stones cascading down to an elaborate center pendant that rested at the apex of the collarbone. Many of the clasps were the simple "spring ring," a tiny circle with a push-pin on a spring which opens and springs shut for closure, but Sarah Coventry also used the "ball and chain" on many of the chokers for adjustment. Plastic is a term applied to a group of synthetic chemical products which can be molded, carved, or pressed into many shapes and sizes, incorporating the looks of tortoise, turquoise, mother-of-pearl, marble, jet, coral, ivory, amber, agate, wood, and many other naturally occurring materials. There are also synthetic gems and pearls in most of the jewelry, and the term generally means a speeded-up way for man to duplicate the natural process, such as the cultured pearl, which is produced by introducing an unnatural irritation within the oyster's shell.

Bracelets have been popular for centuries. What started as jointed, wide-cuff designs quickly evolved to un-jointed bangle types. The bangles were originally called a "bangle ring," since it was a narrow band in the shape of a large wedding ring for the wrist, and they were so popular that artisans soon made them in a variety of colors and widths, molding and carving them from various materials. Bakelike was an early resin process that went out of fashion in the 1950s. Just as Bakelite replaced the highly flammable celluloid of an earlier generation, Lucite and other forms of hard plastic replaced Bakelite. Lucite is a petrochemical product, which can be transparent, translucent, or opaque and once formed, it cannot be bent out of shape. Sarah Coventry used the metal cuff and the plastic bangle, as well as linked chains and fitted band, and many of the bracelet designs were studded with gemstones and pearls, or included charms for added appeal. Charms were once considered "love tokens," and they came in all shapes, including religious symbols, hearts, animals, clocks, signets, beads, and lockets, to name a few. Many of Sarah Coventry's bracelets are signed on the clasp or have a hangtag, but nearly all the plastic bangles are not signed.

Earrings are the foundation stock of any jewelry wardrobe. The designs must be versatile and practical, for daytime or formal wear, and they must flatter the wearer's ear, face, hair, and personality. They date back thousands of centuries. The earliest ones were lightweight, hollow-gold wire hooks designed to pierce the ear lobes, but as artisans used more interesting heavy stones and materials, they needed different methods of attaching them. The post, screw-back, and clip came into being in the 1930s, and they stayed in fashion until the 1970s, when dangling pierced earrings became the fad. Sarah Coventry used the screw-back, clip, fishhook, and the post designs, and they incorporate a wide variety of sizes and styles, from a simple stud centered entirely within the circumference of the ear lobe to dangles measuring around 2-inches or longer. Most of the stones and pearls are glass and synthetic.

CHAPTER ONE

Cardex, 1949-1965

With very few exceptions, all pierced earrings are not signed.

Windswept, 1954, unsigned, necklace, 8540, $50; bracelet, 9540, $40; clip earrings, 7540, $30.

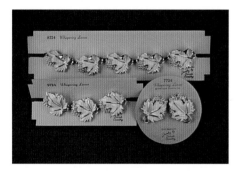

Whispering Leaves, 1959, necklace, 8724, $40; bracelet, 9724, $35; clip earrings, 7724, $22.

Pink Twist, 1954, unsigned, necklace, 8567, $65; bracelet, 9567, $50; screw back earrings, 7567, $30.

Mystery, 1951, unsigned, black in silver metal, necklace, 5372, $50; bracelet, 5472, $35; screw back earrings, 5272, $20; *Arctic Pearl*, 1950, unsigned, white in gold metal, 15-inch necklace, 6300, $50; bracelet, 6400, $35; screw back earrings, 6200, $20; also 17-inch necklace, 6301.

Monte Carlo, 1954, unsigned, necklace, 8554, $30; bracelet, 9554, $30; screw back earrings, 7554, $25.

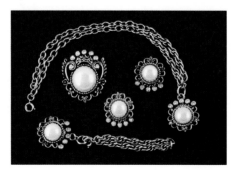

Empress, 1956, unsigned, necklace, 8590, $45; bracelet, 9590, $40; pin, 6590, $30; clip earrings, 7590, $30.

Queen Victoria, 1950, unsigned, necklace, 5334, $60; bracelet, 5434, $75; clip earrings, 5234, $50; also pierced earrings, 5218, from the collection of Karen Walck Haley.

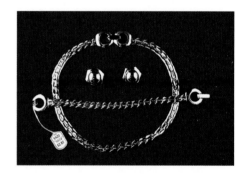

Everlasting Charm, 1949, unsigned, gold or silver necklace, 1321, $55; bracelet, 1421, $25; screw back earrings, 1221, $25; same numbers for both colors; in 1950, numbers changed to gold necklace, 5319, bracelet, 5419, screw back earrings, 5219; silver necklace, 5320; bracelet, 5420; screw back earrings, 5220; from the collection of Karen Walck Haley.

Amber Glory, 1956, necklace, 8595, $45; bracelet, 9595, $55; clip earrings, 7595, $35.

White Rapture, 1951, unsigned, necklace, $50; bracelet, $50; screw back earrings, $35; no numbers given in reference.

Marie Antoinette, 1955, unsigned, necklace, 8575, $80; bracelet, 9575, $55; screw back earrings, 7575, $40.

Turquoise in Crystal, 1949, unsigned, necklace, 1308, $60; bracelet, 1408, $60; screw back earrings, 1208, $30; in 1950, numbers changed and new pieces added: 15-inch necklace, 5308, 17-inch necklace, 5309, bracelet, 5409, screw back earrings, 5208, pierced earrings, 6217, from the collection of Karen Walck Haley.

Antique Medallion, 1950, unsigned, necklace, 5335, $50; bracelet, 5435, $90; screw back earrings, 5235, $25; from the collection of Karen Walck Haley.

Celestial Fire, 1955, unsigned, necklace, 8566, $85; bracelet, 9566, $60; dainty screw back earrings, 7566, $30; in 1956, unsigned daring screw back earrings, 7584, $35; in 1960, signed clip earrings, 7594, $35.

Mandalay, 1954, unsigned, necklace, 8526, $40; bracelet, 9526, $35; screw back earrings, 7526, $25.

Capricorn Jewels, 1950, unsigned, necklace, 5350, $55; bracelet, 5450, $40; pin, 5150, $40; clip earrings, 5250, $35.

Slim Line, 1961, necklace, 8819, $35; bracelet, 9819, $30; clip earrings, 7819, $40.

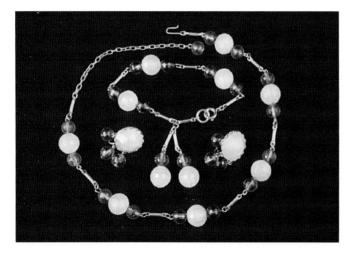

Remembrance, 1955, unsigned, necklace, 8570, $30; bracelet, 9570, $30; clip earrings, 7570, $25; bracelet from the collection of Karen Walck Haley.

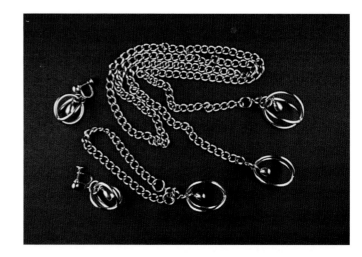

Tailspin, 1956, unsigned, necklace, 8623, $60; bracelet, 9623, $30; screw back earrings, 7623, $35.

Cockle Shells, 1957, unsigned, necklace, 8619, $50; bracelet, 9619, $40; clip earrings, 7619, $30.

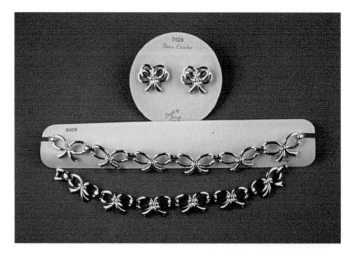

Beau Catcher, 1957, necklace, 8628, $50; bracelet, 9628, $30; clip earrings, 7628, $25.

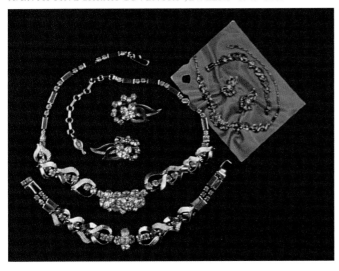

Monte Carlo, 1961, necklace, 8831, $75; bracelet, 9831, $50; clip earrings, 7831, $40.

Golden Bell, 1950, unsigned, necklace, 5352, $50; bracelet, 5452, $30; screw back earrings, 5255, $30; screw back fleur-de-lis earrings, 5268, $30.

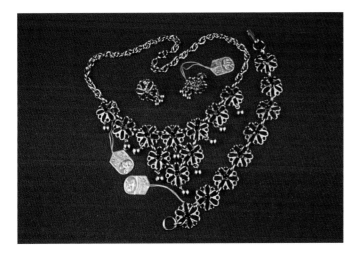

Golden Evergreen, 1950, unsigned, necklace, 5346, $80; bracelet, 5446, $50; screw back earrings, 5246, $25; from the collection of Karen Walck Haley; also pierced earrings, 6216.

Moonlight Serenade, 1958, unsigned, necklace, 8665, $75; bracelet, 9665, $50; clip earrings, 7665, $30.

Emerald Lace, 1951, unsigned, necklace, 5387, $60; bracelet, 5487, $40; screw back earrings, 5287, $35.

Summer Festival, 1959, necklace, 8762, $40; bracelet, 9762, $30; clip earrings, 7762, $25.

Snow Princess, 1962, necklace, 8850, $50; bracelet, 9850, $45; clip earrings, 7850, $30; shown in December 1961 *McCall's*.

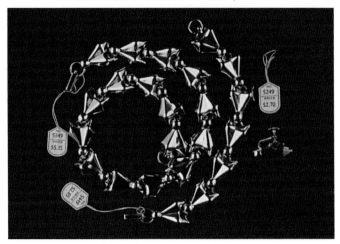

Golden Arrow, 1950, unsigned, necklace, 5349, $50; bracelet, 5449, $25; clip earrings, 5249, $25; one earring shown; from the collection of Karen Walck Haley.

Blue Mystery, 1958, necklace, 8708, $85; bracelet, 9708, $55; clip earrings, 7708, $40; listed in the April 1958 Shopping Guide, same numbers and design as *Blue Champagne*, but having no pin; *Treasure Chest Jewel Box*, 1958, 0003, $15.

Cosmopolitan, 1960, necklace, 8789, $30; bracelet, 9789, $40; clip earrings, 7789, $20.

Blue Champagne, 1958, necklace, 8708, $85; bracelet, 9708, $55; clip earrings, 7708, $40; listed in the August 1958 Shopping Guide, same numbers and design as Blue Mystery; in 1959, pin, 6708, $30.

Windsong, 1959, necklace, 8748, $40; bracelet, 9748, $30; clip earrings, 7748, $25.

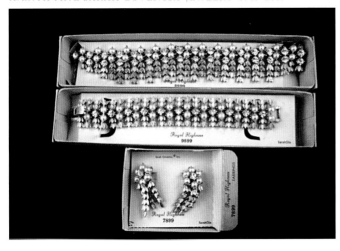

Royal Highness, 1962, necklace, 8899, $75; bracelet, 9899, $50; clip earrings, 7899, $35.

Midnight Magic, 1956, unsigned, necklace, 8605, $80; bracelet, 9605, $120; clip earrings, 7605, $50; in 1959, ring, 5108, $55.

Mood Magic, 1961, necklace, 8829, $40; bracelet, 9829, $55; clip earrings, 7829, $50; bottom part of pendant is detachable and can be added as a dangle to the earrings.

White Magic, 1956, unsigned, necklace, 8578, $60; bracelet, 9578, $45; clip earrings, 7578, $30.

Capri, 1953, unsigned, necklace, 8501, $40; bracelet, 9501, $50; screw back earrings, 7501, $40.

Singing Bells, 1957, unsigned, necklace, 8620, $50; bracelet, 9620, $40; clip earrings, 7620, $25; identical to Monastery Bells; *Monastery Bells*, 1957, unsigned, necklace, 8620, $50; bracelet, 9620, $40; clip earrings, 7620, $25. Shown is the cardex for Monastery Bells. We lack the information to know why this set has two names.

Celebrity, 1962, necklace, 8878, $75; bracelet, 9878, $110; dainty clip earrings, 7917, $35; daring clip earrings, 7878, $45; ring, 5123, $35. Pendant can be worn as pin.

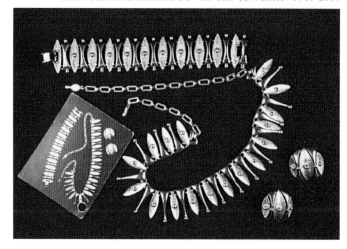

Egyptian Temptress, 1962, necklace, 8893, $45; bracelet, 9893, $40; clip earrings, 7893, $20.

Sabrina Fair, 1959, bracelet, 9699, $40; blue clip earrings, 7699, $20; in 1960, necklace, 8699, $45; cherry clip earrings, 7758, $20; lemon clip earrings, 7759, $20; ring, 5114, $20.

Royal Ballet, 1960, necklace, 8796, $50; bracelet, 9796, $40; clip earrings, 7796, $20.

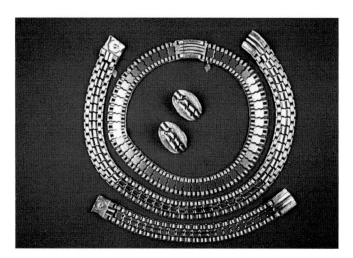

Turn-A-Bout, 1959, reversible, necklace, 8743, $55; bracelet, 9743, $40; clip earrings, 7743, $30. Two necklaces are shown for the reverse pattern.

Gay Adventure, 1953, unsigned, necklace, 5371, $60; bracelet, 5471, $50; screw back earrings, 5271, $35.

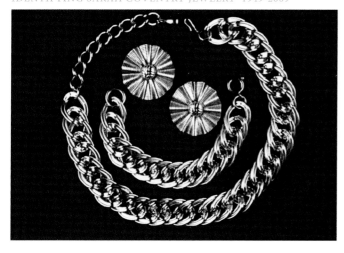

Rhapsody, 1956, unsigned, necklace, 8608, $50; bracelet, 9608, $30; clip earrings, 7608, $30.

Evening Sands, 1960, necklace, 8875, $50; bracelet, 9875, $45; clip earrings, 7875, $40.

Antique Lace, 1956, unsigned, necklace, 8593, $50; bracelet, 9593, $40; clip earrings, 7593, $30.

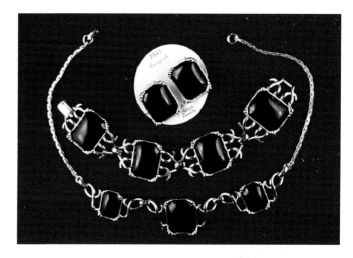

Escapade, 1955, unsigned, necklace, 8541, $55; bracelet, 9541, $50; clip earrings, 7541, $35.

Whispering Leaves, 1953, unsigned, necklace, 8514, $45; bracelet, 9514, $50; pin, 6514, $40; screw back earrings, 7514, $40.

Raspberry Ice, 1955, unsigned, necklace, 8579, $45; bracelet, 9579, $40; clip earrings, 7579, $30.

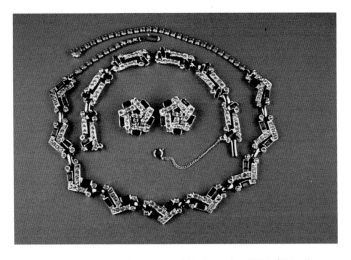

Emerald Ice, 1960, necklace, 8786, $90; bracelet, 9786, $75; clip earrings, 7786, $45.

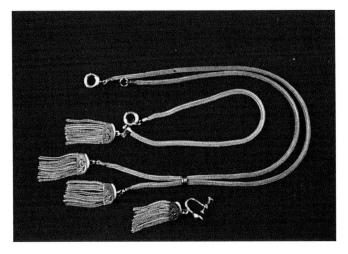

Gold Rope Black Rose, 1949, unsigned, necklace, 3324, $40; bracelet, 3424, $40; screw back earrings, 5233, $30; from the collection of Karen Walck Haley. In 1950, the numbers changed to necklace, 5324, bracelet, 5424, screw back earrings, 5233. This set is listed in references with several different names: *Golden Rope Black Rose, Gold Lariat Black Rose, Black Rose, Gold Rope with Black Rose*.

Golden Links, 1953, unsigned, necklace, $40; bracelet, $30; clip earrings, $25; no numbers give in reference, from the collection of Karen Walck Haley. Shown in the February 1953 *Vogue* as being "named to receive the Fashion Academy Gold Medal Award".

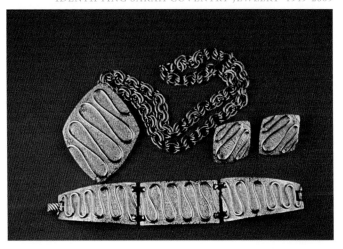

Silvery Nile, 1961, necklace, 8814, $50; bracelet, 9814, $40; clip earrings, 7814, $20.

Chantilly Lace, 1961, necklace, 8845, $45; bracelet, 9845, $45; clip earrings, 7845, $30; modeled by Bess Myerson in March 1962 *McCall's*.

19th Century, 1953, unsigned, necklace, $60; bracelet, $50; screw back earrings, $40; no numbers given in reference, bracelet from the collection of Karen Walck Haley.

Triple Charm, 1950, unsigned, necklace, 5347, $80; bracelet, 5447, $50; screw back earrings, 5247, $25; from the collection of Karen Walck Haley.

Fancy Free, 1960, necklace, 8798, $30; bracelet, 9798, $30; clip earrings, 7798, $20.

Fashion, 1960, necklace, 8763, $40; bracelet, 9763, $30; clip earrings, 7763, $20.

Snow Flower, 1959, unsigned necklace, 8723, $40; signed bracelet, 9723, $30; signed clip earrings, 7723, $20.

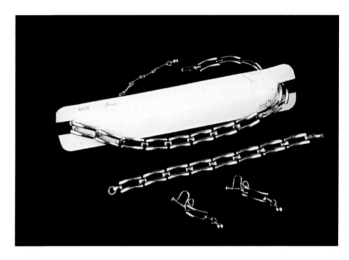

Tango, 1954, unsigned, necklace, 8513, $40; bracelet, 9513, $25; screw back earrings, 7513, $25.

Shimmering Stars, 1958, necklace, 8709, $55; bracelet, 9709, $115; clip earrings, 7709, $40.

Golden Brocade, 1961, necklace, 8822, $50; bracelet, 9822, $45; pin, 6822, $30; clip earrings, 7822, $20.

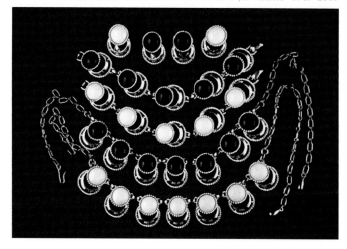

Bold and Beautiful, 1959, black necklace, 8725, $40; bracelet, 9725, $30; clip earrings, 7725, $25; white necklace, 8809, $40; bracelet, 9809, $30; clip earrings, 7809, $25.

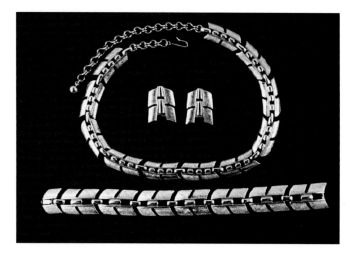

Tailored Lady, 1958, necklace, 8697, $45; bracelet, 9697, $30; clip earrings, 7697, $25.

First Lady, 1951, unsigned, 15-16-inch pearl necklace, 5302, $50; in 1960, bracelet, 9711, $30; clip earrings, 7711, $30; ring, 5113, $25; also 17-inch pearl necklace, 8794.

Sultana, 1959, necklace, 8768, $45; clip earrings, 7768, $40; in 1961, bracelet, 9768, $50.

Fantasia, 1956, unsigned, necklace, 8610, $120; bracelet, 9610, $50; clip earrings, 7610, $40.

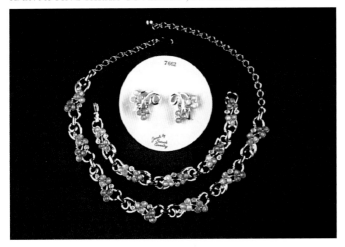

Glamour Tones, 1958, necklace, 8662, $50; bracelet, 9662, $40; clip earrings, 7662, $30.

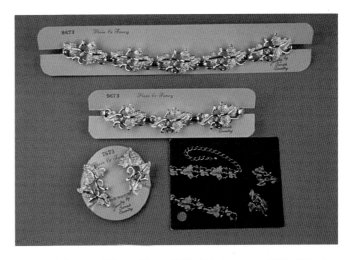

Plain and Fancy, 1958, necklace, 8673, $50; bracelet, 9673, $35; clip earrings, 7673, $30.

Cool Surrender, 1958, necklace, 8671, $60; bracelet, 9671, $45; clip earrings, 7671, $30.

Frosted Feathers, 1961, necklace, 8832, $40; bracelet, 9832, $40; clip earrings, 7832, $20.

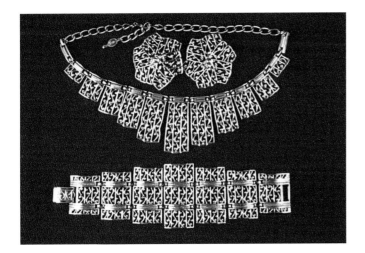

Lady of Spain, 1961, necklace, 8830, $40; bracelet, 9830, $40; clip earrings, 7830, $20.

Chic, 1957, necklace, 8638, $45; bracelet, 9638, $30; clip earrings, 7638, $25.

Merry-Go-Round, 1956, unsigned, necklace, 8609, $50; bracelet, 9609, $40; clip earrings, 7609, $30.

Desert Moon, 1953, unsigned, necklace, 8568, $50; bracelet, 9568, $40; clip earrings, 7568, $25.

Parisienne Nights, 1961, necklace, 8847, $110; bracelet, 9847, $105; clip earrings, 7847, $45; ring, 5118, $40.

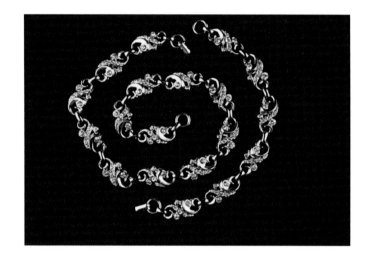

New Yorker, 1951, unsigned, necklace, 5369, $50; bracelet, 5469, $40; also earrings, 5269.

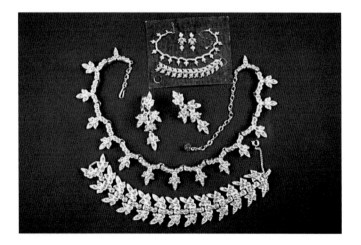

World's Fair, 1964, necklace, 8947, $95; bracelet, 9947, $95; clip earrings, 7947, $45; modeled by Rosemary Clooney in April 1964 *McCall's*.

Gold 'N Glory, 1960, necklace, 8764, $50; bracelet, 9764, $45; clip earrings, 7764, $30.

Candlelight, 1957, unsigned, necklace, 8632, $50; bracelet, 9632, $30; clip earrings, 7632, $25.

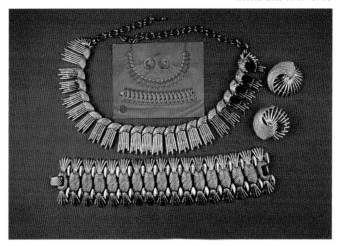

Simply Elegant, 1962, necklace, 8894, $45; bracelet, 9894, $40; clip earrings, 7894, $20.

Crystal Fire, 1965, necklace, 8530, $55; clip earrings, 7530, $35.

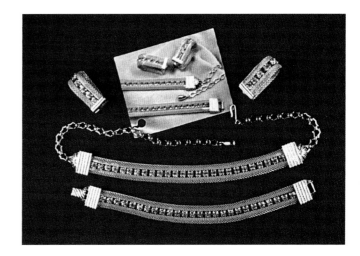

Star-Lighter, 1960, unsigned, necklace, 8744, $45; bracelet, 9744, $45; clip earrings, 7744, $40.

Rhapsody in Blue, 1962, necklace, 8856, $45; clip earrings, 7856, $30.

Fashion Pearl, 1957, unsigned, necklace, 8612, $55; bracelet, 9612, $40; screw back earrings, 7612, $25; *Evening Star*, 1957, unsigned, necklace, 8667, $60; extension 8642, $25; bracelet, 9642, $40; clip earrings, 7642, $30. To make a necklace, you needed the extension and bracelet.

My Fair Lady, 1958, necklace, 8661, $55; bracelet, 9661, $40; clip earrings, 7661, $30.

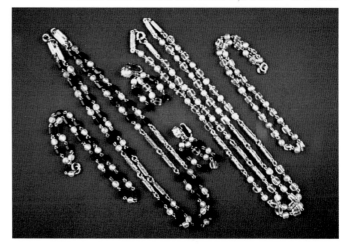

Rope of Fashion, 1959, jet necklace, 8713, $55; choker-let, 9713, $25; clip earrings, 7719, $20; crystal necklace, 8719, $55; choker-let, 9719, $25; clip earrings, 7719, $20. The same earrings were used for both colors. An all jet necklace and an all crystal necklace with same corresponding item numbers exist, and we have no explanation for this.

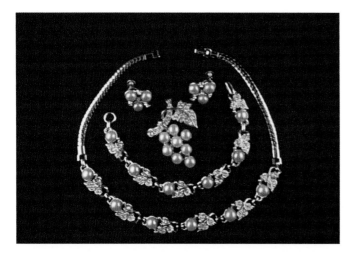

Queen Mary, 1950, unsigned, necklace, 5353, $60; bracelet, 5453, $60; pin, 5153, $50; screw back earrings, 5253, $45.

Carnival, 1953, unsigned, necklace, $40; screw back earrings, $35; no numbers in reference; *Holiday*, 1953, unsigned, necklace, 8534, $40; screw back earrings, 7534, $35.

Tru-Love, 1950, unsigned, necklace, 5354, $40; clip earrings, 5254, $30; pin, 5154, $30.

Sultana, 1953, unsigned, necklace, 5384, $50; bracelet, 5484, $60; pin, 5184, $50; also clip earrings, 5284, pin from the collection of Karen Walck Haley.

Pearls Triple Strand Necklace, 1950, unsigned, 5333, $110; *Pearls Triple Strand Bracelet*, 1949, unsigned, 1400, $40; in 1950, number changed 5401, both from the collection of Karen Walck Haley.

Sweetheart, 1955, unsigned; necklace, 8574, $30; chatelaine pin, 6574, $30; clip earrings, 7574, $30; *South Seas*, 1955, unsigned, necklace, 8571, $40; clip earrings, 7571, $30.

Star Shower, 1965, necklace, 8570, $50; clip earrings, 7570, $30.

Pearl Wardrobe, 1962, 15-inch necklace, 8851, $65; clip earrings, 7851, $45; also 16-1/2-inch necklace, 8923, versatile set with removable section of pearls and reversible clasp and earrings. Two sets are shown. One set is from the collection of Sue Beaver.

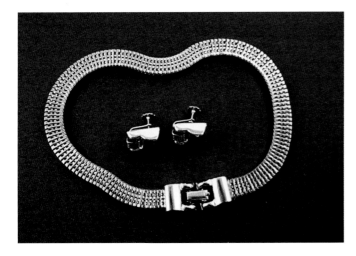

Cobra, 1949, unsigned, necklace, 1305, $30; screw back earrings, 1222, $20; also bracelet, 1405; from the collection of Karen Walck Haley. The necklace and bracelet came in both a regular and longer length and all pieces came in both gold and silver with the same item numbers. In 1950, all numbers changed: gold regular length: necklace, 5341, bracelet, 5441, screw back earrings, 5240; gold longer length: necklace, 5340; bracelet, 5440; screw back earrings, 5240. Silver regular length: necklace, 5343, bracelet, 5443, screw back earrings, 5241; silver longer length: necklace, 5342, bracelet, 5442, screw back earrings, 5241.

Ebony Classic, 1957, unsigned, necklace, 8622, $50; bracelet, 9622, $45; clip earrings, 7622, $45.

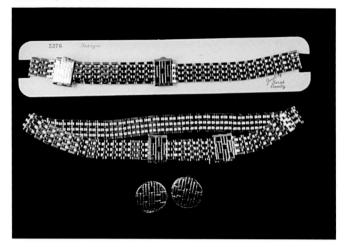

Intrigue, 1953, unsigned, gold necklace, 5376, $40; clip earrings are 5276; item numbers for silver set are not known. Earring values for each color are, $25.

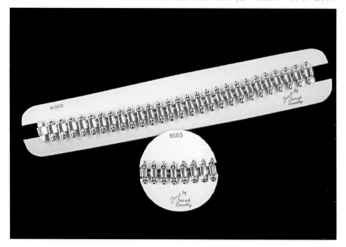

Chatter, 1954, unsigned, necklace, 8505, $30; bracelet, 9505, $25; from the collection of Karen Walck Haley.

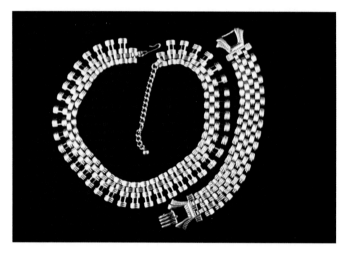

Shanghai, 1956, unsigned, necklace, 8594, $50; bracelet, 9594, $40; also earrings, 7594, bracelet from the collection of Karen Walck Haley.

Contessa, 1964, necklace, 8501, $60; clip earrings, 7501, $35.

Cascade, 1954, unsigned, necklace, 8564, $55; bracelet, 9564, $30; screw back earrings, 7564, $40; from the collection of Pam Eade.

Dancing Magic, 1961, necklace, 8827, $65; clip earrings, 7827, $50; *Color Spray*, 1960, necklace, 8816, $25; clip earrings, 7816, $25; *Chinese Modern*, 1964, necklace, 8938, $45; clip earrings, 7938, $35.

Royal Hawaiian, 1959, necklace, 8817, $40; clip earrings, 7817, $30; *Modern Design*, 1965, necklace, 8517, $50; clip earrings, 7517, $30. In both sets, the pendant can be worn separately as a pin.

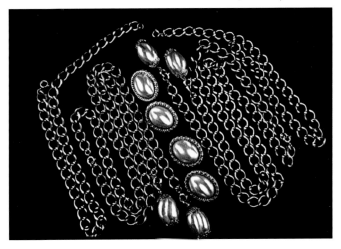

Chain 'O Fashion, 1962, gold necklace, 8867, $75; clip earrings, 7867, $40; silver necklace, 8876, $75; clip earrings, 7876, $40.

Moonlight Madness, 1961, necklace, 8825, $40; dainty clip earrings, 7825, $30; daring clip earrings, 7846, $45; shoe clip earrings, 5825, $30; *Pearl Of The Sea*, 1956, unsigned, necklace or bracelet, 8592, $30; clip earrings, 7592, $30; in 1957, ring, 5103, $20; *Empress*, 1953, unsigned, necklace, 8555, $40; screw back earrings, 7555, $25.

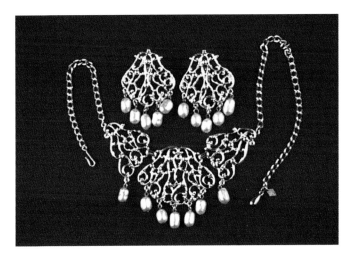

Venetian Lace, 1960, necklace, 8790, $50; clip earrings, 7790, $50.

Fascination, 1965, necklace, 8566, $20; clip earrings, 7566, $30; *Crystal Navette*, 1963, necklace, 8927, $30; clip earrings, 7927, $30; *Twilight Time*, 1959, necklace, 8738, $30; clip earrings, 7738, $30; *Colleen*, 1960, necklace, 8787, $30; clip earrings, 7787, $40.

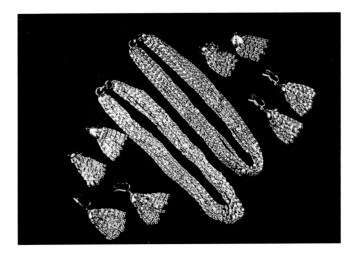

Silvery Cascade, 1960, necklace, 8749, $40; clip earrings, 7749, $35; pierced earrings, 7761, $25; in 1966, 18-inch necklace, 8581; *Golden Cascade*, 1962, necklace, 8896, $40; clip earrings, 7896, $35; pierced earrings, 7897, $25.

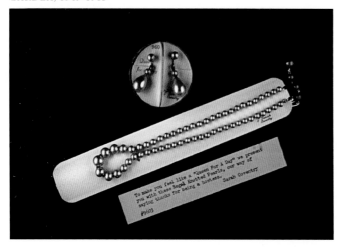

Queen For A Day, 1956, unsigned, necklace, 960, $100; screw back earrings, 9603, $55. The unusual numbers may indicate that this set was one of the first Hostess items.

Cameo Lady, 1960, narrow band ring, 5115, $15; in 1961, narrow band necklace, 8810, $20; wide band clip earrings, 7810, $30; narrow band pierced drops, 7840, $20; in 1962, wide band necklace, 8821, $25; wide band ring, 5121, $20; *Evening Profile*, 1964, necklace, 8951, $35; clip earrings, 7951, $45; ring, 5136, $20.

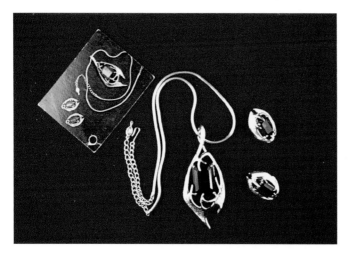

Molten Topaz, 1963, necklace, 8928, $50 clip earrings, 7928, $35.

Goddess of Fashion, 1962, necklace, 8885, $60; clip earrings, 7885, $30.

Sparkling Crystals, 1961, necklace, 8848, $110; unmarked clip earrings, 7848, $40.

First Love, 1958, necklace, 8690, $30; clip earrings, 7690, $30; originally inspired by Queen Elizabeth's first visit to America as a ruling monarch.

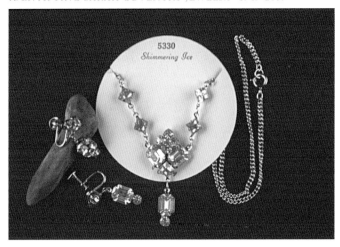

Shimmering Ice, 1951, unsigned, necklace, 5330, $60; screw back earrings, 5223, $40; also pierced earrings, 6215.

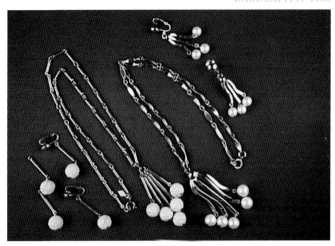

Matinee Elegance, 1962, necklace, 8855, $40; clip earrings, 7855, $20; pierced drops, 7898, $15; *A Touch of Elegance*, 1964, necklace, 8987, $45; clip earrings, 7987, $30.

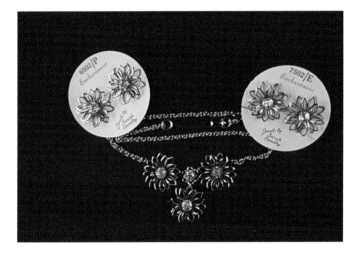

Enchantment, 1953, unsigned, necklace, 8502, $35; pins 6502, $30; screw back earrings, 7502, $30. The pins were sold only in pairs.

Fashion Parade, 1964, necklace, 8941, $60; clip earrings, 7941, $20; ring, 5137, $20; in 1968, stick pin, 6203, $30; shown in November 1963 *McCall's*.

Evening Rose, 1951, unsigned, necklace, 5343, $30; pin, 5143, $25; screw back earrings, 5243, $25; also bracelet, 5443.

Young & Gay, 1959, silver necklace, 8733, $20; bracelet, 9733, $15; clip earrings, 7733, $15; gold bracelet, 9583, $15; there were no other gold pieces; *Satin Glow*, 1965, necklace, 8575, $35; clip earrings, 7575, $35.

Golden Wardrobe, 1964, 3-strand necklace, 8513, $70; 1-strand necklace, 8500, $40; clip earrings, 7500, $30. The necklace can be worn as 3-strands, 2-strands, or 1-strand. Earrings can be worn without dangles. Two sets are shown for illustration.

Desert Flowers, 1960, necklace, 8776, $55; clip earrings, 7776, $30.

Wild Flower. 1953, unsigned, necklace, 5383, $50; bracelet, 5483, $50; clip earrings, 5281, $45; also pin, 5183; the earrings are a different number from the rest of the set, which was common in the early years; the bracelet came with a paper tag having the name printed on the tag, also common in the early years.

Royal Snowflake, 1950, unsigned, necklace, 5351, $35; pin, 5151, $30; screw back earrings, 5251, $40; *Crown Jewels*, 1949, unsigned, screw back earrings, 2202, $20; in 1950, number changed to 5230; in 1951, necklace, 5329, $25.

Hearts and Flowers, 1956, unsigned, necklace, 8606, $15; bracelet, 9606, $10; *White Hearts N' Flowers*, 1964, necklace, 8956, $15; bracelet, 9956, $15.

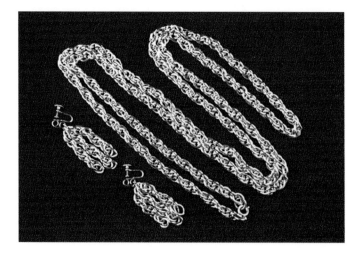

Pink Champagne, 1954, unsigned, necklace, 8542, $60; screw back earrings, 7542, $40; this has a very faint pink color to it.

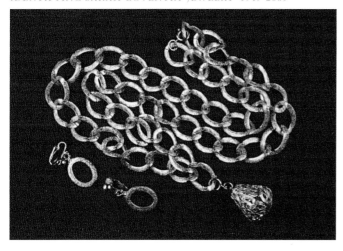

Golden Gypsy, 1964, necklace, 8945, $55; clip earrings, 7945, $20.

Heirloom, 1958, unsigned, necklace, 8678, $45; clip earrings, 7678, $30.

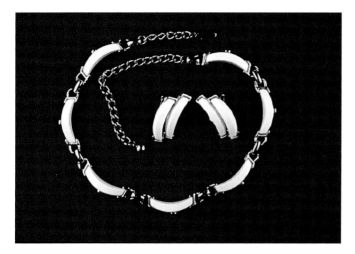

Holiday, 1958, unsigned, necklace, 8660, $45; clip earrings, 7660, $25.

Rainbow Cage, 1957, unsigned, necklace, 8636, $35; screw back earrings, 7636, $30; *Lantern of Love*, 1956, unsigned, bracelet, 9516, $30; in 1958, necklace with dangle, 8712, $45; also necklace without dangle, 8716; in 1959, clip earrings, 7716, $25.

Hidden Pearl, 1962, necklace, 8903, $30; clip earrings, 7903, $30; *Acorn Treasures*, 1964, necklace, 8934, $20; clip earrings, 7934, $20; *Pearl Magic*, 1958, necklace, 8670, $30; screw back earrings, 7670, $40.

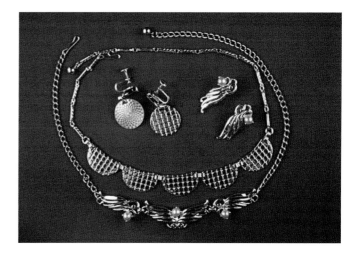

Inside: *Turnabout*, 1953, unsigned, necklace, $40; screw back earrings, $30; no numbers given in reference, one earring is turned to show the reverse pattern; Outside: *Winged Victory*, 1957, unsigned, necklace, 8651, $50; clip earrings, 7651, $25.

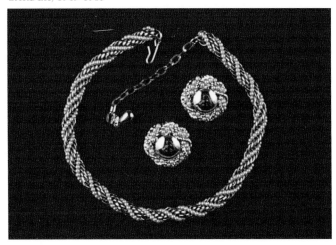

Embraceable, 1958, unsigned, necklace, 8698, $55; clip earrings, 7698, $30.

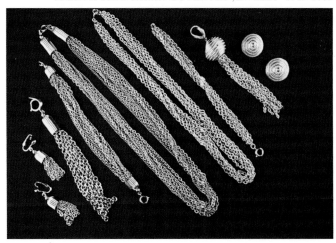

Career Girl, 1964, necklace, 8950, $70; clip earrings, 7950, $30; *Ultra Fashion*, 1960, necklace, 8565, $45; clip earrings, 7565, $30. Both sets are a combination of necklace, bracelet, and tassel pendant, which can be made into various combinations.

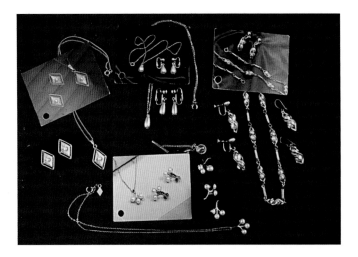

Top: *Debutante*, 1962, necklace, 8869, $20; clip earrings, 7869, $20; *One 'N Only*, 1959, 16-inch necklace, 8726, $20; clip earrings, 7726, $15; in 1960, 18-inch necklace, 8808; also spelled *One and Only*; *Twirling Pearls*, 1958, necklace, 8703, $45; screw back earrings, 7703, $20; in 1959, pierced earrings, 7739, $15; **Bottom:** *Trio*, 1962, necklace, 8902, $20; clip earrings, 7902, $20; tie tac, 5964, $20.

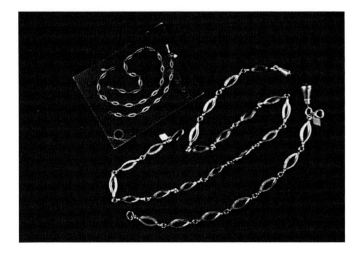

Delightful, 1964, necklace, 8986, $20; bracelet, 9986, $15.

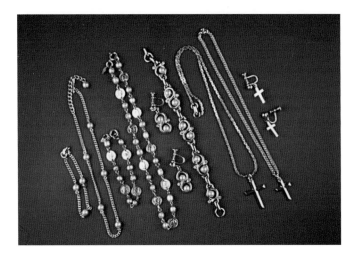

Ballerina, 1955, unsigned, necklace, 8506, $30; bracelet, 9506, $25; *Lucky Penny*, 1961, necklace, 8836, $25; bracelet, 9836, $20; *Mona Lisa*, 1953, unsigned, bracelet, 5483, $35; screw back earrings, 5283, $35; also necklace, 5383; *Simplicity*, 1950, unsigned, necklace, 1313, $45; in 1956, number changed to 5311; *Simplicity Jr*, 1957, unsigned, necklace, 8635, $25; *Simplicity*, 1956, unsigned, screw back earrings, 7631, $25; also pierced earrings, 7677 in 1957.

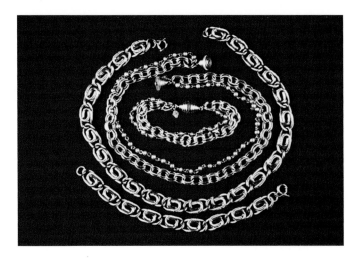

Inside to outside: *Gracious Lady*, 1959, necklace, 8736, $25; bracelet, 9736, $20; *Tailored Lady*, 1964, necklace, 8943, $30; bracelet, 9943, $15.

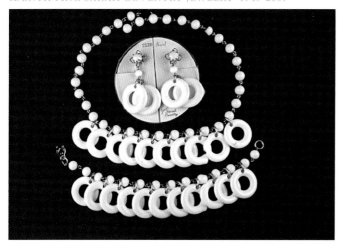

Swirl, 1956, unsigned, necklace, 8539, $50; bracelet, 9539, $40; screw back earrings, 7539, $30.

Reflections, 1957, unsigned tie bar, 5921, $25; unsigned cuff links, 5920, $30; ring, 5105, $25; clip earrings, 7625, $30; scarf holder, 5932, $25; also tie bar and cuff links set, 5092; *Balinese*, 1960, clip earrings, 7775, $30; cuff links, 5938, $30; tie bar, 5937, $25.

Nile Glory, 1955, unsigned, necklace, 8553, $55; bracelet, 9553, $30; *Embraceable*, 1965, reversible, necklace, 8547, $50; bracelet, 9547, $35; bracelet is turned over to show the reverse pattern.

Drum Beats, 1954, unsigned, bracelet, 9569, $30; screw back earrings, 7569, $40; also necklace, 8569, bracelet from the collection of Karen Walck Haley.

Tawny Shadows, 1954, unsigned, necklace, 8563, $55; bracelet, 9563, $30; screw back earrings, 7563, $25.

Dazzling Aurora, 1960, bracelet, 9769, $45; pin, 6737, $40; clip earrings, 7737, $30.

48

Lucky-in-Love, 1960, unsigned, bracelet, 9730, $20; clip earrings, 7730, $20; *Fashionette*, 1963, bracelet, 9921, $35; clip earrings, 7921, $25; *Pearl Flattery*, 1964, bracelet, 9936, $40; clip earrings, 7936, $30.

White Sophisticate, 1957, unsigned, necklace, 8621, $55; bracelet, 9621, $45; clip earrings, 7621, $30; *White Sophisticate*, 1965, bracelet, 9521, $40; clip earrings, 7521, $20.

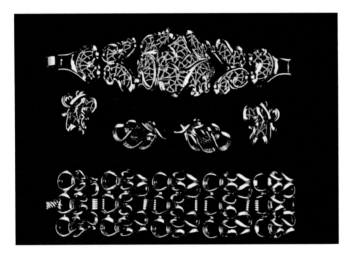

Butterfly Lace, 1962, bracelet, 9913, $35; clip earrings, 7913, $20; *Town and Country*, 1959, bracelet, 9757, $30; clip earrings, 7757, $20.

Frosted Leaves, 1965, pin, 6516, $20; bracelet, 9516, $40; clip earrings, 7516, $35.

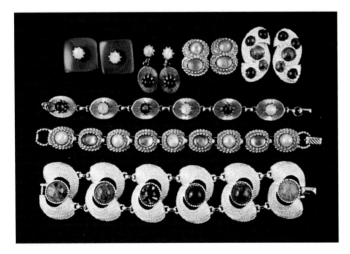

Night and Day, 1958, unsigned, small bracelet, 9626, $30; square clip earrings, 7681, $20; drop clip earrings, 7732, $20; also regular bracelet, 9681, square clip earrings were also sold as *Day and Night*, same date and item number; *Pastel Reflections*, 1962, bracelet, 9858, $45; clip earrings, 7858, $30; *Multi-Swirl*, 1963, bracelet, 9930, $35; clip earrings, 7930, $30.

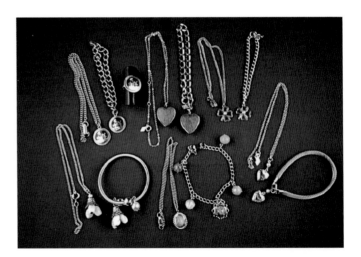

Top: *Dutch Girl*, 1957, unsigned, necklace, 8637, $15; bracelet, 9637, $15; ring, 5106, $20; *Goin' Steady*, 1961, necklace, 8835, $25; bracelet, 9835, $20; *St. Pat's*, 1956, unsigned, necklace, 8607, $15; bracelet, 9607, $10; **Bottom:** *Partytime*, 1962, unsigned, necklace, 8872, $20; bracelet, 9872, $20; *Charming Miss*, 1958, unsigned, necklace, 8696, $15; bracelet, 9696, $20; *Little Love*, 1958, necklace, 8704, $15; bracelet, 9704, $20.

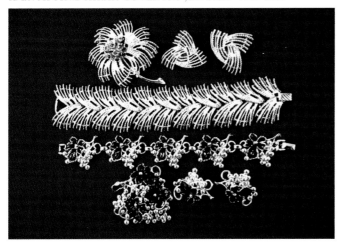

Celestial Spray, 1964, pin, 6946, $30; bracelet, 9946, $40; clip earrings, 7946, $20; *Golden Cluster*, 1961, pin, 6818, $25; bracelet, 9818, $35; clip earrings, 7818, $30.

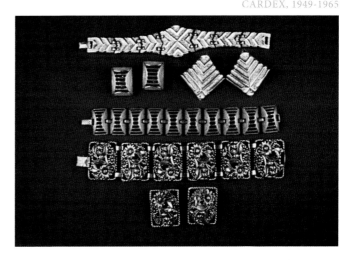

Top to Bottom: *Pyramid Treasures*, 1963, bracelet, 9925, $30; clip earrings, 7925, $20; *Tailored Classic*, 1964, bracelet, 9512, $30; clip earrings, 7512, $20; *Antique Garden*, 1962, bracelet, 9889, $60; clip earrings, 7889, $30.

Top to Bottom: *Sugar 'N Spice*, 1959, bracelet, 9728, $35; clip earrings, 7728, $30; *Happy Holiday*, 1961, bracelet, 9826, $35; clip earrings, 7826, $30; *Frolic*, 1954, unsigned, bracelet, 9577, $50; clip earrings, 7577, $25; also necklace, 8577; *Blue Hawaii*, 1962, bracelet, 9914, $35; clip earrings, 7914, $20; *Indian Treasures*, 1962, bracelet, 9888, $35; clip earrings, 7888, $20.

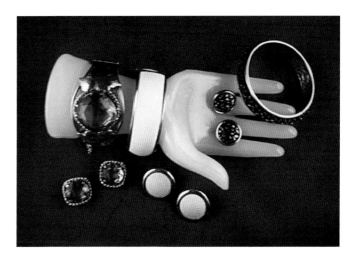

Versailles, 1964, bracelet, 9984, $70; clip earrings, 7984, $35; *Mademoiselle*, 1962, bracelet, 9905, $45; clip earrings, 7905, $30; *Indian Princess*, 1964, bracelet, 9954, $20; clip earrings, 7954, $20.

Carrousel, 1960, bracelet, 9791, $35; green clip earrings, 7791, $25; blue clip earrings, 7792, $25; item numbers for the red and brown clip earrings are presumed to be 7793 and 7794, but we cannot confirm it; *Fiesta*, 1956, unsigned, bracelet, 9596, $45; sea-blue clip earrings, 7596, $30; strawberry red clip earrings, 7647, $30; green clip earrings, 7734, $30.

Charm Converter, 1960, unsigned, gold, 9783, $15; silver, 9784, $15; *Powder Puff*, 1961, bracelet, 9815, $35; clip earrings, 7815, $30; *Frozen Lace*, 1955, unsigned, bracelet, 9565, $35; clip earrings, 7565, $25; *Necklace Extenders*, 1959, unsigned, 7523, $10; set of one gold and one silver chains; *Bracelet Extenders*, 1959, 7522, $10; set of one gold and one silver links.

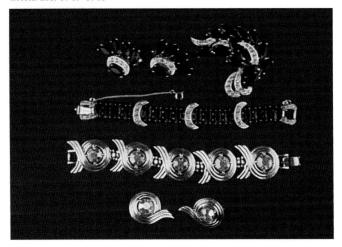

Vienna, 1964, bracelet, 9988, $80; pin, 6988, $50; clip earrings, 7988, $40; *Aurora Swirl*, 1962, bracelet, 9874, $50; clip earrings, 7874, $30.

Woven Classic, 1964, bracelet, 9939, $70; pin, 6939, $55; clip earrings, 7939, $30.

Heart Beats, 1957, unsigned, bracelet, 9627, $40; clip earrings, 7627, $30; also spelled *Heartbeats*.

Top: *Wisteria*, 1962, pin, 6871, $40; clip earrings, 7871, $30; *Raspberry Ice*, 1962, pin, 6852, $30; clip earrings, 7852, $30; *Swirl of Fashion*, 1958, black bracelet, 9658, $30; clip earrings, 7658, $25; blue clip earrings, 7659, $25; also blue bracelet, 9659; **Bottom:** *Alaskan Summer*, 1961, pin, 6854, $40; clip earrings, 7854, $30; bracelet, 9854, $45; modeled by Bess Myerson in March 1962 *McCall's*.

Breath of Spring, 1958, unsigned; bracelet, 9663, $40; pin, 6663, $30; clip earrings, 7663, $30.

Multi-colored Spray, 1949, unsigned, pin, 1109, $110; screw back earrings, 1209, $90; from the collection of Karen Walck Haley.

Golden Oak, 1953, pin, $60 and screw back earrings, $40; no numbers given in the reference, shown in the March 1953 *Vogue* magazine ad, "created in rich leather, golden-edged. Acorn earrings complete the matching set." It was named to receive the Fashion Academy Gold Medal Award for 1953.

Golden Swirl, 1960, pin, 6571, $35; clip earrings, 7571, $30; *Windfall*, 1962, pin, 6870, $30; clip earrings, 7870, $30; *Sun Flower*, 1963, pin, 6937, $35; clip earrings, 7937, $30.

Mardi Gras, 1956, unsigned, pin, 6583, $25; clip earrings, 7583, $30; *Black-Eyed Susan*, 1955, unsigned, pin, 6572, $30; clip earrings, 7572, $25.

Galaxy, 1962, pin, 6880, $40; clip earrings, 7880, $40; shown in 1962 *McCall's*, month unknown.

American Beauty, 1961, pin, 6837, $30; clip earrings, 7837, $30.

Top: *Azure Snowflake*, 1949, unsigned, pin, 1104, $15; in 1950, number changed: pin, 5104, screw back earrings, 5200, $40; *Wedgewood Cameo*, 1949, unsigned, small pin, 1102, $25; large pin, 1101, $50; screw back earrings, 1201, $50; in 1950, numbers changed: small pin, 5102, large pin, 5111, screw back earrings, 5211; *Butterfly*, 1957, unsigned, pin, 6614, $25; clip earrings, 7614, $30; *Bursting Charm*, 1950, unsigned, pin, 5180, $30; screw back earrings, 5280, $35; **Bottom:** *Love Blossoms*, 1958, pin, 6655, $30; clip earrings, 7655, $30.

Chit-Chat, 1959, chatelaine pins, 6771, $20; dainty clip earrings, 7771, $20; daring clip earrings, 7802, $25.

Stardust, 1958, unsigned, pin, 6687, $45; clip earrings, 7687, $90; *Kathleen*, 1964, pin, 6509, $50; clip earrings, 7509, $70; ring, 5151, $35; *Celestial Ice*, 1960, pin, 6882, $45; clip earrings, 7882, $45.

Blue Lagoon, 1964, pin, 6991, $65; clip earrings, 7991, $40.

Camellia, 1962, pin, 6909, $30; clip earrings, 7909, $35.

Heart's Desire, 1958, pin, 6656, $25; clip earrings, 7656, $25.

Fashion Flower, 1961, pin, 6834, $35; daring clip earrings, 7834, $45; dainty clip earrings, 7875, $30.

53

Top: Staburst, 1961, pin, 6838, $30; clip earrings, 7838, $45; also spelled *Star-Burst*, shown in September 1961 *Woman's Day* and modeled by Bess Myerson in March 1962 *McCall's*; **Bottom:** *Mosaic*, 1963, pin, 6940, $45; clip earrings, 7940, $30.

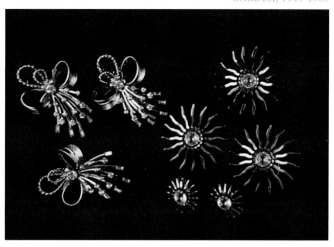

Vogue, 1960, pin, 6797, $30; clip earrings, 7797, $50; *Fascination*, 1959, pin, 6712, $15; dainty clip earrings, 7712, $15; daring clip earrings, 7507, $20.

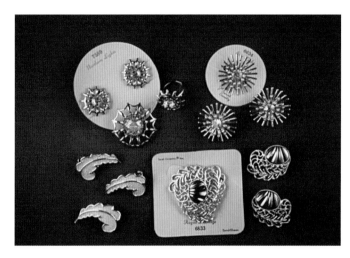

Top: *Northern Lights*, 1956, unsigned, pin, 6589, $30; clip earrings, 7589, $30; in 1957, ring, 5104, $25; *Star Light*, 1957, unsigned, pin, 6634, $25; clip earrings, 7634, $50; **Bottom:** *Sugar Charmers*, 1958, unsigned, pin, 6654, $15; clip earrings, 7654, $30; *Royal Plumage*, 1962, pin, 6833, $30; clip earrings, 7833, $30.

Top: *Sea Treasure*, 1959, unsigned, pin, 6613, $20; clip earrings, 7613, $30; *Ebb Tide*, 1960, pin, 6812, $20; clip earrings, 7812, $30; *Splendor*, 1961, pin, 6839, $20; clip earrings, 7839, $30; **Bottom:** *Bittersweet*, 1962, pin, 6868, $25; clip earrings, 7878, $20; *Coronation*, 1959, pin, 6717, $30; clip earrings, 7717, $30; *Elegance*, 1957, unsigned, pin, 6633, $35; clip earrings, 7633, $35.

Pearl Bloom, 1965, pin, 6518, $20; clip earrings, 7518, $20; *Pearl Elegance*, 1963, pin, 6929, $30; clip earrings, 7929, $35; *Fashion Flair*, 1965, pin, 6533, $35; clip earrings, 7533, $35.

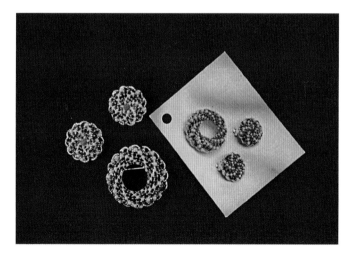

Song of India, 1965, pin, 6576, $40; clip earrings, 7576, $60; shown in January 1966 *Redbook* magazine.

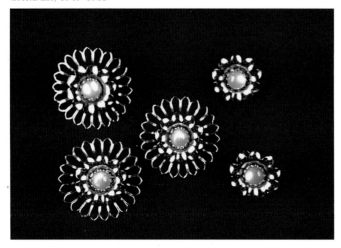

Pink Passion, 1958, unsigned, pin, 6666, $25; dainty clip earrings, 7666, $25; daring clip earrings, 7505, $40.

Eclipse, 1956, unsigned, pin, 6585, $15; screw back earrings, 7585, $25; *Daisy Mae*, 1960, pin, 6793, $35; clip earrings, 7793, $20.

Pinwheel, 1962, pin, 6886, $30; clip earrings, 7886, $20; also spelled *Pin Wheel*; *Feather Fantasy*, 1959, pin, 6765, $30; dainty clip earrings, 7765, $20; daring clip earrings, 7807, $30.

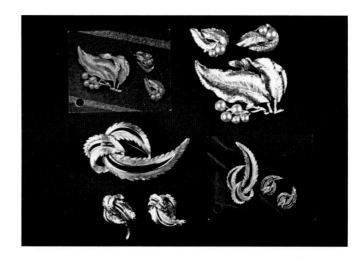

Top: *Silvery Splendor*, 1964, pin, 6953, $30; clip earrings, 7953, $30; **Bottom:** *Feathered Fashion*, 1964, pin, 6505, $30; clip earrings, 7505, $30.

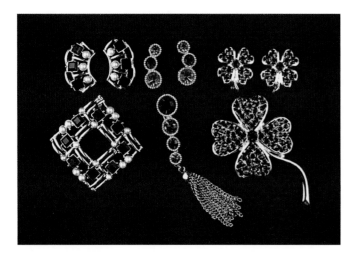

Contessa, 1959, pin, 6745, $30; clip earrings, 7745, $20; *Saucy*, 1965, pin, 6504, $30; in 1966, clip earrings, 7504, $30; *Pink Ice*, 1964, pin, 6503, $35; clip earrings, 7503, $50.

Top: *Satin Petals*, 1964, pin, 6952, $30; clip earrings, 7952, $30; *Peta-Lure*, 1962, pin, 6911, $30; clip earrings, 7911, $30; *Honey Bunch*, 1960, pin, 6799, $30; clip earrings, 7799, $30; **Bottom:** *Cameo Lace*, 1957, pin, 6648, $25; clip earrings, 7748, $25; *Endearing*, 1965, pin, 6564, $50; clip earrings, 7564, $35; *Designer's Choice*, 1962, pin, 6891, $50; clip earrings, 7891, $30; shown in December 1962 *Woman's Day*.

Black Diamond, 1955, unsigned, pin, 6573, $30; clip earrings, 7573, $30; in 1957, ring, 5102, $35.

Harvest Time, 1960, pin, 6782, $30; clip earrings, 7782, $30; *Flair*, 1957, unsigned, pin, 6618, $30; clip earrings, 7618, $30; *Golden Fern*, 1951, unsigned, pin, 5188, $35; in 1956, clip earrings, 7576, $45.

Aqua Swirl, 1956, unsigned, pin, 6624, $15; clip earrings, 7624, $15; in 1958, ring, 5109, $15; also pierced earrings, 7724; *Clover Lights*, 1959, unsigned, pin, 6747, $15; clip earrings, 7747, $20; *Autumn Haze*, 1964, pin, 6511, $30; clip earrings, 7511, $20.

Black Saturn, 1961, pin, 6813, $30; clip earrings, 7813, $35; *Pearlized Perfection*, 1965, pin, 6569, $30; clip earrings, 7569, $30; *Siam*, 1962, pin, 6908, $30; clip earrings, 7908, $30.

Summer Magic, 1964, necklace, 8955, $50; pin, 6949, $35; clip earrings, 7949, $35.

Golden Cherries, 1964, pin, 6507, $20; clip earrings, 7507, $30; *Daisy*, 1964, pin, 6919, $20; clip earrings, 7919, $15.

Top: *Aqua-Fleur*, 1964, pin, 6502, $20; clip earrings, 7502, $20; *Spring Bouquet*, 1957, unsigned, pin, 6617, $30; clip earrings, 7617, $30; **Bottom:** *Shindig*, 1965, pin-barrette 6549, $20; barrette 6550, $20.

Top: *Accent*, 1958, pin, 6640, $20; clip earrings, 7640, $20; *Vogue*, 1955, unsigned, pin, 6531, $25; clip earrings, 7531, $25; *Enchantment*, 1958, pin, 6668, $20; clip earrings, 7668, $20; **Bottom:** *Firefly*, 1951, unsigned, pin, 5190, $55; clip earrings, 5290, $95; *Tantalizing*, 1958, unsigned, pin, 6653, $25; clip earrings, 7517, $35; over and under earrings, 7563, $25.

Prima Donna, 1953, unsigned, necklace, 8510, $50; bracelet, 9510, $60; screw back earrings, 7510, $40; pin, 6510, $50; shown in the November 1, 1953, *Vogue* magazine and "named to receive the Fashion Academy Gold Medal Award".

You and Me, 1950, unsigned, pin, 5101, $50; screw back earrings, 5201, $50; from the collection of Karen Walck Haley; also tie clasp, 5603, and cuff links, 5602.

Black Beauty, 1962, pin, 6863, $20; clip earrings, 7863, $20; ring, 5124, $15.

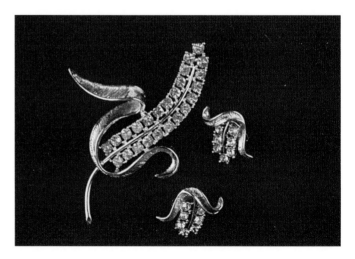

Radiance, 1964, pin, 6932, $30; clip earrings, 7932, $30.

Sunrise, 1958, unsigned, pin, 6701, $20; clip earrings, 7701, $35.

Windsor, 1955, unsigned, pin, 6545, $30; clip earrings, 7545, $30; earrings from the collection of Karen Walck Haley.

Top: *Summer Lace*, 1957, unsigned, pin, 6616, $30; clip earrings, 7616, $40; *Snow Flower*, 1965, pin, 6515, $35; clip earrings, 7515, $35; **Middle:** *Pin Wheel*, 1957, unsigned, pin, 6615, $25; clip earrings, 7615, $20; also spelled *Pinwheel*; **Bottom:** *Lily*, 1956, unsigned, pin, 6581, $15; screw back earrings, 7581, $20; *Symphony*, 1955, unsigned, pin, 6580, $20; screw back earrings, 7580, $20.

Sculptured Cameo, 1951, unsigned, pin, 5161, $15; screw back earrings, 5261, $25; *Golden Sunburst*, 1949, unsigned, pin, 1125, $90; screw back earrings, 1225, $60.

Evening Comet, 1965, pin, 6573, $40; clip earrings, 7573, $40.

Top: *Fashion Leaf*, 1961, pin, 6788, $35; clip earrings, 7788, $30; shown in March 1961 *Woman's Day* magazine; *Nature's Choice*, 1964, pin, 6933, $30; clip earrings, 7933, $30.

Top: *Sunburst*, 1957, unsigned, pin, 6629, $30; daring clip earrings, 7503, $40; dainty clip earrings, 7629, $30; *Star Flower*, 1955, unsigned, pin, 6586, $15; screw back earrings, 7856, $25; *Modern Twist*, 1960, pin, 6766, $20; clip earrings, 7766, $20. **Middle:** *Smart Set*, 1960, pin, 6742, $20; clip earrings, 7742, $20; *Rapture*, 1958, unsigned, pin, 6688, $35; clip earrings, 7688, $35; *Heritage*, 1958, pin, 6693, $20; clip earrings, 7693, $20. **Bottom:** *Trumpet Flower*, 1956, unsigned, pin, 6588, $20; clip earrings, 7588, $25.

Top: *Symphony*, 1964, pin, 6508, $30; clip earrings, 7508, $30; *Pearl Flight*, 1957, pin, 6641, $30; dainty clip earrings, 7641, $30; daring clip earrings, 7684, $50; **Middle:** *Lotus Blossom*, 1962, pin, 6866, $30; clip earrings, 7866, $30; *Precious*, 1964, pin, 6989, $65; clip earrings, 7989, $35; *Sea Whispers*, 1962, pin, 6890, $30; clip earrings, 7890, $20; **Bottom:** *Wind Flower*, 1963, pin, 6924, $30; clip earrings, 7924, $20.

Pink Radiance, 1959, pin, 6715, $30; clip earrings, 7715, $40; *Golden Scepter*, 1959, unsigned, pin, 6714, $30; clip earrings, 7714, $40.

Primrose, 1962, pin, 6910, $30; clip earrings, 7910, $20; *Snow White*, 1964, pin, 6948, $20; clip earrings, 7948, $20.

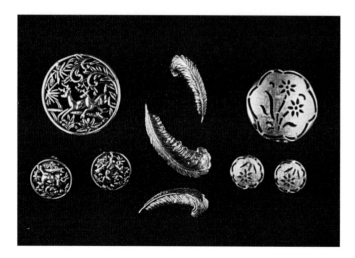

Woodland Flight, 1958, unsigned, pin, 6696, $40; clip earrings, 7696, $30; *Feather Froth*, 1955, unsigned, pin, 6543, $15; clip earrings, 7543, $25; also spelled *Featherfroth*; *Silhouette*, 1960, pin, 6572, $40; clip earrings, 7572, $30.

Aurora Lights, 1965, pin, 6514, $35; clip earrings, 7514, $40; *Amber-Lites*, 1961, pin, 6849, $45; clip earrings, 7849, $30; *Lime-Light*, 1960, pin, 6781, $40; clip earrings, 7781, $30.

Patrician, 1960, unsigned, pin, 6755, $30; clip earrings, 7755, $30.

Crescent, 1964, pin, 6985, $20; clip earrings, 7985, $30; *Satin Flame*, 1960, pin, 6778, $30; clip earrings, 7778, $30.

Evening Snowflake, 1963, pin, 6926, $45; clip earrings, 7926, $45; *Bird of Paradise*, 1965, pin, 6534, $40; clip earrings, 7534, $40; *Evening Accent*, 1965, pin, 6574, $40; clip earrings, 7574, $40.

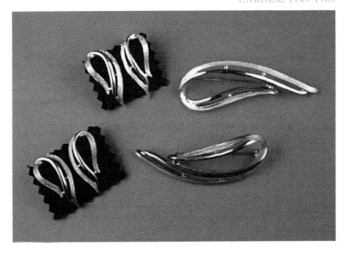

Stunning, 1958, silver clip earrings, 7692, $15; in 1960, silver pin, 6692, $15; gold pin, 6719, $15; gold clip earrings, 7719, $15. The gold set is also found in a F/W 1971 Zone G catalog with numbers 6458 for the pin and 7458 for the earrings. The catalog provides no information on the location of Zone G.

Adam's Delight, 1961, silver pin, 6820, $30; clip earrings, 7820, $20; gold pin, 6900, $30; clip earrings, 7900, $20; shown in December 1961 *Woman's Day* magazine.

Sarah's Circle, 1965, gold pin, 6520, $20; clip earrings, 7520, $20; silver pin, 6582, $20; clip earrings, 7582, $20.

Silvery Maple, 1958, pin, 6689, $20; clip earrings, 7689, $25; *Golden Maple*, 1956, pin, 6587, $20; clip earrings, 7587, $30.

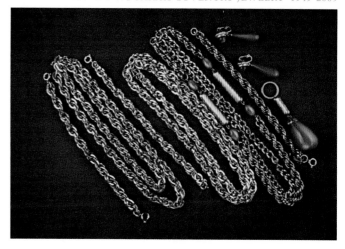

Bib 'N Tucker, 1957, gold necklace, 8630, $50; bracelet, 9630, $25; in 1958, silver necklace, 8705, $45; bracelet, 9705, $20; *Golden Avocado*, 1962, necklace, 8895, $75; clip earrings, 7895, $30; has removable bracelet and dangle.

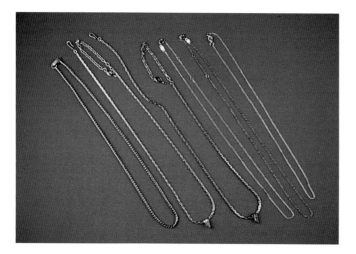

Utility 17-inch Chain, 1951, unsigned, gold, 5339, $20; also in silver, 5338; *Versatility 18-inch Chain*, 1961, gold, 8780, $15; silver, 8779, $15; came with a pendant holder; *Beauty 18-inch Chain*, 1961, 12k gold-filled, 8843, $20; sterling silver, 8844, $20; *Sterling Silver 16-inch Chain*, 1950, unsigned, 5316, $20; same links as *Beauty Chain*.

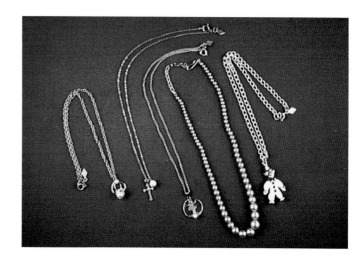

Most Precious, 1960, 8801, $20; *My Choice*, 1964, 8944, $20; *Little Lady*, 1965, 8531, $20; *Little Lady Pearls*, 1957, unsigned, 8652, $25; *Funny Face*, 1962, 8859, $20.

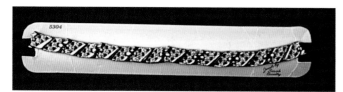

Golden Ice, 1950, unsigned, 5304, $75; from the collection of Karen Walck Haley; also clip earrings, 5204, and bracelet, 5404; originally released in 1949 as necklace, 1304, bracelet, 1404, clip earrings, 1204.

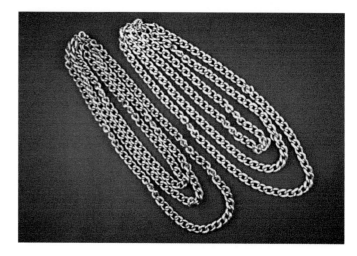

Smart 'N' Snappy, 1961, gold, 8823, $75; silve,r 8824, $75; 3-section chain of 16, 18, and 21-inch chain sections.

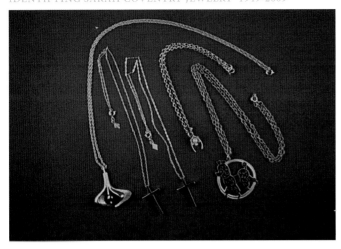

Danish Modern, 1965, unsigned, 8548, $40; *Calvary*, 1962, gold, 8915, $30; silver, 8916, $30; *Promise*, 1956, unsigned, 8600, $30; *Puppy Love*, 1960, unsigned, 8754, $30.

Juke-Box, 1960, 8803, $40; *Picturesque Locket*, 1960, 8751, $40; *Fashion Circle*, 1962, 8904, $50; *Stunning-Plus*, 1964, unsigned, 8935, $40; *Classic*, 1962, 8912, $45; shown in January 1963 *Redbook*.

Birthstone Pendant, 1965, 8535-8546, $45; Back: February, March, August; Front: September, October, December, April, May, June, July, November. Not shown: January.

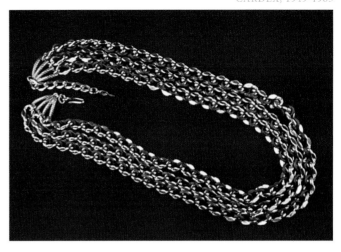

Bib O' Fashion, 1965, 8567, $45.

Fashion Twist Necklace/Bracelet, 1965, unsigned, 8532, $50.

Quick Silver, 1955, unsigned, necklace, 8552, $30; also bracelet, 9552; *Slave Chain*, 1958, unsigned, necklace, 8669, $40; also bracelet, 9669.

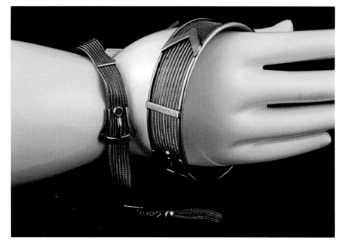

Golden Weave, 1949, unsigned, bracelet, 3423, $50; also necklace, 3323 and screw back earrings, 3324; in 1950, earrings discontinued and numbers changed for necklace to 5223 and bracelet to 5423; *Golden Cavalier*, 1949, unsigned, 3425, $60; discontinued in 1950. Both are from the collection of Karen Walck Haley.

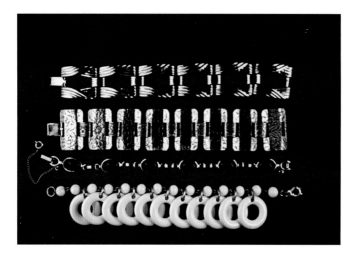

Gad-A-Bout, 1964, 9510, $30; *Brocade*, 1955, unsigned, 9556, $25; from the collection of Karen Walck Haley; *Harmony*, 1964, 9983, $30; *Swirl*, 1956, unsigned, 9539, $40; also necklace, 8539 and earrings, 7539.

International Belt, 1964, unsigned, large 26-32 inch, 9993, $105; also small 22-28 inch, 9992.

Sea Charms, 1964, 9990, $30; shown in July 1964 *Woman's Day*.

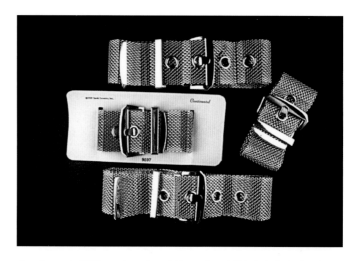

Continental, 1956, unsigned, gold bracelet, 9597, $50; belt, 9613, $120; silver bracelet, 9649, $50; belt, 9654, $120.

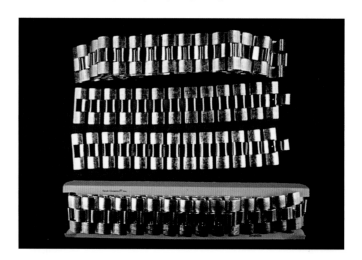

Four Seasons, 1962, gold belt, 5960, $110; bracelet, 9883, $35; silver belt, 5961, $110; bracelet, 9884, $35.

Pert 'N Saucy, 1958, unsigned, silver, 9685, $30; gold, 9686, $30; can be worn as earrings, bracelet, or sweater guard; also known as the *Saucy Sweater Guard*.

Golden Bangle, 1965, bracelet, 9568, $40; in 1966, clip earrings, 7568, $35.

English Echo, 1955, unsigned, 9558, $25; *Wheel of Fortune*, 1960, unsigned, 9795, $50.

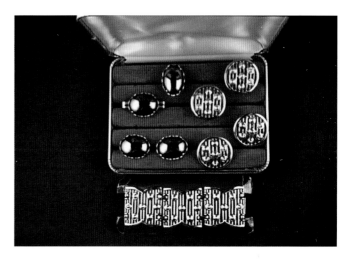

Reflections, 1957, clip earrings, 7925, $30; scarf holder, 5932, $25; ring, 5105, $25; *Golden Rain*, 1957, unsigned, bracelet, 9639, $40; clip earrings, 7639, $25; cuff links 5916, $25.

Memory Locket, 1951, unsigned, 5402, $35; in 1953, number changed to 9542; *Playmate*, 1962, unsigned, 9879, $20.

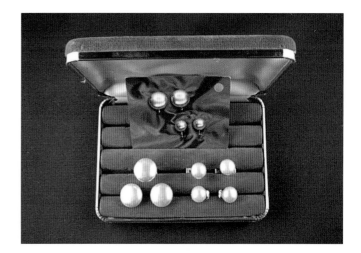

Button Pearl, 1960, unsigned, dainty clip earrings, 7646, $15; cuff links, 5946, $35; daring clip earrings, 7805, $20; cuff links 5948, $35; one daring cuff link shown; the dainty clip earrings were first released in 1957 as *Petite Pearls* clip earrings, same item number.

Top: *Golden Mist*, 1957, unsigned, ring, 5107, $30; in 1958, drop, 6679, $30; clip earrings, 7657, $50; *Tie Tac Set*, 1963, unsigned, 6750, $35; designed for "him" and for "her" or they can be worn in pairs; Bottom: *Confetti*, 1959, clip earrings, 7710, $20; ring, 5110, $15; *Carnival*, 1962, clip earrings, 7901, $20; ring, 5134, $15.

Golden Stallion, 1950, unsigned, 5123, $50; *Joyful Joe*, 1953, unsigned, 6503, $40; *Joy*, 1953, unsigned, 6546, $40.

Beauty Buttons, 1957, clip earrings, 7644, $30; cuff links, 5922, $30; *Queen of the Nile*, 1958, cuff links, 5927, $25; also clip earrings, 7707, and tie bar, 5929.

Top: *Sunrise*, 1951, unsigned, 5189, $30; *Petite*, 1954, unsigned, 6523, $30; Bottom: *Opal Star*, 1951, unsigned, 5117, $20. You could order one pin, 5117, or you could order two pins and chain, 5087, or you could order just the chain, 5339; *Night Owl*, 1959, 6777, $30; *Cloisonné*, 1949, unsigned, 1106, $15; in 1950, number changed to 5107.

Laurel Wreath Initial, 1949, unsigned, 1116-1141, $20; all 26 letters available, from the collection of Karen Walck Haley.

Top: *Sapphire Snowflake*, 1949, unsigned, 1108, $15; in 1950, number changed to 5108; *Black-Eyed Susan*, 1953, unsigned, 6572, $30; also earrings, 7572; *Fleur-de-Lis*, 1949, unsigned, 1123, $20; Middle: *Lady Bug*, 1956, 6598, $15; *Lucky Leaf*, 1949, unsigned, emerald, 1106, $15; aqua, 1105, $15; in 1950, numbers changed to emerald, 5106, aqua, 5105; Bottom: *Sittin' Pretty*, 1962, unsigned, 6857, $10; *Whimsey*, 1953, unsigned, pin, $25; also necklace and earrings, and all are shown in early literature without item numbers; *Ruby Tipped Snowflake*, 1949, unsigned, 5103, $15.

Starlit Trio, 1962, 6853, $60; two are shown to illustrate how it can be worn as three separate pins.

Renaissance, 1953, unsigned, 6516, $40.

Sea Star, 1954, unsigned, 6544, $25; released again in 1956 as *Sand Star*, 6582; *Melody*, 1953, unsigned, 5119, $25; *Crescent*, 1959, 6746, $25.

Blue Lilys, 1950, unsigned, 5152, $30; from the collection of Karen Walck Haley; also earrings, 5252; *Heartbeat*, 1953, unsigned, 6517, $40; *Wishbone*, 1955, unsigned, 6518, $20; *Jupiter*, 1950, unsigned, 5128, $30; also necklace, 5328, and earrings, 5228; *Moonglow*, 1949, unsigned, 1115, $25; in 1950, number changed to 5115.

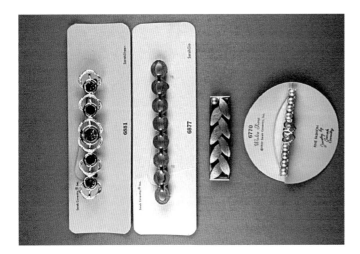

Left to right bar pins: *Amber-Jet*, 1961, 6881, $20; *Chanel-Bar*, 1960, 6877, $20; *Pin-Barrette*, 1964, 6506, $30; *Waltz Time*, 1959, 6770, $20.

Top: *Royal Crest*, 1958, silver, 6695, $30; gold, 6694, $30; can be worn as a pendant; *Griffin*, 1959, no number in reference, $30; **Middle:** *Little Doe*, 1964, 6931, $20; *Spring Bouquet*, 1965, 6519, $35; **Bottom:** *Mardi Gras*, 1956, unsigned, 6583, $20; also earrings, 7583; *Tropicana*, 1962, 6873, $35; shown in June 1962 *Woman's Day*; *Flirtation*, 1963, 6942, $30.

Top: *Fantasy*, 1962, 6887, $30; *High Fashion*, 1962, 6892, $50; **Bottom:** *Flirtation*, 1959, 6735, $30; *Solitude*, 1962, 6906, $20; *Sheath*, 1950, unsigned, 5113, $25.

Top: *Heirloom*, 1953, unsigned, 5185, $20; *Royal Scepter*, 1960, 6800, $60; *Ivy Swirl*, 1950, unsigned, 5149, $30; **Bottom:** *Queen Mary*, 1950, unsigned, 5153, $50; *Symphonette*, 1953, unsigned, 6530, $50.

Bow Knot, 1950, unsigned, 5101, $50.

Sarah's A.B.C.'s, 1964, 6957 – 6982, $20; all 26 letters available. They were sold for many years and can be found in various shades of gold.

Back Row: *Amethyst Pearl*, 1950, unsigned, 5224 (one shown), $20; *Moonglow*, 1949, unsigned, 2204, $20; in 1950, number changed to 5232; *Bit of Ireland*, 1949, unsigned, 1210, $30; in 1950, number changed to 5210; **Middle Row:** *Simulated Pearl Studded Helmet*, 1950, unsigned, 1218, $15; *Jade Moonstone*, 1949, unsigned, 2203, $15; in 1950, number changed to 5213; *Gayety*, 1950, unsigned, 5245, $30; also necklace, 5345 and bracelet, 5445; **Front Row:** *Midnight*, 1950, unsigned, 5221, $25; *Misty Dew Drop*, 1949, unsigned, 1215, $15; in 1950, number changed to 5213. All are screw back and from the collection of Karen Walck Haley.

Top: *Coffee Break*, 1958, unsigned, clip earrings, 7683, $20; *Love and Marriage*, 1958, unsigned, clip earrings, 7682, $20; *Bud 'N Bloom*, 1960, clip earrings, 7760, $30; **Middle:** *Trio*, 1954, unsigned, screw back, 7504, $20; *Color Frame*, 1959, clip earrings, gold, 7772, $30; silver, 7827, $30; **Bottom:** *Pierced Classics*, 1965, unsigned, gold, 7529, $30; pearl 7528, $30; *Pearl Contour*, 1963, clip earrings, 7920, $30.

Top: *Saucy*, 1961, clip earrings, 7841, $30; *Fan-Fare*, 1959, clip earrings, 7756, $20; *Delicate Lace*, 1959, clip earrings, 7821, $20; **Row 2:** *Golden Allure*, 1958, clip earrings, 7706, $20; **Row 3:** *Flair*, 1962, clip earrings, 7862, $25; *Portrait*, 1961, clip earrings, 7842, $25; **Bottom:** One earring each, all unsigned: *Bewitching*, 1958, screw back, 7509, $30; *Gay Chandelier*, 1958, screw back, 7702, $25; *Palmetto*, 1956, clip earrings, 7591, $30; *Tangerine*, 1955, clip earrings, 7521, $30.

Mardi-Gras, 1959, clip earrings, 7773, $25; *Around the World*, 1958, unsigned, clip earrings, 7664, $35; also bracelet, 9664; *Jubilee*, 1953, unsigned, clip earrings, 7515, $40; from the collection of Karen Walck Haley; also necklace, 8515.

Top: *Wedding Bell*, 1953, unsigned, screw back, 7525, $30; *Demure*, 1961, clip earrings, 7752, $15; *Exotic*, 1962, clip earrings, 7864, $25; **Middle:** *Hidden Fire*, 1960, clip earrings, 7731, $30; *Contoura*, 1962, clip earrings, 7865, $25; *Moonburst*, 1955, unsigned, clip earrings, 7550, $20; **Bottom:** *Jet Flight*, 1961, clip earrings, 7811, $45; *Mystic*, 1963, clip earrings, 7922, $30.

Top: *Gypsy*, 1956, unsigned, screw back, silver, 7519, $40; gold, 7672, $40; reverse from a shiny side to a patterned side; *Trapeze*, 1959, unsigned, clip earrings, 7720, $40; a 3-piece set that can be worn with one, two, or all three pieces: **Middle:** *Thunderbird*, 1960, clip earrings, 7774, $30; *Summer Frost*, 1956, clip earrings, 7727, $30; also pin, 6727; *He Loves Me*, 1958, unsigned, clip earrings, 7506, $30; *Balinese*, 1960, clip earrings, 7775, $30; *Summer Frost*, 1953, unsigned, clip earrings, $25; no number given in reference; **Bottom:** *Shooting Star*, 1960, clip earrings, 7740, $20; *Danger*, 1955, unsigned, clip earrings, 7548, $30.

Blue Blossom, 1953, unsigned, screw back, 7547, $40; from the collection of Karen Walck Haley.

Top: *Pearl Duet*, 1965, 5152, $35; *Blush Pearl*, 1960, 5116, $30; **Bottom:** *Pearl Mates*, 1959, unsigned, 5110, $20; *Sweet & Lovely*, 1961, 5119, $20.

Top: *Whirling Flame*, 1953, unsigned, screw back, 7551, $30; *Senorita*, 1953, unsigned, screw back, 7549, $15; *Sorcery*, 1962, clip earrings, 7861, $20; **Middle:** *Dancing Pearl*, 1960, clip earrings, 7729, $30; *Wings of Fashion*, 1957, unsigned, clip earrings, 7643, $30; *Sorcery*, 1954, unsigned, screw back, 7508, $20; *Golden Treasure*, 1956, unsigned, screw back, 5222, $20; **Bottom:** *Glamour Rings*, 1958, screw back, 7691, $20; *Prima Donna*, 1953, unsigned, screw back, 7510, $40; also necklace, 8510; bracelet, 9510; and pin, 6510; shown in the November 1, 1953, *Vogue* magazine and "named to receive the Fashion Academy Gold Medal Award"; *Slim 'N' Trim*, 1962, clip earrings, 7860, $20; *Cockle Shells*, 1957, unsigned, clip earrings, 7619, $30; *Petite Pearls*, 1957, clip earrings, 7646, $15; released again in 1960 as the dainty Button Pearl clip earrings, same item number.

Celebrity, 1962, 5123, $35; *Parisienne Nights*, 1961, 5118, $35; *Midnight Magic*, 1959, unsigned, 5108, $30.

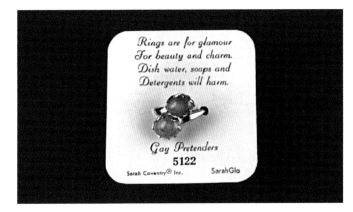

Gay Pretenders, 1962, 5122, $20.

Top: *Black Diamond*, 1957, unsigned, 5102, $20; *Bewitching*, 1965, 5153, $40; *Nite Lites*, 1961, unsigned, 5117, $35; also spelled *Night Lites*; **Middle:** *Black Beauty*, 1962, 5124, $15; *After-Five*, 1964, 5135, $30; *Northern Lights*, 1957, unsigned, 5104, $25; *Aqua Swirl*, 1956, unsigned, 5109, $15; *Night 'N' Day*, 1962, 5120, $20; *Dutch Girl*, 1957, unsigned, 5106, $20; **Bottom:** *Moonlight Cascade*, 1957, 5101, $30; *Kathleen*, 1964, 5151, $35; *First Lady*, 1960, 5113, $25.

Reflections, 1957, unsigned, 5105, $25; *Sabrina Fair*, 1960, 5114, $20; *Fashion Parade*, 1964, 5137, $20; *Pearl Of The Sea*, 1957, unsigned, 5103, $30.

Carnival, 1962, 5134, $15; *Golden Mist*, 1957, unsigned, 5107, $30; *Confetti*, 1959, 5111, $15.

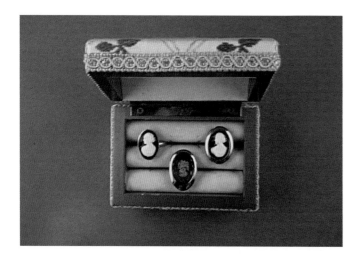

Cameo Lady, 1960, unsigned, 5115, $15; *Evening Profile*, 1964, 5136, $20; *Cameo Lady*, 1962, 5121, $20.

Row 1: *Birthstone Ring*, 1964, 5138-5149, $50; Front: January – March; **Row 2:** April – July; **Row 3:** August – September; Back: October – December.

Men's Jewelry

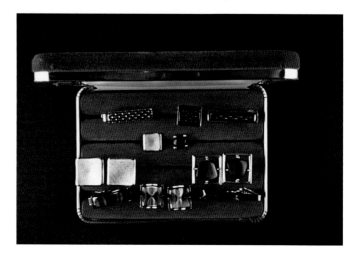

Top: *Debonair*, 1956, unsigned, tie bar, 5905, $20; also cuff links, 5906; *Debonair*, 1965, tie bar, 5988, $20; cuff links, 5989, $25; **Middle:** *Times Square*, 1963, tie tac, 5962, $20; cuff links, 5963, $25; *The New Yorker*, 1965, tie tac, 5979, $20; cuff links, 5980, $35; **Bottom:** *Smart Set*, 1962, tie bar, 5958, $20; cuff links, 5959, $30; *Olympic*, 1960, tie bar, 5939, $15; also cuff links, 5940.

Fidelity, 1957, unsigned, 5924, $15; *Diplomat*, 1955, tie bar, 5901, $20; cuff links, 5902, $30; *Windsor-Tip*, 1950, unsigned, tie bar, 5665, $25; cuff links (one shown) 5675, $40; from the collection of Karen Walck Haley; *Tie Magic*, 1959, unsigned, 5923, $20.

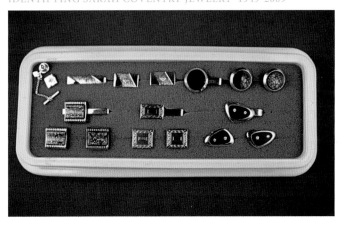

Top: *Aristocrat*, 1965, tie tac, 5982, $20; tie bar, 5983, $20; cuff links, 5984, $30; *Ambassador*, 1958, tie bar, 5951, $30; cuff links, 5952, $40; **Bottom:** *Mr. Wonderful*, 1956, unsigned, tie bar, 5911, $25; cuff links, 5912, $30; *Fashion Plate*, 1959, tie bar, 5933, $15; cuff links, 5934, $20; *Star-Jet*, 1961, tie bar, 5941, $30; cuff links, 5942, $40.

Prestige, 1964, tie tac and cuff links set, 5000, $65.

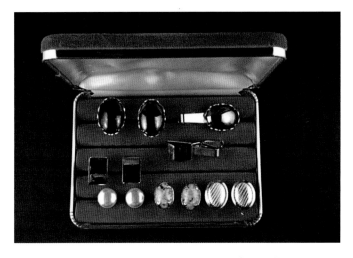

Top: *Reflections*, 1957, unsigned, tie bar, 5921, $25; cuff links, 5920, $30; also tie bar and cuff links set, 5092; **Middle:** *Cavalier,* 1960, tie bar, 5925, $20; cuff links, 5936, $30; **Bottom:** *Tie Tac Set*, 1963, unsigned, 6750, $35; designed for "him" and for "her" or they can be worn in pairs; *Sunday Best*, 1959, cuff links, 5929, $25; also tie bar, 5928; *Executive*, 1956, unsigned, cuff links, 5908, $40; also tie bar, 5907.

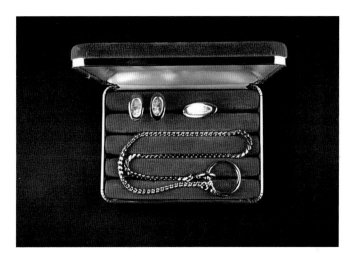

Tailored Elegance, 1963, silver tie bar, 5967, $15; cuff links, 5968, $20; also gold tie bar, 5969 and cuff links, 5970; *Key Magic Key Chain*, 1957, unsigned, 5915, $15.

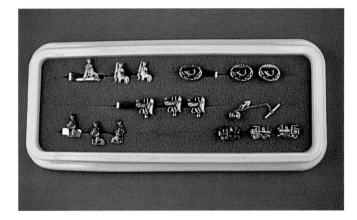

Top: *Tom Sawyer*, 1959, tie bar, 5930, $15; cuff links, 5931, $20; *Sportsman*, 1960, tie bar, 5943, $25; cuff links, 5944, $30; **Middle:** *Woofer*, 1956, unsigned, tie bar, 5903, $15; cuff links, 5904, $20; **Bottom:** *Royal Mountie*, 1963, tie bar, 5965, $20; cuff links, 5966, $20; *The Santa Fe*, 1964, tie tac, 5973, $15; cuff links, 5974, $20.

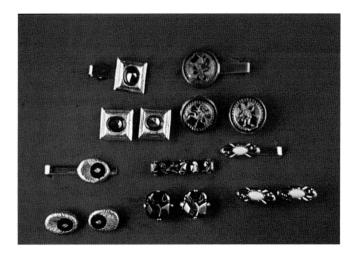

Top: *Esquire*, 1962, tie bar, 5955, $30; cuff links, 5956, $35; *Balinese*, 1960, tie bar, 5937, $25; cuff links, 5938, $30; **Bottom:** *Comet*, 1956, unsigned, tie bar, 5909, $20; cuff links, 5910, $30; *Charcoal Classic*, 1961, tie bar, 5953, $20; cuff links, 5954, $30; *Prestige*, 1957, unsigned, tie bar, 5913, $20; cuff links, 5914, $30.

Lord and Lady Coventry.

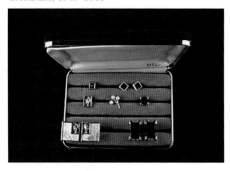

Top: *V.I.P.*, 1957, tie tac, 5919, $15; also tie bar, 5917 and cuff links, 5918; *On The Square*, 1962, gold, 5957, $20; silver, 5981, $20; **Bottom:** *Heraldic*, 1964, tie tac, 5971, $20; cuff links, 5972, $25; *Trio*, 1962, tie tac, 5964, $20; *Bold Knight*, 1964, tie tac, 5977, $20; cuff links, 5978, $40.

Queen of the Nile, 1958, unsigned, tie bar, 5929, $25; cuff links, 5927, $25; also earrings, 7707. Cardex photo shows the Queen facing left on the tie bar, and we are not able to explain this anomaly.

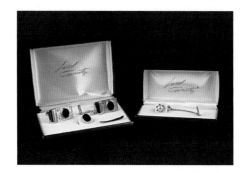

Oxford Tie Tac and Cuff Links Set, 1965, 5092, $85; *Pearl Classic Tie Tac*, 1965, 5987, $35.

Circle Charm, 1965, 9557, $70.

Sterling Remembrance, 1965, 9558, $70.

Flowered Circle Set, 1965, 5091, $70.

Theater Set, 1965, 5090, $105.

Lady Coventry Pearls, 1965, unsigned, 8551, $70; comes in satin-lined black leather case.

Star Bright, 1965, 15-inch, 8554, $50; also 18-inch, 8578 in 1966; *Solitude*, 1965, 8555, $50; *Trinity*, 1965, 8553, $50.

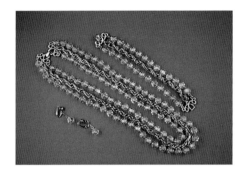

Golden Ice, 1976, necklace, 8728, $80; bracelet, 9728, $55; clip earrings, 7728, $25.

Camelot, 1966, necklace, 8647, $140; bracelet, 9647, $50; earrings, 7647, $40.

Wild Honey, 1970, necklace, 8356, $55; bracelet, 9356, $80; clip earrings, 7356, $35; pierced earrings, 7368, $40; ring, 5166, $25.

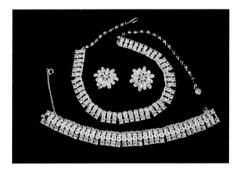

Premier, 1966, necklace, 8652, $105; bracelet, 9652, $70; clip earrings, 7652, $35.

Crystal Snowflakes, 1969, necklace, 8277, $95; bracelet, 9277, $75; pin, 6277, $50; clip earrings, 7277, $40; also spelled *Crystal Snow Flakes*.

Shangri-La, 1972, necklace, 8526, $150; bracelet, 9256, $150; pin, 6256, $80; clip earrings, 7256, $80; ring, 5372, $55.

Taffy Tones, 1975, necklace, 8179, $60; bracelet, 9179, $45; pierced earrings, 7179, $30; *Castaway*, 1981, necklace, 8188, $50; bracelet, 9073, $30; pierced earrings, 7132, $25.

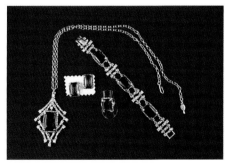

Twilight, 1973, necklace, 8827, $65; bracelet, 9827, $75; clip earrings, 7827, $35; ring, 5457, $30.

Enchantress, 1967, necklace, 8728, $90; bracelet, 9728, $70; clip earrings, 7728, $35.

Petite Accent, 1979, necklace, 8148, $40; bracelet, 9038, $30; pierced earrings, 7034, $35.

Winsome, 1966, necklace, 8589, $45; bracelet, 9589, $40; clip earrings, 7589, $25.

Military Brass, 1968, belt, 8754, $80; bracelet, 9754, $25; clip earrings, 7754, $25.

Goldenlinks, 1974, 36-inch chain necklace, 8166, $60; bracelet, 9166, $25; pierced earrings, 7166, $30.

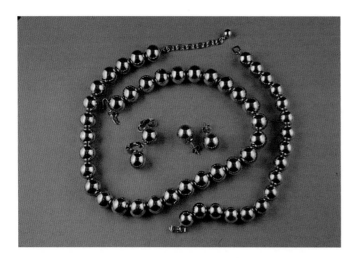

Headliner, 1980, necklace, 8366, $95; bracelet, 9053, $40; clip earrings, 7096, $20; pierced earrings, 7095, $20.

Golden Sunset, 1973, bracelet, 9855, $50; in 1974, necklace, 8855, $45; clip earrings, 7855, $30.

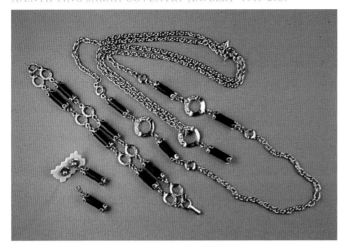

Emberwood, 1975, 20-inch and 32-inch chains necklace, 8271, $85; bracelet, 9271, $60; convertible pierced earrings, 7271, $35.

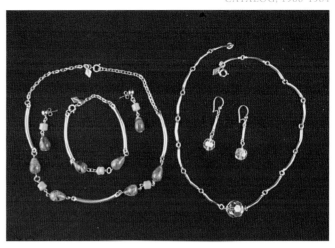

Oriental Mood, 1976, necklace, 8726, $65; bracelet, 9726, $40; pierced earrings, 7726, $45; modeled by Liberty Williams in August 1976 *Seventeen* magazine; *Mirage*, 1975, necklace, 8285, $45; pierced earrings, 7285, $40.

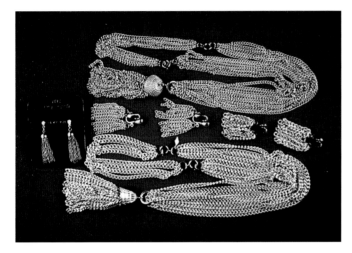

Golden Tassel, 1970, necklace, 8349, $70; clip earrings, 7349, $35; in 1971, pierced earrings, 7437, $50; shown in 1971 *Vogue* magazine; *Tassel Magic*, 1976, silver necklace, 8628, $85; clip earrings, 7628, $35; also gold necklace, 8629 and clip earrings, 7629. All have a removable bracelet section.

Minuet, 1972, bracelet, 9506, $45; in 1973, necklace, 8506, $25; pierced earrings, 7506, $40; *Bluebird of Happiness*, 1970, necklace, 8345, $20; bracelet, 9345, $20; in 1973, pierced earrings, 7345, $45.

Fashion Flip, 1975, entire set is reversible, necklace, 8249, $65; bracelet, 9249, $30; pierced earrings, 7249, $40; two sets shown.

Fashionette, 1966, gold necklace, 8596, $55; clip earrings, 7596, $30; silver necklace, 8597, $55; clip earrings, 7597, $30.

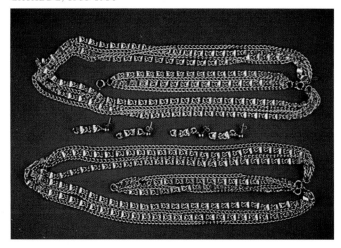

Four Dimensions, 1973, 33-inch multi-chains necklace with detachable bracelet section, silver necklace, 8107, $60; gold necklace, 8660, $65; in 1975, silver pierced earrings, 7107, $35; gold pierced earrings, 7660, $35.

Fashion-Rite, 1972, necklace, 8541, $60; clip earrings, 7541, $25.

Spanish Moss, 1972, silver necklace, 8475, $55; gold necklace, 8476, $55; in 1973, silver clip earrings, 7475, $40; gold clip earrings, 7476, $40.

Safari, 1978, 37-inch beads and 29-inch chain necklace, 8984, $85; clip earrings, 7987, $25; pierced earrings, 7984, $25.

Texture Links, 1975, necklace, 8112, $60; bracelet, 9112, $60; clip earrings, 7112, $30; *Golden Leaf*, 1981, necklace, 8203, $80; bracelet, 9076, $50; pierced earrings, 7123, $20.

Ming Garden, 1972, necklace, 8521, $40; clip earrings, 7521, $30; *Tea House*, 1977, necklace, 8657, $55; clip earrings, 7657, $35.

Golden Lanterns, 1972, necklace, 8523, $80; clip earrings, 7523, $30; *Golden Embers*, 1967, necklace, 8643, $55; clip earrings, 7643, $25; ring, 5161, $35.

Majorca, 1969, necklace, 8217, $40; clip drop earrings, 7217, $40; clip button earrings, 7269, $40; pierced earrings, 7260, $40; ring, 5189, $35.

Catherine, 1972, pin, 6525, $45; can be worn as pendant, clip earrings, 7525, $40; in 1973, necklace, 8525, $30; pierced earrings, 7598, $35; ring, 5387, $40.

Light N' Bright, 1969, 36-inch necklace, 8216, $35; pin, 6216, $20; clip earrings, 7216, $35; pierced earrings, 7285, $20.

Light of the East, 1968, necklace, 8212, $30; pin, 6212, $45; drop clip earrings, 7212, $35; in 1969, pierced earrings, 7267, $40 (shown on necklace card), button clip earrings, 7268, $40; ring, 5216, $35.

Deep Burgundy, 1966, necklace, 8613, $35; pin, 6613, $40; clip earrings, 7613, $40; ring, 5155, $30.

Over the Rainbow, 1971, necklace, 8427, $45; clip earrings, 7427, $45; unsigned ring, 5265, $40; *Marigold*, 1970, necklace, 8357, $35; clip earrings, 7357, $35; ring, 5165, $35.

Princess, 1974, necklace, 8900, $30; clip earrings, 7900, $30; ring, 5488, $25; in 1975, pierced earrings, 7286, $35; *Papillion*, 1973, necklace, 8591, $25; in 1974, pierced earrings, 7907, $40; ring, 5499, $25.

Symphony, 1968, ring, 5186, $35; in 1969, necklace, 8279, $35; clip earrings, 7279, $40.

Exclusive, 1978, reversible necklace, 8501, $40 two shown; ring, 5783, $30; *Filigree Hoop*, 1978, pierced earrings, 7255, $30; *Carameltone*, 1973, necklace, 8850, $60; clip earrings, 7850, $40; *Jupiter*, 1974, ring, 5523, $30; *Directions*, 1976, necklace, 8691, $30; pierced earrings, 7691, $30; ring, 5729, $30.

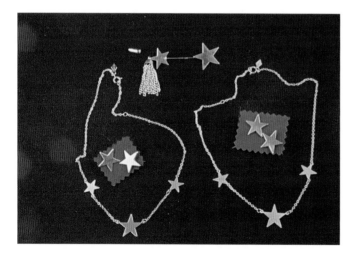

Star Shower, 1976, gold necklace, 8729, $40; gold stickpin, 6729, $40; gold pierced earrings, 7729, $35; silver necklace, 8528, $40; silver pierced earrings, 7528, $35; there was no silver stickpin.

Hidden Rose, 1976, necklace, 8668, $60; clip earrings, 7668, $70; pierced earrings, 7669, $55; ring, 5679, $50.

Rosette, 1972, necklace, 8514, $30; pierced earrings, 7537, $30; ring, 5341, $30; *Royal Crown*, 1971, necklace, 8381, $40; clip earrings, 7381, $40; ring, 5257, $35; in 1973, pierced earrings, 7394, $35.

Lovers Knot, 1969, ring, 5221, $35; in 1970, necklace, 8366, $25, no reference found; pierced earrings, 7366, $55; *Dream Boat*, 1973, necklace, 8856, $25; in 1974, pierced earrings, 7856, $30; ring, 5512, $25.

Scarlet Tears, 1973, necklace, 8822, $50; clip earrings, 7822, $35; *Hi-Style*, 1977, necklace, 8538, $70; pierced earrings, 7538, $35; *Dynasty*, 1973, necklace, 8656, $60; clip earrings, 7656, $40.

Jet Elegance, 1968, necklace, 8206, $30; clip earrings, 7206, $40; ring, 5182, $35; *Male Elegance*. 1967, tie bar, 5999, $25; cuff links, 5998, $40; also tie tac, 5997.

My Valentine, 1975, necklace, 8178, $35; pierced earrings, 7178, $35; ring, 5606, $30.

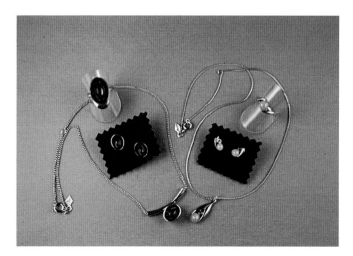

Fire-Lite, 1976, necklace, 8398, $55; pierced earrings, 7398, $40; ring, 5676, $55; *Angel*, 1980, necklace, 8322, $35; pierced earrings, 7089, $20; ring, 5300, $45.

Azure Skies, 1972, necklace, 8524, $35; clip earrings, 7524, $35; ring, 5371, $35; in 1973, pin, 6575, $55; *Czarina*, 1971, necklace, 8404, $35; clip earrings, 7404, $45; ring, 5261, $25 shown in May 1971 *Family Circle*.

Duchess, 1976, necklace, 8250, $70; clip earrings, 7250, $35; *Cleopatra*, 1979, necklace, 8025, $60; convertible pierced earrings, 7025, $25; *Harlequin*, 1980, necklace, 8362, $40; pin, 6059, $25; ring, 5345-5347, $60, size 5-7.

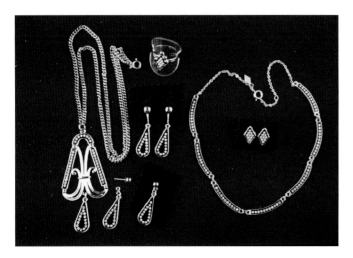

Polonaise, 1975, necklace, 8644, $70; clip earrings, 7644, $50; pierced earrings, 7645, $55; ring, 5666, $30; *New Polonaise*, 1976, necklace, 8956, $70; pierced earrings, 7956, $30.

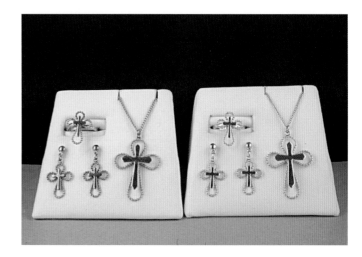

Serenity Cross, 1974, gold necklace, 8108, $40; silver necklace, 8109, $40; in 1975, gold pierced earrings, 7253, $45; gold ring, 5612, $30; silver pierced earrings, 7252, $45; silver ring, 5611, $30.

Coraline, 1974, necklace, 8924, $55; pendant can be worn as a pin as shown, clip earrings, 7924, $35; ring, 5495, $35.

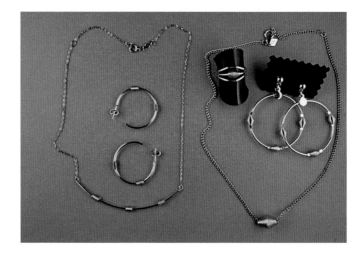

Chimes, 1977, necklace, 8715, $35; pierced earrings, 7715, $30; *New Design*, 1976, necklace, 8700, $25; pierced earrings, 7709, $40; ring, 5680, $20.

Summer Magic, 1966, pin, 6586, $20; clip earrings, 7586, $45; *New Summer Magic*, 1970, 36-inch beads and 36-inch chain necklace, 8290, $50; pin, 6290, $30; clip earrings, 7290, $35; modeled by Stephanie Powers in August 1970 *Good Housekeeping* magazine.

Spellbound, 1980, necklace, 8403, $105; pierced earrings, 7104, $35; *LaSoiree*, 1980, necklace, 8342, $60; with *Stargazer*, 1980, clip earrings, 7092, $35; pierced earrings, 7093, $35; *Golden Gypsy*, 1969, necklace, 8276, $35; clip earrings, 7276, $40.

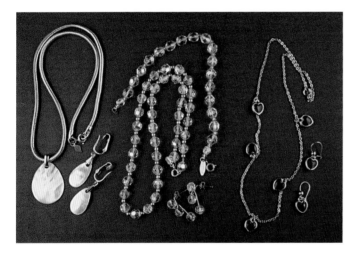

South Seas, 1968, necklace, 8781, $40; clip earrings, 7781, $35; *Aurora Borealis*, 1981, necklace, 8730, $125; pierced earrings, 7730, $45; in 1982, bracelet, 2125, $55; *Candied Heart*, 1976, necklace, 8688, $45; pierced earrings, 7688, $20.

Holiday Ice, 1969, necklace, 8230, $40; pin, 6230, $40; clip earrings, 7230, $45; *Touch of Elegance*, 1970, necklace, 8326, $35; pin, 6326, $60; clip earrings, 7326, $35; in 1971, pierced earrings, 7396, $40.

Misty Morning, 1981, necklace, 8831, $75; pin, 6831, $25 (has hook to be used as enhancer on necklace); pierced earrings, 7831, $30; *Affection*, 1982, gold, 17-inch necklace, 2033, $65; clip earrings, 2036, $35; pin, 2032, $40; also 30-inch necklace, 2221, pierced earrings, 2035; ring, 2029-2031, size 6-8; and silver, 17-inch necklace, 2209, 30-inch necklace, 2222, clip earrings, 2212, pierced earrings, 2211, ring, 2205-2207, size 6-8.

Three Cheers, 1973, necklace, 8561, $55; clip earrings, white 7579, $25; blue 7632, $25; red 7631, $25; in 1976, ring, 5671, $20.

Sunburst, 1976, pendant/pin, 8686, $65; pin, 6933, $35; pierced earrings, 7686, $40; also clip earrings, 7933; *Golden Tulip*, 1974, necklace, 8903, $35; pin, 6903, $50; clip earrings, 7903, $45.

Ultra-Versatile, 1976, amber/black/green necklace, 8596, $70; clip earrings, 7596, $70; red/white/blue necklace and earrings drops 8597, $20.

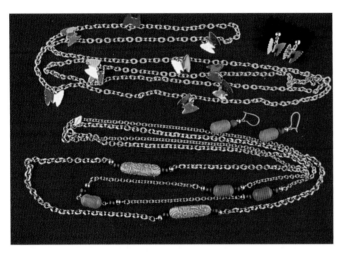

Top: *Flutter Byes*, 1975, 20-inch and 32-inch chain necklace, 8199, $45; pierced earrings, 7199, $20; **Bottom:** *Bittersweet*, 1975, 31-inch and 36-inch chain necklace, 8275, $75; pierced earrings, 7275, $25.

Wisteria, 1973, necklace, 8592, $75; clip earrings, 7592, $25; in 1974, pierced earrings, 7134, $40; *Lilac Time*, 1975, 50-inch necklace, 8208, $75; has 16-inch removable section, clip earrings, 7208, $30; *Pastel Glo*, 1971, 52-inch necklace, 8402, $45; clip earrings, 7402, $30.

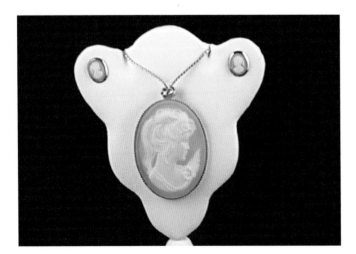

Lasting Impressions, 1981, necklace, 8191, $55; pierced earrings, 7169, $25.

Sea Star, 1977, necklace, 8349, $40 bracelet, 9349, $40; clip earrings, 7371, $35; pierced earrings, 7349, $30; ring, 5771, $35; in 1978, stick pin, 6349, $25.

Glitter Bits, 1976, necklace, 8100, $40; pierced earrings, 7100, $30; *Snowdrop*, 1984, silver necklace, 8929, $25; silver pierced earrings, 7929, $25; also gold necklace, 8928, there are no gold earrings; *Sterling Rose*, 1984, unsigned, necklace, 3814, $45; pierced earrings, 3975, $35; *Satin Glo*, 1976, necklace, 8588, $35; pierced earrings, 7588, $45.

Vintage, 1973, ring, 5467, $35; in 1974, necklace, 8948, $35; pierced earrings, 7948, $35; *Amber Light*, 1982, necklace, 8031, $45; pierced earrings, 7278, $50; ring, 5429-5433, $60, sizes 5-9.

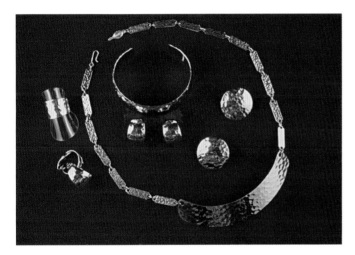

Scandia, 1977, necklace, 8835, $50; wide cuff bracelet, 9244, $25; hoop clip earrings, 7944, $25; hoop pierced earrings, 7244, $25; button clip earrings, 7857, $25; ring, 5764, $30.

Mini-Midi-Maxi, 1971, necklace, 8405, $55; clip earrings, 7405, $30; *Fashion Mobile*, 1971, necklace, 8423, $35; clip earrings, 7423, $35; *Jet Ice*, 1973, necklace, 8832, $60; clip earrings, 7832, $25.

Tranquility, 1970, necklace, 8319, $60; clip earrings, 7319, $40; *Lites*, 1974, necklace, 8031, $45; clip earrings, 7031, $30; earring drops 7061, $30.

Shell-Cor, 1981, unsigned, 17-inch peach cord and 34-inch beige cord necklace, 8189, $75; *Shell*, 1981, clip earrings, 7117, $35; *Shell*, 1981, necklace, 8190, $35; pierced earrings, 7116, $30; ring, 5377-5379, $25, sizes 5-7; ring from the collection of Joy Robson.

Old Vienna, 1975, necklace, 8123, $85; clip earrings, 7123, $60; ring, 5567, $45; bottom dangle of necklace can be removed and worn as a pin; *Blue Cloud*, 1977, necklace, 8529, $45; pierced earrings, 7529, $40; ring, 5753, $30.

Piccadilly Circle, 1974, necklace, 8989, $60; clip earrings, 7989, $45; *Golden Petals*, 1971, necklace, 8400, $40; clip earrings, 7400, $35; shown in 1971 *Vogue* magazine; *Flamenco*, 1971, unsigned necklace, 8435, $40; clip earrings, 7435, $50.

Angel Pink, 1973, necklace, 8563, $25; clip earrings, 7563, $30; ring, 5386, $30; *Victorian Bouquet*, 1975, necklace, 8111, $35; earring drops 7111, $30; in 1976, ring, 5603, $30.

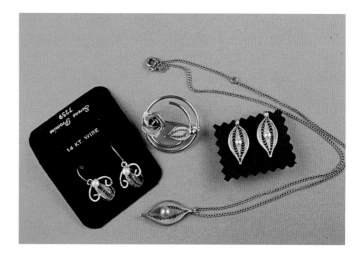

Serene Promise, 1969, pierced earrings, 7259, $50; *Promise*, 1967, pin, 6700, $30; *Serene*, 1966, necklace, 8648, $25; clip earrings, 7648, $20.

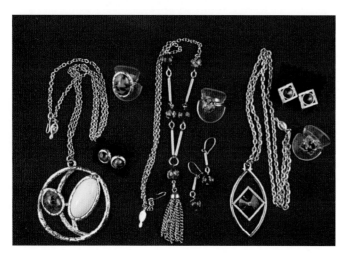

Desert Flower, 1974, necklace, 8032, $55; pierced earrings, 7060, $30; ring, 5517, $30; *Venetian Treasure*, 1974, necklace, 8939, $55; pierced earrings, 7939, $30; in 1976, ring, 5640, $25; *Volcano*, 1975, necklace, 8191, $50; clip earrings, 7191, $30; ring, 5604, $30.

Top: *Lustre*, 1984, 28-inch bead necklace, 8950, $65; *Matchmaker*, 1982, silver clip earrings, 7203, $30; also pierced earrings, 7202, and gold clip earrings, 7201, pierced earrings, 7200; both from the collection of Joy Robson; **Bottom:** *Fancy Free*, 1982, 36-inch bead necklace, 8509, $50; clip earrings, 7261, $30; also pierced earrings, 7267; earrings from the collection of Joy Robson.

Fashion Fortune, 1969, unsigned necklace, 8252, $65; clip earrings, 7252, $40; *Fashion Loops*, 1967, reversible necklace, 8672, $55; clip earrings, 7672, $40; *Golden Coin*, 1975, necklace, 8237, $55; earring drops 7237, $30.

Hercules, 1975, necklace, 8360, $65; in 1976, pierced earrings, 7360, $30; *Aloha*, 1974, necklace, 8041, $65; clip earrings, 7041, $35; *Embassy*, 1975, necklace, 8198, $60; clip earrings, 7198, $35.

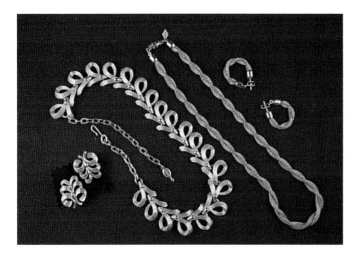

Golden Braid, 1966, necklace, 8617, $50; clip earrings, 7617, $30; *Golden Braids*, 1976, necklace, 8953, $50; pierced earrings, 7211, $40.

Lotus Blossom, 1974, necklace, 8935, $55; clip earrings, 7935, $30; *Pyramid Treasure*, 1971, necklace, 8451, $55; in 1972, clip earrings, 7503, $35; pierced earrings, 7502, $15.

Socialite, 1981, necklace, 8206, $30; *Opaline*, 1981, pierced earrings, 7133, $20; *Love Knots*, 1977, necklace, 8569, $45; pierced earrings, 7569, $30; *Portrait*, 1984, necklace, 8904, $25; pierced earrings, 7904, $30.

Golden Rope, 1976, tortoise necklace, 8413, $60; clip earrings, 7413, $35; white necklace, 8396, $60; clip earrings, 7396, $35; *Inca Fire*, 1976, necklace, 8368, $80; clip earrings, 7368, $45; bottom of pendant can be removed and worn as a pin.

Snow Lace, 1975, necklace, 8193, $60; clip earrings, 7193, $25; in 1976, pierced earrings, 7934, $25; *Fanfare*, 1974, necklace, 8899, $60; clip earrings, 7899, $35; presented on the 25th anniversary of Sarah Coventry jewelry; *Sassy*, 1975, necklace, 8120, $30; clip earrings, 7120, $45.

Enchantress, 1971, necklace, 8416, $95; clip earrings, 7416, $85; shown in 1971 *Vogue* magazine.

Candlelight, 1972, necklace, 8464, $55; pendant, 8463, $30; clip earrings, 7463, $30.

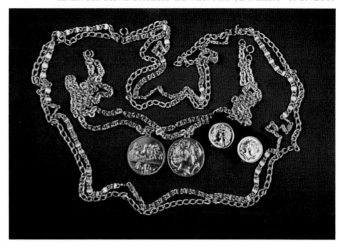

Romanesque, 1969, reversible, multi-chain necklace, 8270, $75; clip earrings, 7270, $30; usually found as a single chain pendant necklace only, two pendants shown for the reverse side.

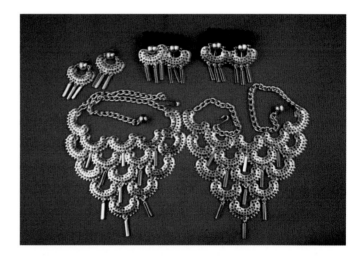

Charisma, 1973, silver necklace, 8650, $75; clip earrings, 7650, $45; in 1975, gold necklace, 8391, $65; clip earrings, 7391, $35; silver pierced earrings, 7373, $45; also gold pierced earrings, 7392.

Rock Trio, 1971, unsigned hoop necklace with interchangeable drops, 8419, $55; pierced earrings with interchangeable drops, 7455, $45; *Summer Skies*, 1976, necklace, 8055, $45; in 1977, pierced earrings, 7066, $25.

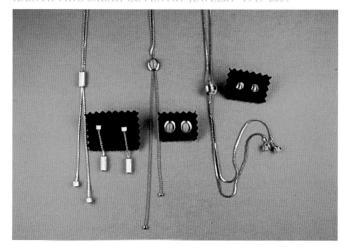

Finesse, 1980, necklace, 8321, $40; pierced earrings, 7085, $30; *Mint Delight*, 1980, necklace, 8241, $45; pierced earrings, 7091, $25; *Forget Me Knot*, 1982, necklace, 8584, $45; pierced earrings, 7168, $25.

Pastel Parfait, 1973, 36-inch beads and 38-inch chain necklace, Kelly green, 8600, $40; 36-inch beads and no chain necklace, yellow/Kelly green, 8602, $40; clip earrings, yellow/white/green, 7580, $45; pink/lilac/white, 7581, $45; pierced earrings, 7593, $40.

Pastel Parfait, 1972, 36-inch beads and 38-inch chain necklace, white, 8474, $40; pink, 8485, $40; yellow, 8486, $40; lilac, 8487, $40; avocado, 8488, $40.

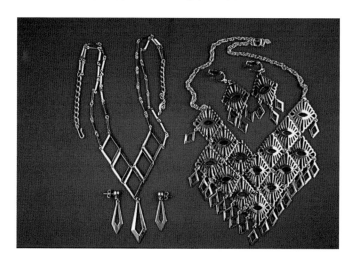

Goddess, 1977, necklace, 8582, $65; pierced earrings, 7582, $40; *Mandarin Magic*, 1974, necklace, 8990, $80; clip earrings, 7990, $30; pierced earrings, 7991, $35; shown in September 1974 *Lady's Home Journal*.

Pastel Parfait, 1972, 36-inch beads and no chain necklace, yellow/avocado, 8495, $40; lilac/pink, 8496, $40.

Starburst, 1974, necklace, 8040, $80; in 1975, clip earrings, 7040, $30; *Caprice*, 1984, necklace, 8910, $35; clip earrings, 7910, $25; earrings from the collection of Joy Robson; *Crusader*, 1971, necklace, 8403, $45; in 1973, pierced earrings, 7663, $35.

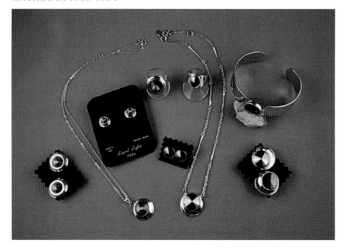

Liquid Lights, 1971, necklace, 8382, $35; pierced earrings, 7444, $35; ring, 5258, $35; in 1972, clip earrings, 7516, $45; *Jet Set*, 1976, necklace, 8267, $50; bracelet, 9267, $55; clip earrings, 7267, $55; pierced earrings, 7268, $40; ring, 5723, $35; shown in 1976 *Vogue* magazine.

Nature's Choice, 1979, 7010, $30; set of butterfly tac pin and mushroom pierced earrings; *Mushroom*, 1975, necklace, 8125, $35; pierced earrings, 7125, $35; *Luv*, 1972, necklace, 8480, $30; pierced earrings, 7483, $20; *Unforgettable*, 1981, necklace, 8187, $40; pierced earrings, 7130, $20; *Intimate*, 1982, necklace, 8034, $45; pierced earrings, 7279, $30.

Jonquil, 1974, ring, 5518, $30; in 1976, necklace, 8269, $30; pierced earrings, 7269, $35.

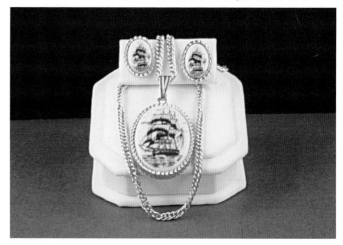

Legend, 1975, 22-inch and 30-inch chains necklace, 8289, $70; pierced earrings, 7289, $45.

Folklore, 1971, necklace, 8420, $50; clip earrings, 7420, $30; *Silvery Moon*, 1977, 29-inch necklace, 8768, $40; *Blue Moon*, 1977, 16-inch pendant necklace, 8769, $40; pierced earrings, 7768, $30; *Aztec*, 1972, necklace, 8470, $25; clip earrings, 7470, $30.

Overture, 1980, necklace, 8367, $45; pendant can be worn as pin, pierced earrings, 7094, $35; *Hi-Lo Elegance*, 1972, 36-inch and 28-inch chain necklace, 8478, $85; clip earrings, 7478, $40.

Talisman of Love, 1973, necklace, 8560, $50; bracelet, 9560, $35; clip earrings, 7560, $35; *Jet Set*, 1970, versatile necklace, 8312, $75; bracelet, 9312, $50; clip earrings, 7312, $30; ring, 5227, $30; necklace can be worn several ways; modeled by Lee Meriwether in *Northwest Orient Airlines*.

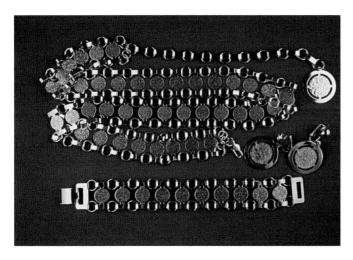

Disco-Tek, 1974, belt, 8875, $75; bracelet, 9875, $30; clip earrings, 7875, $25.

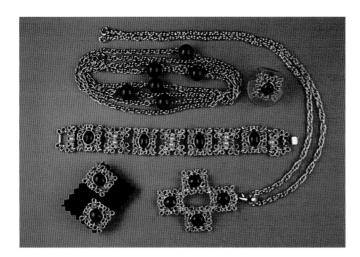

Victoria Blue, 1975, bead necklace, 8197, $55; pendant necklace, 8202, $65; bracelet, 9197, $75; clip earrings, 7197, $40; ring, 5597, $30.

Indian Maiden, 1973, necklace, 8823, $50; bracelet, 9823, $55; clip earrings, 7823, $25; pierced earrings, 7824, $35; ring, 5481, $25.

Preview, 1978, necklace, 8512, $50; *Midnight*, 1978, pierced earrings, 7580, $15; *Egyptian*, 1976, necklace, 8461, $60; clip earrings, 7461, $35; pierced earrings, 7462, $35.

Chain-Ability, 1971, 42-inch chain necklace with removable drops and adjustable stations, silver necklace, 8453, $70; clip earrings, 7453, $35; pierced earrings, 7533, $35; gold necklace, 8454, $70; clip earrings, 7454, $35; pierced earrings, 7534, $35; *Fashion Wrap*, 1975, 40-inch chain necklace with removable drops, silver necklace, 8798, $50; gold necklace, 8797, $50.

Royal Lace, 1978, necklace, 8776, $60; in 1979, pierced earrings, 7776, $25; *Elegante*, 1972, necklace, 8551, $45; clip earrings, 7551, $30.

Magic Spell, 1978, necklace, 8544, $50; pierced earrings, 7544, $25; *Bow Tie*, 1980, necklace, 8044, $55; clip earrings, 7044, $35; pierced earrings, 7045, $20; ring, 5064, $35.

Midnight Cameo, 1970, necklace, 8297, $35; clip earrings, 7297, $45; *Tiny Garden*, 1975, necklace, 8994, $25; pierced earrings, 7766, $25; *Cupid's Touch*, 1976, necklace, 8384, $40; in 1978, pierced earrings, 7384, $30.

Chain-O-Lites, 1969, necklace, 8220, $60; removable bracelet section, pierced earrings, 7265, $30; clip earrings, 7220, $30; *Serenade*, 1978, 21-inch and 32-inch chain necklace, 8826, $65; pierced earrings, 7826, $25.

Young Love, 1977, necklace, 8318, $25; pierced earrings, 7318, $20.

Swingalong, 1972, composed of bracelet, pin, and 20-inch chain necklace, 8494, $100; clip earrings, 7494, $35; *Casual Classic*, 1971, necklace, 8425, $45; clip earrings, 7425, $25.

Night Garden, 1976, necklace, 8589, $45; pierced earrings, 7613, $50; also clip earrings, 7589; *Polka*, 1974, necklace, 8043, $60; clip earrings, 7043, $25.

Carousel, 1968, blue/green necklace, 8765, $55; clip earrings, 7765, $25; pink/orange necklace, 8766, $55; clip earrings, 7766, $25; citrus necklace, 8762, $55; clip earrings, 7762, $25.

Heart to Heart, 1974, necklace, 8904, $55; pierced earrings, 7904, $40.

Fashion Frost, 1976, two strands of 36-inch beads, black and gray necklace, 8328, $40; black clip earrings, 7328, $30; pink and dark pink necklace, 8327, $40; dark pink clip earrings, 7327, $30; brown and beige necklace, 8326, $40; brown clip earrings, 7326, $30; blue and green necklace, 8325, $40; blue clip earrings, 7325, $30.

Triple Treat, 1974, 8873, $65; *Fiesta*, 1974, clip earrings, 7047, $60; in 1975, pierced earrings, 7183, $75.

Top: *Rain Flower*, 1975, necklace, 8287, $65; pierced earrings, 7287, $50; **Bottom:** *Ember Tears*, 1975, 18-inch necklace, 8272, $50; clip earrings, 7272, $30; also 16-inch necklace, 8296.

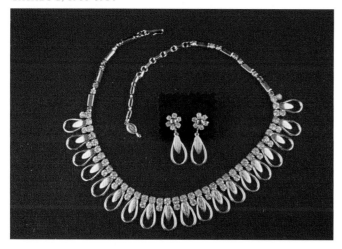

Chan-Di-Lites, 1966, necklace, 8644, $70; clip earrings, 7644, $35.

Heliotrope, 1972, necklace, 8547, $40; clip earrings, 7547, $45.

LaBelle, 1976, necklace, 8983, $55; clip earrings, 7983, $45; ring, 5716, $35; *Debut*, 1978, necklace, 8407, $75; pierced earrings, 7407, $30; ring, 5795, $25.

Hi-Fashion, 1974, necklace, 8898, $45; clip earrings, 7898, $25; *White Satin*, 1967, 54-inch beads with detachable 17-inch section 8682, $50; clip earrings, 7682, $30; *Summer Scheme*, 1977, necklace, 8770, $45; *Milky Way*, 1977, bracelet, 9577, $45; *Spring Fever*, 1977, ring, 5734, $25.

Oriental Lanterns, 1978, 17-inch green necklace, 8410, $35; 33-inch green necklace, 8387, $45; 27-inch tortoise necklace, 8411, $60; pierced earrings, 7387, $30.

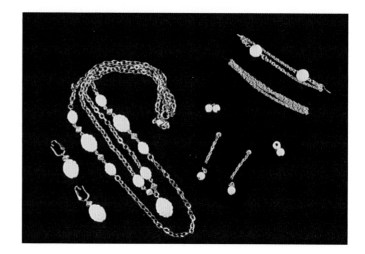

Summer Flirt, 1976, 22-inch and 29-inch chain necklace, 8604, $80; clip earrings, 7604, $30; *LaBelle*, 1980, necklace, 8236, $55; pierced earrings, 7236, $25.

Empress, 1972, necklace, 8515, $70; clip earrings, 7515, $45; *Aura*, 1974, necklace, 8928, $45; clip earrings, 7928, $30; *Double Choice*, 1976, necklace, 8393, $70; clip earrings, 7393, $55.

Dawn to Dusk, 1967, reversible, necklace, 8671, $30; clip earrings, 7671, $30; both necklace and earrings reverse to rhinestones, necklace is turned over to show the rhinestone side.

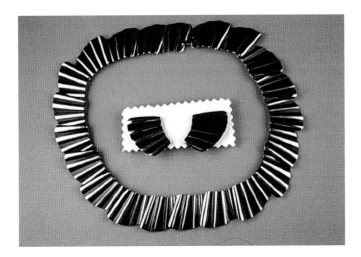

Fame, 1983, necklace, 2255, $200; clip earrings, 2252, $45.

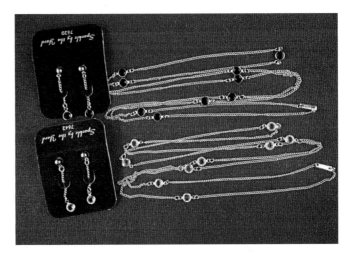

Sparkle by the Yard, 1976, unsigned, 36-inch jet necklace, 8620, $60; pierced earrings, 7620, $25; 36-inch ice necklace, 8642, $60; pierced earrings, 7642, $25.

Heirloom Treasure, 1968, necklace, 8800, $30; clip earrings, 7800, $40; pierced earrings, 7801, $40; *The Big Apple*, 1975, silver necklace, 8113, $30; pierced earrings, 7113, $20; gold necklace, 8114, $30; pierced earrings, 7114, $30.

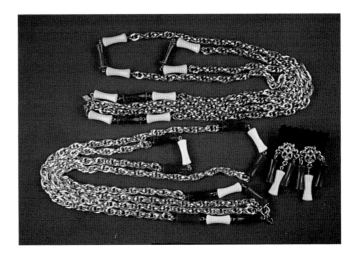

Applause, 1975, 28-inch and 35-inch chains, tortoise necklace, 8117, $65; red/white/blue necklace, 8136, $65; clip earrings, 7136, $45. There are no tortoise earrings.

Honeycomb, 1975, necklace, 8124, $45; convertible pierced earrings, 7124, $40; *Autumn Trio*, 1975, necklace, 8247, $55; clip earrings, 7247, $40; *Sara-Zade*, 1970, necklace, 8293, $30; clip earrings, 7293, $25.

Ember Chains, 1970, 55-inch beads and 110-inch chain necklace, 8327, $65; clip earrings, 7327, $30; *Rustic Charmer*, 1977, 42-inch necklace with adjustable clasp 8880, $50; clip earrings, 7880, $35; pierced earrings, 7893, $25; *Tortoise Fashions*, 1968, 30-inch chain and 30-inch beads with removable bracelet section, 8802, $55; clip earrings, 7802, $25.

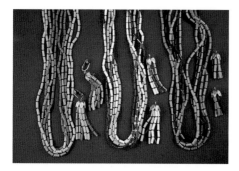

Sun 'n Fun, 1967, yellow/orange/green necklace, 8685, $50; clip earrings, 7675, $40; *Pool Side*, 1967, red/white/blue necklace, 8686, $50; clip earrings, 7686, $40; *Midnight Multi*, 1967, pink/turquoise/black necklace, 8687, $50; clip earrings, 7687, $40. This group is known as the *Cruise Line* series. They were offered on the same undated flyer as the Bold Gypsy sets, but unlike the Bold Gypsy, which first appears in the January 1967 catalog, the Cruise Line sets are not in any catalogs or Shopping Guides that we have. The only provenance we have for them is the flyer. The earrings all came with illusion clips, as shown on the *Sun 'n Fun* earrings.

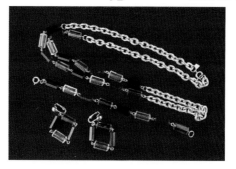

Vogue, 1975, 43-inch necklace/bracelet, 8196, $85; clip earrings, 7196, $40.

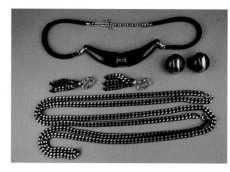

New Yorker, 1976, necklace, 8401, $50; clip earrings, 7401, $30; *Bewitchery*, 1967, unsigned, necklace, 8731, $55; clip earrings, 7731, $25.

White Magic, 1978, necklace, 8394, $45; clip earrings, 7511, $25; pierced earrings, 7510, $25; *Sensation*, 1977, necklace, 8566, $40; *Anything Goes*, 1977, clip earrings, 7502, $30; pierced earrings, 7566, $30; *Perfection*, 1977, 32-inch necklace, 8502, $70; convertible pierced earrings, 7503, $35.

White Charmer, 1975, necklace, 8248, $65; clip earrings, 7248, $30; *Black Charmer*, 1976, necklace, 8381, $65; pendant can be worn as a pin, clip earrings, 7381, $30; *Mystic Lady*, 1976, necklace, 8617, $55.

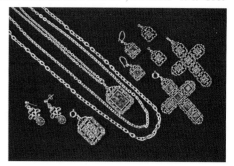

Roman Holiday, 1973, 24-inch, 30-inch, and 37-inch chains with removable and reversible drop pendant, 8637, $70; in 1975, pierced earrings, 7180, $60; *Tudor*, 1976, reversible cross drop 8607, $40; reversible pierced earrings, 7607, $35.

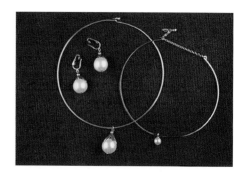

New Mode, 1970, unsigned necklace, 8358, $35; clip earrings, 7358, $30; *Petite Pearl*, 1971, necklace, 8448, $30.

Ultima, 1969, necklace/bracelet/pins, 8211, $75; clip earrings, 7211, $45.

Special Dream, 1981, 8458, $25; *Classic*, 1981, clip earrings, 7501, $10; also pierced earrings, 7500; *Mayfair*, 1979, necklace, 8140, $35; pierced earrings, 7023, $35; *Pearl Swirl*, 1966, necklace, 8615, $30; bracelet, 9615, $20; clip earrings, 7615, $20; also pierced earrings, 7812.

Autumn Leaves, 1982, necklace, 2247, $150; bracelet, 2246, $70; also pierced earrings, 2244.

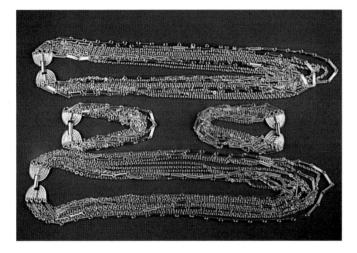

Chiffon, 1977 silver necklace, 8445, $75; in 1978, silver bracelet, 9445, $35; gold necklace, 8439, $75; gold bracelet, 9439, $35.

Mood Magic, 1974, necklace, 8988, $60; clip earrings, 7988, $25; pierced earrings, 7992, $25; *Candlelight*, 1975, bracelet, 9276, $60.

On Stage, 1972, 38-inch chain and 38-inch pearls necklace, 8499, $70; removable dangles, clip earrings, 7499, $35; *Exquisite Lady*, 1976, 36-inch pearls 8612, $55; clip earrings, 7612, $45; *Patrician*, 1975, 36-inch necklace, 8118, $45; pierced earrings, 7118, $35.

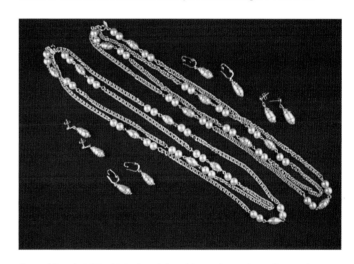

Caged Pearl, 1970, 50-inch gold necklace, 8320, $55; clip earrings, 7320, $25; pierced earrings, 7338, $25; 50-inch silver necklace, 8340, $55; clip earrings, 7340, $25; pierced earrings, 7339, $25.

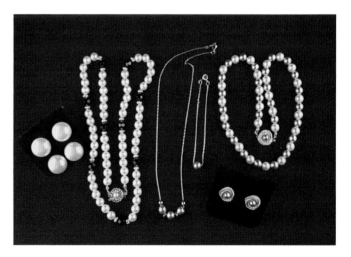

Rhapsody, 1981, necklace, 8196, $50; *Moonfrost*, 1981, clip earrings, 7103, $25; pierced earrings, 7102, $25; *Cassandra*, 1981, necklace, 8193, $40; bracelet, 9072, $15; uses Contessa earrings; *Contessa*, 1981, necklace, 8194, $75; pierced earrings, 7128, $20.

Sweetwater Magic, 1980, necklace, 8392, $40; pierced earrings, 7099, $30; also stickpin, 6058; *Starburst*, 1979, necklace, 8180, $45; pin, 6040, $40; convertible pierced earrings, 7037, $35; necklace and pin from the collection of Joy Robson; *Sabrina*, 1975, 19-inch and 34-inch chains necklace, 8292, $60; pierced earrings, 7294, $30.

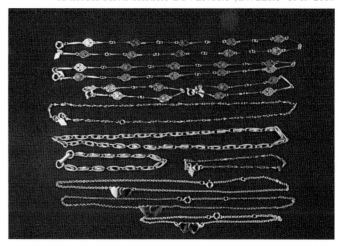

Top to Bottom: *Infinity*, 1980, silver necklace, 8356, $30; in 1981, silver bracelet, 9059, $20; gold necklace, 8357, $35; gold bracelet, 9060, $20; *Whisper*, 1977, necklace, 8930, $35; bracelet, 9930, $25; *Counterpoint*, 1977, necklace, 8598, $30; bracelet, 9598, $20; *Flirting Heart*, 1976, silver necklace, 8279, $30; ankle bracelet, 8.75-inch, 9279, $25; also 9.75-inch, 9283; in 1977, gold necklace, 8782, $25; there is no gold ankle bracelet.

Fashion Flirt, 1967, 36-inch necklace, 8703, $50; bracelet, 9703, $25; clip earrings, 7703, $10; necklace and bracelet have removable dangles.

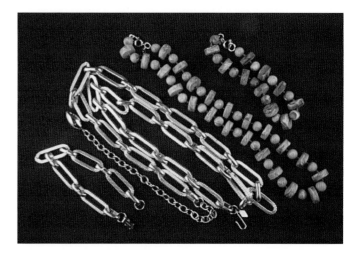

Tailored Accent, 1976, necklace, 8590, $55; bracelet, 9590, $25; *Stone Age*, 1977, necklace, 8443, $25; bracelet, 9443, $20.

Umber Tones, 1974, necklace, 8042, $55; clip earrings, 7042, $20.

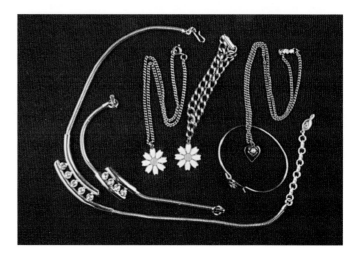

Holiday Lites, 1977, necklace, 8456, $72, bracelet, 9456, $55; *Lazy Daisy*, 1966, necklace, 8649, $20; bracelet, 9649, $20; *Rosebud*, 1976, necklace, 8430, $20; unsigned bracelet, 9430, $25.

Pal-ette, 1968, necklace, 8202, $20; bracelet, 9202, $20; *Little Sweetheart*, 1971, necklace, 8445, $25; bracelet, 9445, $25; *Primrose*, 1972, necklace, 8536, $20; bracelet, 9536, $20.

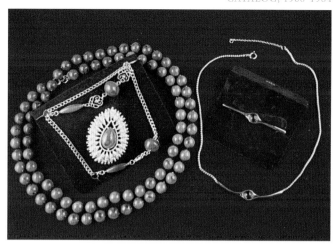

Granada, 1979, 37-inch beads and 29-inch chain necklace, 8996, $60; pin, 6995, $25; *Norwegian Ice*, 1980, necklace, 8408, $50; pin, 6057, $25.

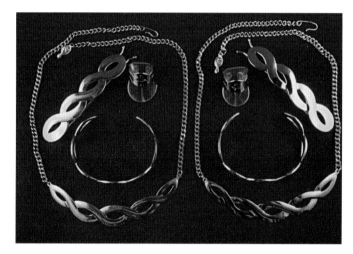

Fashion Braid, 1975, gold bracelet, 9281, $25; silver bracelet, 9280, $25; in 1976, gold necklace, 8281, $40; barrette 6281, $25; ring, 5731, $20; silver necklace, 8280, $40; barrette 6280, $25; ring, 5730, $20.

Fanfare, 1982, necklace, 8026, $140; pierced earrings, 7286, $45; earrings from the collection of Pam Eade.

Ember Light, 1967, necklace, 8702, $30; *Golden Autumn*, 1968, bracelet, 9752, $40; *Golden Embers*, 1967, ring, 5161, $35; *Coronation*, 1975, necklace, 8126, $65; bracelet, 9126, $65; ring, 5566, $30.

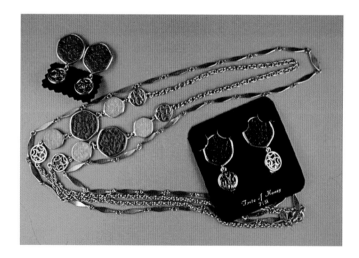

Taste of Honey, 1974, 38-inch and 40-inch chain necklace, 8951, $70; clip earrings, 7951, $30; in 1975, pierced earrings, 7238, $35.

Triple Feature, 1982, 26-28-30-inch necklace, 8020, $110; 7-inch bracelet, 9110, $40; from the collection of Joy Robson; *Going Places*, 1982, pierced earrings, 2039, $40.

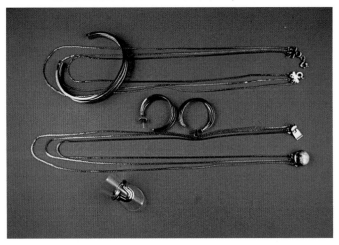

Elegant Trio, **Top:** 1979, necklace, 8077, $50; bracelet, 9035, $45; pierced earrings, 7035, $40. **Bottom:** in 1980, necklace was released again with a new clasp, same item number 8077, $50; set of rings 5307-5309, $30, sizes 5-7.

Festival, 1983, bracelet, 9832, $90; with *Chain-A-Bead Chain*, 1982, 34-inch necklace, 8643, $30; also 16-inch, 8369, originally called *Add-A-Bead Chain* in 1980 with same item numbers, and *Beads*, 1984, 8832, $40; sold only in packets of six; *Summer Wind*, 1982, necklace, 8096, $45; pierced earrings, 7273, $25.

Indian Pride, 1982, necklace, 8041, $70; *Matchmaker*, 1982, clip earrings, 7203, $30; both from the collection of Joy Robson.

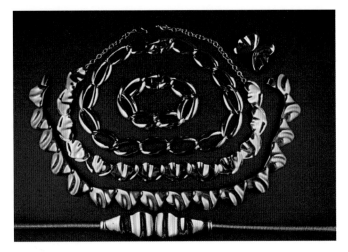

Inside to outside: *Accent*, 1984, necklace, 8941, $40; bracelet, 9941, $25; bracelet from the collection of Joy Robson; *Wave Length*, 1982, necklace, 8065, $60; pierced earrings, 7310, $30; earrings from the collection of Joy Robson; *Rich Girl*, 1982, necklace, 2014, $165; belt, 2018, $100; also bracelet, 2016 and pierced earrings, 2015.

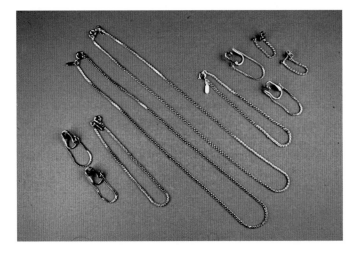

Classic Partners, 1978, gold necklace, 8418, $15; gold bracelet, 9418, $15; silver bracelet, 9419, $10; also *Classic Partners Going Steady* gold pierced earrings, 7418; in 1980, silver necklace, 8419, $20; *Classic Partners Going Steady* gold clip earrings, 7090, $25; silver clip earrings, 7086, $25; silver pierced earrings, 7419, $20.

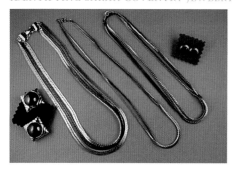

Night & Day, 1982, 16-inch silver necklace, 2157, $90; also gold tones 2156; *Dramatic*, 1984, clip earrings, 7949, $55; from the collection of Joy Robson; *Midnight Magic*, 1982, gold, 18-inch necklace, 2167, $50; 30-inch necklace, 2166, $70; also bracelet, 2170; stack ring set, 2174-2176, sizes 5-7; also silver, 18-inch necklace, 2169, 30-inch necklace, 2168, bracelet, 2171, stack ring set, 2177-2179, sizes 5-7; *Eclipse*, 1983, pierced earrings, 7811, $30; from the collection of Joy Robson.

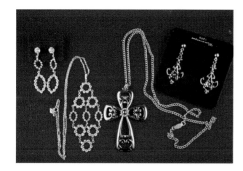

Vienna, 1970, necklace, 8376, $55; clip earrings, 7376, $30; *Romanesque*, 1975, cross necklace, 8270, $75; pierced earrings, 7370, $50.

Summer White, 1982, necklace, 8532, $40; from the collection of Joy Robson; *Matchmaker*, 1982, clip earrings, 7203, $30; from the collection of Joy Robson; *Show Stopper*, 1984, necklace, 8873, $70; *Times Square*, 1984, clip earrings, 7914, $30; also pierced earrings, 7912, and gold clip earrings, 7913, pierced earrings, 7911, from the collection of Joy Robson.

Prairie Princess, 1982, necklace, 2241, $80; pierced earrings, 2242, $50; ring, 2238-2240, sizes 5-9, $55.

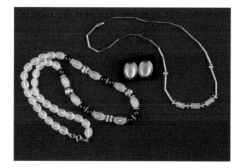

Elegance, 1982, necklace, 2202, $75; pierced earrings, 2203, $40; necklace from the collection of Joy Robson; *Sugarfrost*, 1977, necklace, 8773, $35.

Starlite, 1979, necklace, 8850, $40; ring, 5799, $25; *Premier*, 1977, necklace, 8638, $50; ring, 5755, $40; *Festive*, 1979, necklace, 8460, $75; removable drop, ring, 5798, $35; *Lovely Lady*, 1976, ring, 5650, $35; in 1977, necklace, 8266, $50.

Moon Beam, 1977, necklace, 8594, $25; ring, 5748, $25; *Java*, 1974, necklace, 8026, $45; ring, 5511, $35; *Sierra*, 1979, necklace, 8062, $45; ring, 5859, $30; *Tapestry*, 1973, necklace, 8618, $45; ring, 5391, $40; *Cameo Lady*, 1973, necklace, 8833, $25; ring, 5462, $20; *Rose Cameo*, 1966, necklace, 8653, $45; in 1967, ring, 5162, $40.

Flattery, 1974, necklace, 8945, $45; ring, 5506, $30; *Moon Cloud*, 1974, necklace, 8906, $30; ring, 5492, $30; *Navajo*, 1973, necklace, 8651, $40; ring, 5399, $35; *Imperial*, 1974, pin-pendant, 8940, $65; ring, 5503, $30.

Sea Treasure, 1977, necklace, 8551, $50; ring, 5733, $35; *Winsome*, 1974, necklace, 8905, $35; ring, 5491, $30; *Sara*, 1980, necklace, 8255, $45; ring, 5095-5097, sizes 5-7, $20; *Katrina*, 1977, necklace, 8243, $60; in 1978, ring, 5782, $30; *Melissa*, 1978, necklace, 8632, $40; ring, 5781, $40.

Folklore, 1977, necklace, 8541, $30; ring, 5756, $35; *Continental*, 1977, necklace, 8242, $60; ring, 5765, $20; *Pink Lady*, 1973, necklace, 8830, $45; in 1974, ring, 5500, $30.

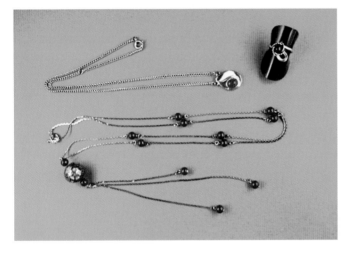

Top: *Spice Island*, 1977, necklace, 8711, $30; *Spice*, 1982, ring, 2141-2143, $55, sizes 5-7; from the collection of Joy Robson; **Bottom:** *Trade Winds*, 1982, necklace, 2180, $55.

Holiday Beads, 1974, 36-inch necklace, all came with a detachable 36-inch silver chain; Bermuda blue, 8896; jet, 8097; ice, 8099; navy, 8895; chalk, 8897; $40 each.

Holiday Beads, 1974, 36-inch necklace, all came with a detachable 36-inch gold chain; tortoise, 8098; satin sand, 8894; melon, 8893; $40 each.

Holiday Beads, 1974, 36-inch necklace, came as sets shown without chains; jet and ice, 8103; satin sand and melon, 8930; navy and chalk, 8929; $40 each.

Holiday Beads, 1975, 36-inch necklace, no chains; red, 8212; yellow, 8213; lavender, 8214; pink, 8215; blue, 8216; white, 8217; jet, 8388; tortoise, 8389; ice, 8390; $25 each; *Holiday Circles*, 1975, clip earrings, 7647, $40 (black, ice, tortoise set); *Holiday*, 1975, pierced earrings dangles, red/gold, 7220; white/silver, 7229; yellow/silver, 7221; pink/silver, 7225; lavender/gold, 7224; $25 each; also red/silver, 7219; white/gold, 7230; yellow/gold, 7222; pink/gold, 7226; lavender/silver, 7223; blue/silver, 7227; blue/gold, 7228; *Chicken Clip*, 1974, earrings, 7056, $20, one pair silver and one pair gold; *Ear Wires*, 1974, pierced earrings, 7053, $15, one pair silver and one pair gold.

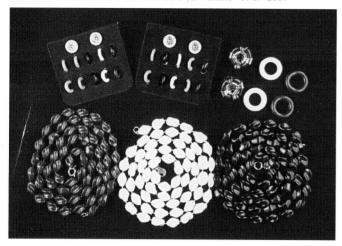

Holiday Beads, 1976, 36-inch necklace, no chains, red, 8799; white, 8800; navy, 8801; $25 each; *Holiday Circles*, 1976, pierced silver, 7820, $30; pierced gold, 7819, $30; *Holiday Circles*, 1976, clip earrings, 7804, $40 (red, white, blue set).

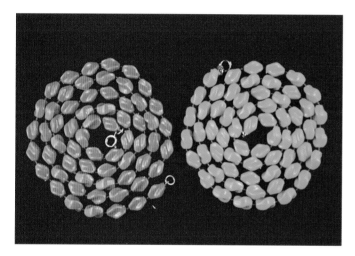

Holiday Beads, 1977, 36-inch necklace, no chains, melon, 8330; Bermuda blue, 8331; $20 each.

Holiday Garden, 1976, 33-inch and 36-inch chains, white, 8380; black, 8379; tortoise, 8374; aqua and eggshell, 8378; melon and eggshell, 8377; $55 each; *Flip Set*, 1976, pierced earrings, 7619, $25.

Starstruck, 1983, necklace, 2184, $55; ring, 2188-2190, $40, sizes 5-7; *Jazzy*, 1983, pin, 2298, $145; from the collection of Joy Robson; *Sassy*, 1983, clip earrings, 2249, $60; from the collection of Joy Robson; *Snowflower*, 1982, pierced earrings, 2192, $50; ring, 2194-2196, $55, sizes 5-7; also necklace, 2191, ring from the collection of Joy Robson.

Holiday, 1966, bracelet, red, 9621, $45; clip earrings, 7621, $30; black, 9620, $45; clip earrings, 7620, $30; white, 9590, $45; clip earrings, 7590, $30; blue, 9622, $45; clip earrings, 7622, $30; green, 9619, $45; clip earrings, 7619, $30.

Atlantis, 1976, bracelet, 9369, $40; clip earrings, 7369, $35; *Sea Scroll*, 1974, bracelet, 9874, $40; clip earrings, 7874, $35; *Cosmic Wrap-Around*, 1971, bracelet, copper, 9429, $40; silver, 9384, $40; silver ring, 5260, $30; gold, 9383, $40; gold ring, 5259, $30; there was no copper ring; *Florentine*, 1972, bracelet, silver, 9466, $50; clip earrings, 7466, $40; gold, 9465, $50; clip earrings, 7465, $40.

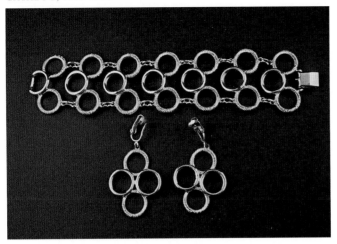

Fancy Free, 1971, bracelet, 9412, $45; clip earrings, 7412, $30.

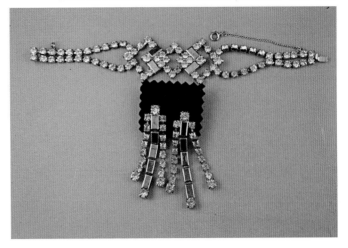

Golden Ice, 1972, bracelet, 9550, $85; clip earrings, 7550, $55.

Goldenrod, 1976, bracelet, 9997, $60; clip earrings, 7997, $25; *Soft Swirl*, 1973, bracelet, 9567, $40; clip earrings, 7567, $20; ring, 5390, $25.

Strawflower, 1975, bracelet, 9194, $60; pin, 6194, $30; clip earrings, 7194, $30; ring, 5602, $30; *Wood Nymph*, 1970, bracelet, 9334, $30; in 1972, ring, 5339, $25.

Acapulco, 1969, bracelet, 9275, $55; pin, 6275, $30; clip earrings, 7275, $15; *One and Only*, 1984, necklace, 8909, $20; pierced earrings, 7909, $15; *Garland*, 1968, bracelet, 9209, $30; pin, 6209, $20; clip earrings, 7209, $25.

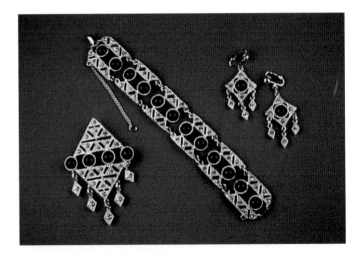

Operetta, 1973, bracelet, 9828, $80; pin, 6828, $50; clip earrings, 7828, $45.

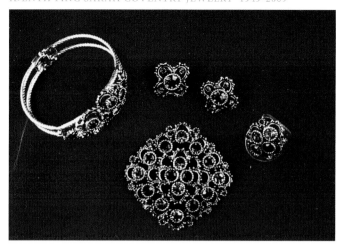

Austrian Lites, 1973, bracelet, 9633, $50; pin, 6633, $50; clip earrings, 7633, $40; ring, 5392, $40.

Leading Lady, 1970, bracelet, 9355, $60; pin, 6355, $50; clip earrings, 7355, $35.

Black Reflections, 1972, bracelet, 9507, $45; clip earrings, 7507, $30; *Mystique*, 1974, bracelet, 9030, $60; ring, 5504, $30; *Nocturne*, 1972, bracelet, 9484, $50; in 1974, pierced earrings, 7878, $30; ring, 5485, $25.

Serenade, 1970, bracelet, 9354, $60; pin, 6354, $50; clip earrings, 7354, $30; *Moon-Lites*, 1970, bracelet, 9287, $40; pin, 6287, $35; clip earrings, 7287, $35.

Crescent, 1969, bracelet, 9273, $40; pin, 6273, $40; clip earrings, 7273, $40.

Valencia, 1970, bracelet, 9291, $45; pin, 6291, $30; clip earrings, 7291, $20; *Inca*, 1974, bracelet, 9879, $45; pin, 6879, $30; clip earrings, 7879, $35.

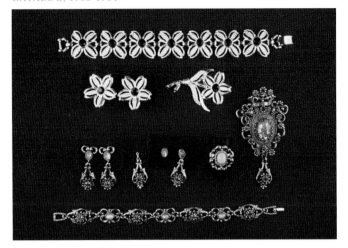

Black Beauty, 1967, bracelet, 9734, $45; pin, 6734, $25; clip earrings, 7734, $25; *Contessa*, 1974, bracelet, 9936, $55; pin-pendant,6936, $60; clip earrings, 7936, $40; in 1975, convertible pierced earrings, 7184, $50; ring, 5608, $45.

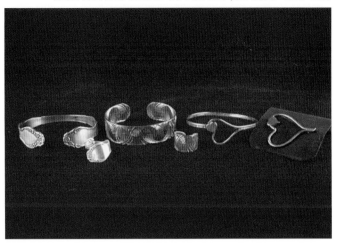

Personal Choice, 1975, bracelet, 9129, $45; ring, 5527, $30; *Golden Swirls*, 1976, bracelet, 9459, $40; ring, 5667, $25; *Open Heart*, 1980, bracelet, 9052, $25; pin, 6055, $25.

Antique Rose, 1971, bracelet, 9439, $40; pin, 6439, $25; clip earrings, 7439, $30; pierced earrings, 7440, $30; in 1972, ring, 5377, $25.

Cleopatra, 1972, bracelet, 9479, $75; clip earrings, 7479, $50; ring, 5329, $40; *Fashion Cuff*, 1973, pewter, 9634, $40; also bronze, 9635; *Fashion Hold Barrette*, 1972, unsigned bronze, 6544, $30; also pewter, 6545; *Golden Nile*, 1971, bracelet, 9452, $45; necklace, 8452, $50.

Blue Lady, 1973, bracelet, 9636, $40; pierced earrings, 7636, $30; ring, 5393, $25; *Northern Lights*, 1973, bracelet, 9576, $60; clip earrings, 7576, $35; ring, 5388, $40.

Nocturne, 1966, pin, 6614, $40; clip earrings, 7614, $40; *Nature's Pearl*, 1970, pin, 6318, $25; clip earrings, 7318, $25.

Wooded Beauty, 1968, pin, 6753, $25; clip earrings, 7753, $25; *Whispering Leaf*, 1967, pin, 6701, $25; clip earrings, 7701, $25; *Amber Petal*, 1982, pin/pendant, 8027, $40; pierced earrings, 7277, $40.

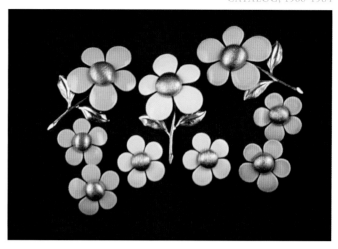

Flower Flattery, 1968, yellow pin, 6744, $35; clip earrings, 7744, $35; white pin, 6743, $35; clip earrings, 7743, $35; pink pin, 6745, $35; clip earrings, 7745, $35.

Tahitian Flower, 1969, salmon pin, 6224, $40; clip earrings, 7224, $40; white pin, 6225, $40; clip earrings, 7225, $40; blue pin, 6226, $40; clip earrings, 7226, $40.

Ivy, 1968, silver pin, 6783, $20; clip earrings, 7783, $20; gold pin, 6782, $20; clip earrings, 7782, $20.

Dogwood, 1969, pink pin, 6221, $30; clip earrings, 7221, $30; white pin, 6222, $30; clip earrings, 7222, $30; black pin, 6223, $30; clip earrings, 7223, $30.

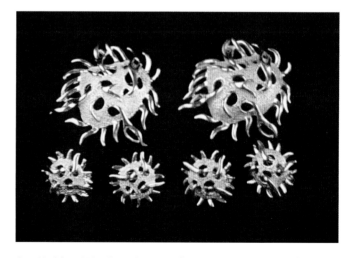

Sea Urchin, 1970, silver pin, 6317, $25; clip earrings, 7317, $25; gold pin, 6316, $25; clip earrings, 7316, $25.

Fantasy, 1967, pin, 6705, $40; clip earrings, 7705, $40; *Placid Beauty*, 1967, pin, 6680, $30; clip earrings, 7680, $30.

Remembrance, 1968, pin, 6798, $45; clip earrings, 7798, $25; in 1969, pierced earrings, 7266, $35; in 1970, stick pin, 6350, $45.

Fashion In Motion, 1969, pin, 6251, $45; clip earrings, 7251, $40; *Silvery Maple*, 1967, pin, 6679, $40; clip earrings, 7679, $30.

Top: *Festival*, 1975, pin, 6122, $50; clip earrings, 7122, $40; *Burgundy*, 1972, pin, 6485, $25; clip earrings, 7485, $35; *Moonlight*, 1973, pin, 6841, $50; clip earrings, 7841, $40; **Bottom:** *Lite Touch*, 1982, pin, 6836, $25; *Snow Blossom*, 1982, pierced earrings, 7266, $35; belt, 7266, $65; belt from the collection of Joy Robson; *Masterpiece*, 1972, pin, 6497, $55; stickpin, 6498, $35.

Fashion Petals, 1968, green pin, 6737, $35; clip earrings, 7737, $35; orange pin, 6738, $35; clip earrings, 7738, $35; jet black pin, 6741, $35; clip earrings, 7741, $35; blue pin, 6740, $35; clip earrings, 7740, $35; hot pink pin, 6739, $35; clip earrings, 7739, $35; white pin, 6742, $35; clip earrings, 7742, $35.

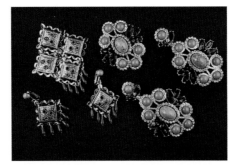

Temple Lites, 1969, pin, 6254, $45; clip earrings, 7254, $35; *Maharani*, 1969, pendant, 8284, $50; pin, 6284, $50; clip earrings, 7284, $30. This was Sarah's special 20th Anniversary set. The pendant came with a hook on the back for attaching a chain, which was not included. Two pendants could be attached to a loop on the earrings, shown, for the exotic look.

Fashion Round, 1970, silver pin, 6314, $25; clip earrings, 7314, $25; gold pin, 6315, $25; clip earrings, 7315, $25; *Foxtail*, 1981, gold pin, 6094, $35; pierced earrings, 7109, $30; silver pin, 6093, $35; also pierced earrings, 7108.

Strawberry Festival, 1966, pin, 6640, $50; clip earrings, 7640, $35; *Tangerine*, 1973, pin, 6638, $40; clip earrings, 7638, $35; *Westminster*, 1972, pin, 6529, $55; clip earrings, 7529, $45.

Pastel Petals, 1967, pin, 6669, $40; clip earrings, 7669, $40; *Candy Land*, 1973, pin, 6557, $25; clip earrings, 7557, $25; *Americana*, 1971, pin, 6387, $40; clip earrings, 7387, $30; pierced earrings, 7428, $35.

Bold Gypsy, 1967, burnt orange pin, 6673, $35; clip earrings, 7673, $40; poison green pin, 6690, $35; clip earrings, 7690, $40; Wedgwood blue pin, 6689, $35; clip earrings, 7689, $40; go-go pink pin, 6688, $35; clip earrings, 7688, $40.

White Petals, 1972, pin, 6462, $40; clip earrings, 7462, $35; *Golden Mum*, 1969, pin, 6219, $55; clip earrings, 7219, $55; *Water Lily*, 1966, pin, 6587, $35; clip earrings, 7587, $30.

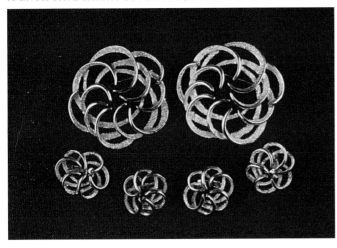

Tailored Swirl, 1967, silver pin, 6722, $25; clip earrings, 7722, $25; gold pin, 6723, $25; clip earrings, 7723, $25.

Flair, 1970, silver pin, 6351, $20; clip earrings, 7351, $25; gold pin, 6352, $20; clip earrings, 7352, $25; *Madam Butterfly*, 1971, silver pin, 6441, $25; gold pin, 6442, $25; in 1973, silver pierced earrings, 7707, $25; gold pierced earrings, 7706, $25; in 1976, silver ring, 5659, $20; gold ring, 5658, $20.

Ribbonette, 1971, silver pin, 6421, $30; clip earrings, 7421, $30; gold pin, 6422, $30; clip earrings, 7422, $30; *Scarf Keeper*, 1970, unsigned, gold, 6295, $25; silver, 6296, $25; shown in January 1970 *Cosmopolitan*; *Roman Coins*, 1971, clip earrings, gold, 7399, $35; silver, 7398, $35.

Ember Flower, 1972, pin, 6513, $45; clip earrings, 7513, $35; *Allusion*, 1968, pin, 6208, $55; clip earrings, 7208, $35.

Sea Sprite, 1972, gold pin, 6508, $25; clip earrings, 7508, $25; silver pin, 6509, $25; clip earrings, 7509, $25; *Demi-Flower*, 1969, gold pin, 6249, $25; clip earrings, 7249, $25; silver pin, 6250, $25; clip earrings, 7250, $25.

Sunflower, 1969, gold pin, 6227, $20; clip earrings, 7227, $25; silver pin, 6228, $20; clip earrings, 7228, $25.

Baroque Goddess, 1969, pin, 6256, $30; clip earrings, 7256, $40; *Fashion Flower*, 1967, pin, 6721, $45; clip earrings, 7721, $30; *Fashion Splendor*, 1970, pin, 6286, $40; clip earrings, 7286, $35.

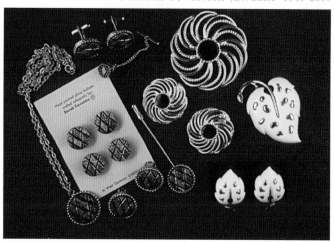

Mosaic, 1972, necklace, 8522, $45; stick pin, 6522, $30; clip earrings, 7522, $45; button covers 6554, $25; tie tac, 5941, $30; cuff links, 5942, $45; also tie tac and cuff links set, 5081, shown in October 1972 *Family Circle* magazine; *Mystic Swirl*, 1966, pin, 6641, $30; clip earrings, 7641, $35; *White Velvet*, 1971, pin, 6430, $30; clip earrings, 7430, $30.

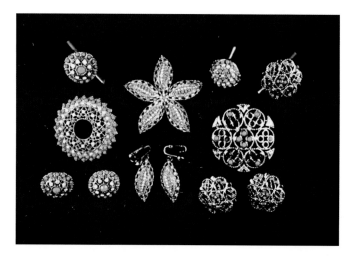

Aquarius, 1970, pin, 6360, $60; clip earrings, 7360, $40; ring, 5170, $45; *Ocean Star*, 1968, pin, 6799, $30; clip earrings, 7799, $30; ring, 5181, $30; shown in April 1968 *Redbook* magazine; *Ceylon*, 1971, pin, 6409, $40; clip earrings, 7409, $45; ring, 5262, $45.

Venetian, 1969, pin, 6274, $25; clip earrings, 7274, $25; *Silvery Mist*, 1971, pin, 6407, $25; clip earrings, 7407, $25; *Circlet*, 1973, pin, 6825, $25; clip earrings, 7825, $25; *Birds in Flight*, 1967, pin, 6704, $40; clip earrings, 7704, $30.

Centurion, 1975, pin, 6342, $55; clip earrings, 7342, $30; *Peking*, 1972, pin, 6548, $55; clip earrings, 7548, $45.

Swan Lake, 1972, necklace, 8540, $55; with *Sparkle Circle*, 1972, pin, 6540, $30; clip earrings, 7540, $35; *Crystal Fern*, 1967, pin, 6724, $35; clip earrings, 7724, $35.

107

Golden Trillium, 1969, pin, 6253, $45; clip earrings, 7253, $40; *Tinsel Twist*, 1976, pin, 6603, $40; clip earrings, 7603, $40.

Strawberry Ice, 1968, pin, 6736, $25; clip earrings, 7736, $20; in 1970, pierced earrings, 7735, $30; *Criss Cross*, 1971, pin, 6388, $30; clip earrings, 7388, $25; *Trellis*, 1973, pin, 6826, $25; clip earrings, 7826, $25.

Summer Frost, 1966, pin, 6616, $30; clip earrings, 7616, $30; *Petite*, 1966, pin, 6627, $20; clip earrings, 7627, $20; *Modern Leaf*, 1968, pin, 6201, $35; clip earrings, 7201, $35.

Blue Snowflake, 1973, pin, 6659, $55; clip earrings, 7659, $55; *Star Fire*, 1967, pin, 6720, $50; clip earrings, 7720, $35; modeled by Cyd Charisse in 1973 *Woman's Day* magazine; *Anniversary*, 1973, pin, 6840, $75; clip earrings, 7840, $40; ring, 5465, $30.

Tropics, 1966, pin, 6610, $30; clip earrings, 7610, $30; *Filigree Clover*, 1972, pin, 6461, $25; clip earrings, 7461, $25; *Windfall*, 1978, pin, 6547, $30; clip earrings, 7547, $30.

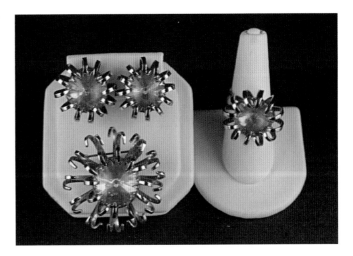

Mystic Blue, 1969, pin, 6281, $50; clip earrings, 7281, $60; ring, 5218, $35.

Simplicity, 1966, pin, 6612, $20; clip earrings, 7612, $20; *Sun Flower*, 1966, pin, 6645, $25; clip earrings, 7645, $20.

Polynesian, 1967, pin, 6668, $40; clip earrings, 7668, $40.

Flirtation, 1974, pin, 6902, $20; clip earrings, 7902, $20; *Oriental*, 1971, pin, 6443, $30; clip earrings, 7443, $30.

Enchanted Forest, 1967, pin, 6699, $40; clip earrings, 7699, $40; *Autumn Splendor*, 1976, pin, 6601, $50; clip earrings, 7601, $50.

Delicious, 1970, pin, 6292, $30; large clip earrings, 7292, $40; medium clip earrings, 7374, $35; pierced earrings, 7373, $40.

Carnival, 1970, pin, 6313, $35; clip earrings, 7313, $30.

Springtime, 1972, pin, 6493, $55; clip earrings, 7493, $40; in 1973, pierced earrings, 7657, $30.

Orbit, 1970, turquoise pin, 6348, $30; clip earrings, 7348, $30; coral pin, 6347, $30; clip earrings, 7347, $30.

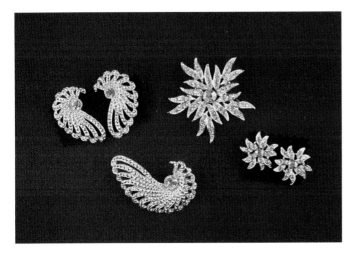

Evening Splendor, 1968, pin, 6750, $25; clip earrings, 7750, $25; *Aurora Blaze*, 1967, pin, 6725, $70; clip earrings, 7725, $40; modeled by Lesley Ann Warren in October 1967 *McCall's*.

Top: *Sparkle Lites*, 1970, pin, 6323, $30; clip earrings, 7323, $25; *Mountain Flower*, 1968, pin, 6210, $45; clip earrings, 7210, $40; **Bottom:** *Evening Star*, 1966, pin, 6629, $30; clip earrings, 7629, $20; earrings from the collection of Sue Beaver.

Persian Princess, 1971, pin, 6386, $65; clip earrings, 7386, $45.

Silvery Sunburst, 1969, pin, 6255, $30; clip earrings, 7255, $30.

Moon Flower, 1966, pin, 6584, $40; clip earrings, 7584, $30.

Royal Velvet, 1972, pin, 6553, $80; clip earrings, 7553, $70; ring, 5381, $40.

Heritage, 1976, pin-pendant,8383, $60; 15-inch detachable chain, clip earrings, 7383, $60; ring, 5727, $40; *Daisy Time*, 1971, pin, 6385, $35; clip earrings, 7385, $30; *Blue Note*, 1967, pin, 6732, $25; clip earrings, 7732, $25.

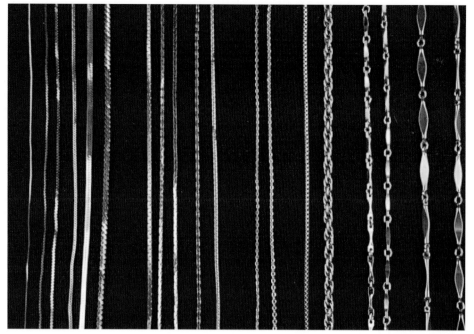

Left to Right: *Ultra Fine 21-inch Serpentine Chain*, 1981, 14kt gold, necklace, 3000, $110; also 18-inch, 3001, 16-inch, 3002, 7-inch, 3003; *Fine Serpentine 16-inch Chain*, 1983, necklace, 3626, $20; also 15-inch, 3627, 18-inch, 3625, 21-inch, 3624, 24-inch, 3623, 27-inch, 3622, 7-inch, 3628; *Serpentine 16-inch Chain*, 1982, sterling silver necklace, 3872, $25; also 15-inch, 3873, 18-inch, 3871, 7-inch, 3874; *Serpentine 16-inch Chain*, 1980, 14kt gold necklace, 6234, $190; also 7-inch, 6208; *Bold Serpentine 18-inch Chain*, 1983, 14kt gold, necklace, 3536, $450; also 16-inch, 3537, 24-inch, 3535, 7-inch, 3538; *Serpentine 32-inch Chain*, 1979, necklace, 8060, $55; *"C" 16-inch Chain*, 1984, sterling silver necklace, 3877, $30; also 15-inch, 3878, 18-inch, 3876, 21-inch, 3875, 7-inch, 3879; *Cobra 24-inch Chain*, 1979, silver, necklace, 8185, $50; also18-inch, 8184, 15-inch, 8183, pierced earrings, 7185; and gold, 24-inch, 8133, 18-inch, 8132, 15-inch, 8131; pierced earrings, 7131; *Cobra 15-inch Chain*, 1982, gold necklace, 8563, $25; also 18-inch, 8565, 24-inch, 8567, 30-inch, 8569, 7-inch, 9105, 9-inch, 9107; and silver, 15-inch, 8564, 18-inch, 8566, 24-inch, 8568, 30-inch, 8570; 7-inch, 9106, 9-inch, 9108; *Peanut 15-inch Chain*, 1980, necklace, 8441, $30; also 18-inch, 8440; *Banana 15-inch Chain*, 1980, gold necklace, 8371, $15; also silver, 8372; *Dainty Lady 16-inch Chain*, 1976, gold necklace, 8652, $15; silver, 8653, $15; *Ripple 18-inch Chain*, 1977, necklace, 8315, $25; also 27-inch, 8314; *Antiqued 24-inch Chain*, 1975, gold necklace, 8336, $25; also silver, 8343; *Fashion Basic 30-inch*, 1979, silver necklace, 8852, $30; gold, 8851, $30; *Fashion Accent 30-inch*, 1977, silver necklace, 8035, $35; gold, 8036, $35.

Slicker 18-inch Chain, 1979, gold necklace, 8298, $35; also silver, 8299; *Coventry Square 20-inch Chain*, 1979, necklace, 8064, $35; *Aaron 15-inch Chain*, 1978, necklace, 8121, $20; *Gentry 20-inch Chain*, 1978, necklace, 8518, $25; *Sparkle 24-inch Chain*, 1972, necklace, 8473, $20; also silver, 8472; *Herringbone 20-inch Chain*, 1980, gold necklace, 8462, $40; also16-inch, 8466, 18-inch, 8464; pierced earrings, 7097; silver, 20-inch, 8463, 16-inch, 8467, 18-inch ,8465; pierced earrings, 7098; *Stretched Cable 36-inch Chain*, 1980, gold necklace, 8364, $35; also silver, 8365; *Caravan 33-inch Chain*, 1978, necklace, 8017, $40; *Dream Weaver 16-inch Chain*, 1983, necklace, 2304, $45; also 18-inch, 2303, 24-inch, 2302, 30-inch, 2301, 7-inch, 2306, 8-inch, 2305; *French Rope 32-inch Chain*, 1981, necklace, 8720, $75; also 16-inch, 8716, 18-inch, 8717, 20-inch, 8718, 24-inch, 8719, 7-inch, 9716, 8-inch, 5984.

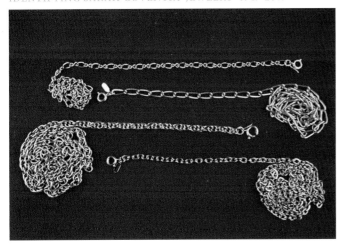

Golden Chain, 1974, top to bottom, 18-inch, 8170, $25; from the collection of Joy Robson; 24-inch, 8167, $30; 30-inch, 8168, $35; 36-inch, 8169, $35.

Bostonian Link 30-inch Chain, 1981, silver necklace, 8216, $40; also gold, 8215; *Bostonian Classic*, 1974, gold bracelet, 9028, $30; silver bracelet, 9029, $30; in 1975, 24-inch gold necklace, 8273, $60; silver, 8274, $60; *Fashion Tie-Up 36-inch Chain*, 1972, necklace, 8549, $65; removable tassels; *Fantastic 30-inch Chain*, 1976, gold necklace, 8683, $35; silver, 8682, $35.

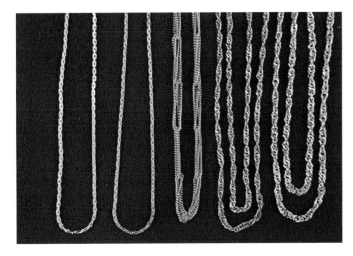

Left: *Embraceable 16-inch Chain*, 1974, silver, 8910, $25; gold, 8909, $25; **Right:** *Simply Elegant 18-inch Chain*, 1976, 8732, $30; *Delicate Twist 36-inch*, 1976, gold, 8332, $40; silver, 8498, $40; shown doubled.

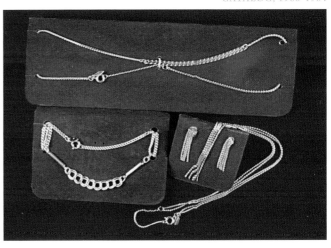

Vari-Chain, 1980, 16-18-inches, 8350, $30; *Double Links*, 1980, 8319, $30; *Free Fall*, 1979, 8174, $45; pierced earrings, 7003, $25.

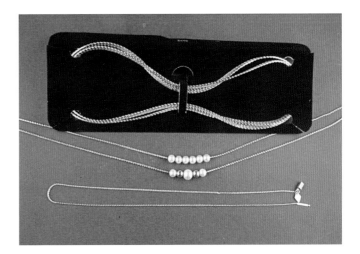

Top: *Endless Herringbone 36-in Chain*, 1981, gold, 8422, $45; also silver, 8423; **Bottom:** *Add-A-Bead Chain*, 1980, 16-inch, 8369, $25; 34-inch, 8643, $35; name changed in 1982 to Chain-A-Bead Chain. Available beads in 1980 were: *Simulated Pearls*, 8646, $15, shown on top chain; *Graduated Beads & Simulated Pearls* 8645, $15, shown on bottom chain; also Graduated Goldentone Beads, 8644, and Goldentone Beads, 8647. All beads came in packages of six for making many different combinations.

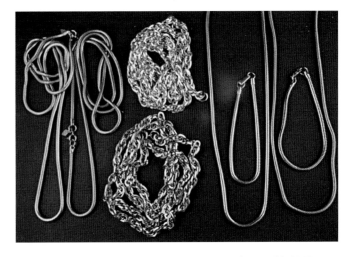

Fashion Rope 37-inch Chain, 1974, silver, 8942, $45; gold, 8943, $45; *Holiday 36-inch Chain*, 1975, silver, 8219, $25; gold, 8220, $25; *Fashion Rope 36-inch Chain*, 1976, gold necklace, 8640, $50; bracelet, 9640, $20; silver necklace, 8641, $50; bracelet, 9641, $20.

Exclamation, 1984, 8998, $85; from the collection of Joy Robson.

Splendor, 1982, 8081, $40; also pierced earrings with removable leaf 7270; *Eternity*, 1982, 2197, $55; *Lucky Lady*, 1980, 30-inch with green stations 8373, $35; *Center Attraction*, 1979, 8536, $35; reversible and removable squares; *Expressions*, 1983, 2285, $45; also pierced earrings, 2276, all from the collection of Joy Robson.

Spectator, 1984, red, 8889, $40; also blue, 8888, from the collection of Joy Robson; *Bamboo*, 1984, turquoise, 8908, $40; coral, 8907, $40.

Spangle Bangles, 1974, red/white/blue, 8923, $55; amber/brown/gold, 8105, $55; *Bangles*, 1974, 8106, $10.

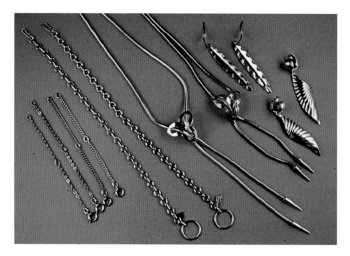

Necklace Extenders Set, 1984, 8908, $20; *Chain Extenders Set*, 1977, 8599, $15; *Choker Chain Set*, 1971, 9415, $30; *Imagination*, 1978, unsigned, 39-inch silver, 8521, $55; gold, 8522, $55; *Spirit*, 1982, pierced earrings, 7272, $35; from the collection of Joy Robson; *Sunburst*, 1983, clip earrings, 2293, $50; also pierced earrings, 2292, from the collection of Joy Robson.

Swingin' Bear, 1971, 8449, $30; *Dancin' Bear*, 1976, 8333, $30; *Skip*, 1976, 8670, $30; *Cheshire*, 1976, 8781, $30; *Magical Unicorn*, 1983, 3917, $50; from the collection of Joy Robson; *Chicken Little*, 1976, 8049, $30; from the collection of Pam Eade; *Swingin' Bear*, 1976, 8806, $30; *Guppy*, 1975, 8288, $20; also bracelet, 9288, from the collection of Fay Williquette; *First Star*, 1977, 8696, $35.

Flight, 1983, 8816, $65; *Fancy Free*, 1978, 8830, $30; *Pandora*, 1978, 8404, $40; from the collection of Joy Robson; *Fly Away*, 1976, 8101, $50; *Brilliant Butterfly*, 1979, 8147, $40; *Windy*, 1978, 8546, $40; *Frolic*, 1979, 8119, $25; reversible, two shown; *Two-Tone Butterfly*, 1980, 8283, $45; gold on one side and silver on the other.

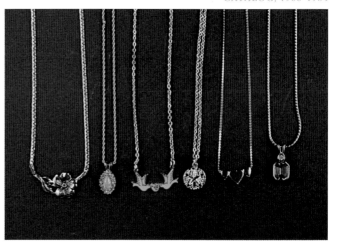

Spring Posie, 1979, 8122, $40; *Heavenly*, 1984, 8803, $50; *Love Birds*, 1984, 8949, $15; *Sand Dollar*, 1980, 8138, $15; *Love Notes*, 1983, 8789, $25; *Calendar Girl*, 1982, 8001-8012, $30; shown is August; also pierced earrings, 7288-7299.

Rajah, 1976, 8405, $90; removable drop; *Athena*, 1977, 8648, $30; *Evening Mist*, 1982, 25-inch, 8067, $50; also 16-inch, 8068.

All unsigned. *Escapade*, 1980, 30-inch cord, 8363, $50; *Orchid*, 1980, 24-inch cord, 8320, $40; *Contemporary*, 1979, 17-inch cord, 8145, $50; *Batik*, 1979, 24-inch rust cord and 44-inch black cord, 8144, $50.

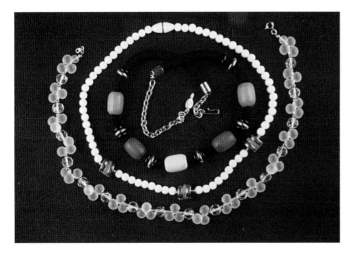

Inside to outside: *On The Move*, 1977, 8849, $60; *Melon Accent*, 1979, 8052, $40; *Frostfire*, 1984, 8943, $50.

Trendsetter, 1977, 8593, $35; *Spinner*, 1976, 8690, $35; *Mizpah*, 1984, gold, 8124, $35; also silver, 5990; traditional coin cut into halves for lovers, engraved, "The Lord watch between me and thee while we are absent one from another." *Twisted Knot*, 1980, 36-inch lariat, 8134, $40.

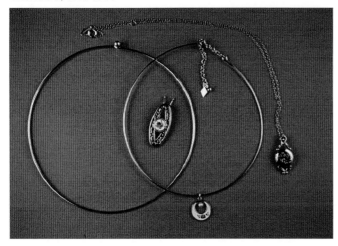

Magic Hoop, 1976, unsigned, silver, 8720, $20; also gold ,8721; *Tracy Hoop*, 1976, 8431, $20; in 1978, barrette, 6431, $20; *Remembrance Locket*, 1980, 8424, $40.

Cinema, 1976, reversible, 8406, $70; both sides shown; *Sand Dune*, 1977, 8513, $45; *Silhouette Perfume*, 1978, 8517, $70; *Viva*, 1984, 8896, $35; from the collection of Joy Robson; *Monogram Coin*, 1980, 8329, $70.

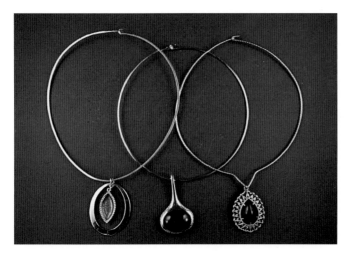

Danish Modern Hoop, 1975, 8204, $50; *Mahogany Hoop*, 1976, 8058, $50; *Golden Teardrop Hoop*, 1974, 8872, $25.

Top to Bottom: *Spring Moods*, 1978, 40-inch, 8834, $25; *Regency*, 1980, 36-inch beads and 29-inch pendant chain, 8252, $80.

Nile Queen, 1977, 8446, $95; *Chinatown*, 1976, 8703, $75.

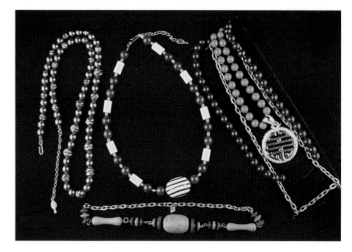

Bronze Glow, 1982, 8021, $75; also clip earrings, 7305; *Cinnamon Swirl*, 1979, 8074, $55; *Fashion Flair*, 1976, 8051, $70; **Bottom:** *Zulu*, 1976, 8334, $60.

All unsigned. *Broadway*, 1978, 24-inch cord, 8500, $50; *Surfside*, 1982, 30-inch cord, 2232, $235; came with shell dangles (not shown); also pierced earrings, 2236, belt, 25-28-inch, 2234, and belt, 29-32-inch, 2235; *Sunset Elegance*, 1979, 18-inch cord, 8013, $55; pendant can be worn as pin.

Broken Heart, 1980, 8284, $40; *Queen of Hearts*, 1977, 8567, $40; *Heart Beam*, 1978, 8557, $35; *Fashion Heart*, 1980, 8141, $50.

Pastel Beads, 1978, pink, 8351, $30; blue, 8352, $30; yellow, 8353, $30; detachable bracelet.

Sea Shell Lariat, 1979, unsigned 8070, $55; *Creamy Shell*, 1982, 2227, $65; *Starfish*, 1982, 2224, $40; *Seaswept*, 1981, 8198, $35; *Gentle Breeze*, 1982, 2225, $60; **Bottom:** *Sea Spray*, 1983, clip earrings, 7837, $40; also pierced earrings, 7836, from the collection of Joy Robson.

Krackle Beads, 1980, 36-inch, purple, 8338, $25; yellow, 8339, $20; *Sierra*, 1977, 18-inch, blue, 8548, $30; flame, 8549, $30.

Personally Yours, 1974, necklace, 8957-8982, $35; all initials available; also pierced earrings, 1975, 7957-7974.

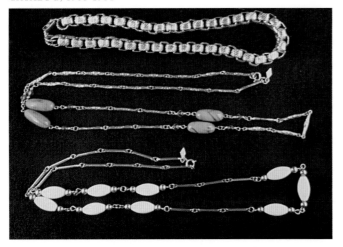

Top to Bottom: *Golden Nugget*, 1977, 8530, $45; *Lucky Lady*, 1976, 8335, $65; *High Society*, 1977, 8658, $55.

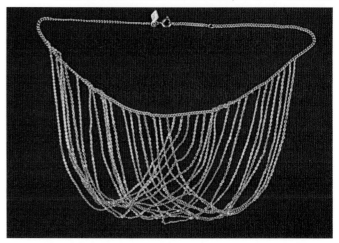

Caprice Bib, 1977, 8837, $85.

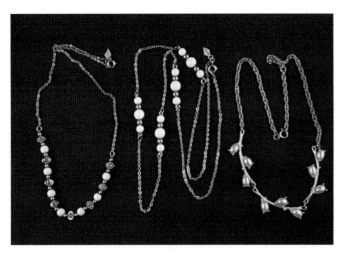

Summer Mist, 1978, 8545, $45; *White Elegance*, 1979, 8066, $45; *Springtime*, 1975, 8203, $60.

Dedication Cross, 1978, 8453, $25; *Heavenly Cross*, 1978, 8261, $20; *Innocence Cross*, 1976, 8689, $20; *Heaven Sent Cross*, 1982, 3619, $95.

Top to Bottom: *Easy Elegance*, 1977, 8516, $40; *Park Avenue*, 1977, 8783, $45; *Update*, 1979, 8047, $45; *Valerie*, 1979, 8023, $45; *Carmel Twist*, 1978, 8523, $40; *Beau Time*, 1976, 8265, $65.

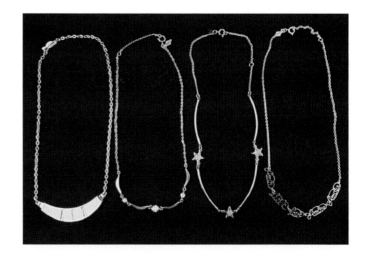

Summer Lites, 1978, 8524, $45; *Gentle Moods*, 1979, 8053, $25; *Enchantment*, 1976, 8455, $50; *Words of Love*, 1979, 8022, $25.

Ice Age, 1976, 8324, $45; *Infinity*, 1978, 8316, $30; *Eclipse*, 1978, 8560, $45; *Splash*, 1975, 8282, $30; *Tri-Tone*, 1977, 8554, $50; *Egyptian Scarab*, 1976, 8409, $35; *Sweetheart*, 1977, 8663, $50.

Coventry Cameo, 1981, 8427, $35; *Pretty Portrait*, 1978, 8579, $25; *Cameo*, 1979, 8102, $50; *Essence*, 1978, 8562, $35; *Magnolia Locket*, 1976, 8337, $45.

Confetti, 1984, red, 8948, $15; also black, 8898, and pearl, 8944; *Will 'O Wisp*, 1978, 8828, $20; *Merrymaker*, 1983, 8784, $45 with three interchangeable sections; *My Three Loves*, 1977, 8848, $30; *Sophisticate*, 1977, 8609, $40.

School Days Initial, 1976, 8472-8497, $35.

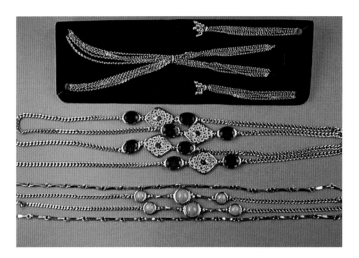

Top to Bottom: *Elegant Links Lariat*, 1979, 5-chains, each 37-inches, 8177, $65; *Lavender 'n Lace*, 1976, 54-inch chain, 8687, $55; *Pink Parfait*, 1979, 33-inch and 36-inch chains, 8057, $75.

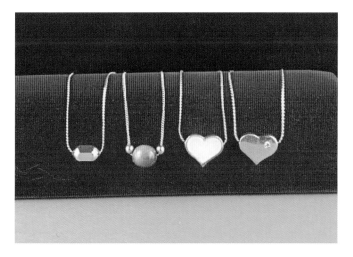

On The Go, 1980, 8354, $30; *Trapeze*, 1974, 8949, $30; *Turn-a-bout*, 1979, 8175, $50; reversible, two are shown.

Jade Accent, 1967, 8683, $40; *Secrets Locket*, 1972, 8535, $20; *Tenderly*, 1977, 8853, $40; *Seashore*, 1979, 8171, $35; *Field Flower*, 1974, 8039, $35; *Viewpoint*, 1979, 8038, $30.

Ann 'N Andy, 1975, 8127, $25; *Hooty Owl*, 1979, 8033, $25; *Myrtle*, 1972, 8643, $25; *Froggy*, 1974, 8987, $30; *Ellie*, 1978, 8542, $20; *Yearling*, 1980, 8416, $30; *Hot Dog*, 1976, 8779, $30.

Endearing, 1976, 8673, $35; *Wildflower*, 1983, 8804, $35; *Demure*, 1966, 8618, $25; *Sarah Ann*, 1977, 8571, $20; *Starlet*, 1977, 8533, $20.

Littlest Angel, 1977, 8931, $40; *Our Secret*, 1977, 8444, $35; two are shown with one opened to reveal the secret; *Calvary Cross*, 1976, 8692, $30.

Charade Set, 1984, 5644-5646, $55 ring sizes 6-8; set of 3 interchangeable ring heads that clip onto a ring shank and also slide onto the chain as a pendant.

Lariat, 1979, 8024, $55, released in January; *Lariat*, 1979, 8080, $55, released in August; the difference in the two Lariat necklaces is the chain; *French Scroll Lariat*, 1980, 8257, $65; *Hi 'N Lo Lariat*, 1979, 37-inch necklace and 29-inch lariat, 8151, $50; *Twister Lariat*, 1980, gold, 8294, $55; also silver, 8295.

Going My Way Lariat, 1979, 8681, $45; *Golden Dove*, 1975, 8201, $35; *Image*, 1979, 8028, $60; interchangeable black and ivory centers; *Candle-Glo*, 1972, 8527, $25; *Mademoiselle*, 1977, 8840, $45.

Moon Luv, 1976, 8734, $35; *Heather*, 1978, 8514, $35; *#1 Mom*, 1981, 14kg, 3272, $75; *Ambrosia*, 1983, 8795, $45; *Tinker Bell*, 1984, 8895, $20; *Confection*, 1983, 8839, $40; also pierced earrings, 7839.

Lovable, 1982, silver, 8623, $35; also gold, 8622; *Change of Heart*, 1976, 8534, $55.

Fashion Melody, 1975, 18-inch and 40-inch chains, 8209, $80; *Designer Links*, 1973, 54-inch chain with detachable bracelet, 8658, $130; *Goldenwood*, 1978, 18-inch beads and 36-inch chain, 8656, $50.

Blue Horizon, 1980, 17-inch and 18-inch chains, 8150, $35; *Glamour*, 1978, 8698, $50; *Glitter*, 1982, 8097, $60; also bracelet, 9114, and pierced earrings, 7251; *Scalloped Lace*, 1978, 8902, $35; *White 'N Bright*, 1979, 8071, $55.

Raspberry Ice, 1977, 21-inch and 29-inch chains, 8505, $65; *Concord*, 1977, 8665, $50; *Touch of Class*, 1976, 37-inch and 40-inch chains, 8429, $80.

Love Story, 1976, 8881-8892, $45.

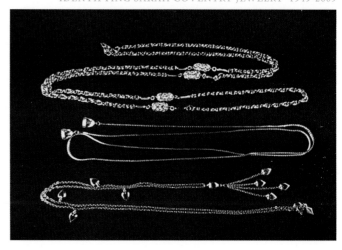

Top to Bottom: *Four Seasons*, 1977, 8778, $45; *Austrian Crystal Lariat*, 1980, 8417, $65; *Jubilee*, 1979, 8153, $75.

Top to Bottom: *Pizzazz*, 1975, 8278, $40; *Fifth Avenue*, 1978, 8833, $65; *Silverspin*, 1977, 8630, $45; *Timely*, 1975, 8341, $50; *Scampi*, 1974, 8027, $40; also bracelet, 9027.

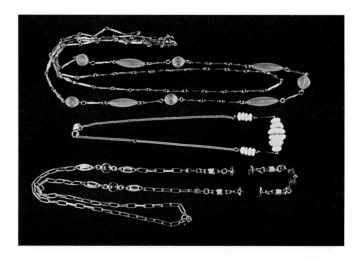

Top to Bottom: *Frosted Ice*, 1979, 35-inch beads and 30-inch chain, 8046, $65; *Puka Beads*, 1976, 8947, $40; *Emberglo*, 1977, 8839, $50.

Heartline, 1977, 8587, $30; *Monogram Heart*, 1980, 8129, $40; *Jealous Heart*, 1976, 8262, $30; *Small Puffed Heart*, 1982, 14kt, 3355, $90; also pendant drop, 3049; *Petite Heart*, 1967, T802, $20; *Monogram Heidi Locket*, 1981, 8186, $30.

Butterflies, 1983, unsigned, 10-inch satin cords, 2273, $80; each necklace has different ways of sorting and attaching the butterflies.

Diamond Buttercup, 1982, 14kt gold-filled, 3750, $25; also pierced earrings, 3751; *Sapphire Buttercup*, 1982, 14kt gold-filled, 3754, $25; also pierced earrings, 3755; *Sparkle Magic*, 1979, 8636, $30; *Cube*, 1980, 16-inch, 8347, $30; also 28-inch, 8348 (has 7 cubes on it); *Cameo*, 1967, T817, $35.

Jewelfish, 1971, 8434, $35; *Thunderstruck*, 1977, 8507, $40; *Coventry Square*, 1977, 8534, $40; *Danish Mood*, 1979, 8994, $45; *Autumn Beauty*, 1979, 8929, $40; *Mystique*, 1978, 8452, $40.

Spring Beauty, 1978, 8605, $40; *Thea*, 1976, 8425, $60; *Pierre*, 1974, 8984, $30; *Cosmopolitan*, 1980, 8137, $50; *Morning Blossoms*, 1979, 8059, $40; *Paradise*, 1978, 8402, $40; *Brocade*, 1981, 8435, $45; *Raindrop*, 1982, 2199, $55; also pierced earrings, 2200 and clip earrings, 2201; *Nostalgia*, 1983, 8817, $40; *Monogram Unisex*, 1981, 8377, $35; *Solitude*, 1978, 8699, $30.

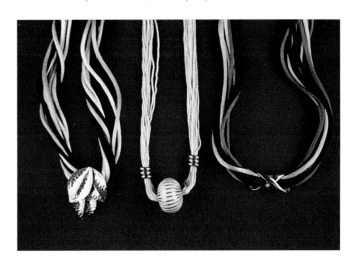

Wind Song, 1982, 20-inch satin cords, 8061, $60; also pierced earrings, 7309; *Milky Way*, 1982, 20-inch cords, 8113, $65; *Vogue*, 1981, 17-inch satin cords 8197, $50.

Fifi, 1975, 8264, $35; *Amulet*, 1979, 8181, $55; *Fantasia*, 1978, 8985, $60; *Blaze*, 1977, 8346, $45; *Marriage Cross*, 1979, 8019, $55; *Front Row*, 1977, 8578, $45; *Angelique*, 1979, 8905, $45.

Copenhagen, 1978, 8822, $60; *Flight*, 1975, 8115, $45; *Royal Flair*, 1975, 8116, $55; *Safari*, 1974, 8954, $55.

Rosary, 1967, 8696, $85; crystal aurora borealis beads with sterling centerpiece and crucifix, offered only once on a flyer at the back of the August 1967 catalog for the Holiday Season as part of Sarah's Religious Jewelry.

St. Christopher Medal, 1967, 17-inch or 24-inch, 8692, $65; *Protestant Medal*, 1967, 17-inch or 24-inch, 8695, $60. These were offered only once on a flyer at the back of the August 1967 catalog for the Holiday Season as part of Sarah's Religious Jewelry. Also available was a Sterling Servicemen's St. Christopher Medal with Land Sea Air, 8694.

Star of David Medal, 1967, 8693, $65; offered only once on a flyer at the back of the August 1967 catalog for the Holiday Season as part of Sarah's Religious Jewelry.

Silvery Zodiac, 1974, 8154-8165, $45.

Multi-Fashion, 1967, 32-inch beads and 30-inch chain, 8684, $25; *Spring Melody*, 1980, 17-inch and 30-inch chains, 8253, $60; shown in June 1980 *Woman's Day*; *Aqua Chain*, 1971, 42-inch beads and 43-inch chain, 8401, $45.

Egyptian Goddess, 1979, reversible, 8139, $45; both sides shown.

Breezy, 1982, 36-inch brown satin cord 8042, $55; may be worn as pin; also pierced earrings, 7275; *Nicole*, 1981, 20-inch blue cord, 8128, $30; *Spring Fever*, 1982, unsigned, reversible 30-inch pink satin cord, 8069, $55; single pendant shows the other side and is from the collection of Joy Robson.

Top to Bottom: *Chain Reaction*, 1984, 8955, $45; *Reflections*, 1984, 17-inch pink baroque pearls, 8812, $35; also lavender, 8823; from the collection of Joy Robson; *Glitter and Smoke*, 1982, 24-inch braid, 8049, $65.

Memories, 1976, 8048, $50; *New Memories*, 1978, 8018, $50; removable locket.

Christina Locket, 1979, 8135, $80; *Tapestry*, 1976, 8672, $55; *Country Roads Locket*, 1977, 8573, $60.

Timeless Beauty, 1977, 22-inch and 30-inch chains, 8559, $60; offered as a special presentation to each Hostess with $100 or more Buying Guest Total as Item Number 0224 during the period of April 11-23 ,1977 before being sold in the August 1977 catalog; *Golden Splendor*, 1977, 8037, $45; *Omega*, 1978, 8448, $45; *Outer Space*, 1976, 8595, $35.

Springtime Lilac, 1979, 33-inch and 36-inch chains, 8094, $80; *Monterey*, 1978, 33-inch and 36-inch chains, 8842, $75; *Golden Classic*, 1977, 22-inch, 24-inch, and 26-inch chains, 8838, $90.

Fashion Duet, 1974, 21-inch and 34-inch chains, 8950, $60; *Primrose,* 1979, 36-inch beads, 8075, $60; 30-inch chain pendant, 8073, $50; *Nature's Treasures*, 1975, 19-inch and 34-inch chains, 8290, $65.

Rose-Marie, 1977, 8317, $50; *Lotus Blossom*, 1979, 8030, $55; *Evergreen*, 1978, reversible, 8832, $50; two shown; *Spring Bouquet*, 1978, 8651, $55; *Spring Song*, 1977, 8553, $60; *Desert Scene*, 1978, 8543, $50.

Grecian, 1976, 8671, $75; includes hook to make bracelet from removable chains; *Today*, 1973, 8834, $60; *Antique Lady*, 1975, 8207, $70.

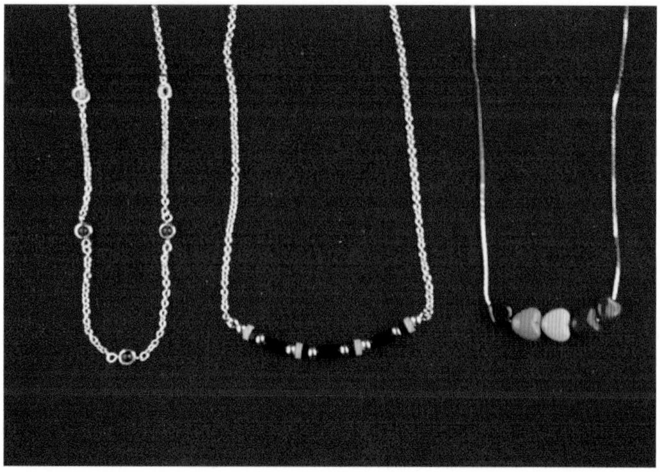

Top to Bottom: *Jamie*, 1977, 8576, $25; *Gigi*, 1977, 8635, $55; *Happy Hearts*, 1983, 8793, $35.

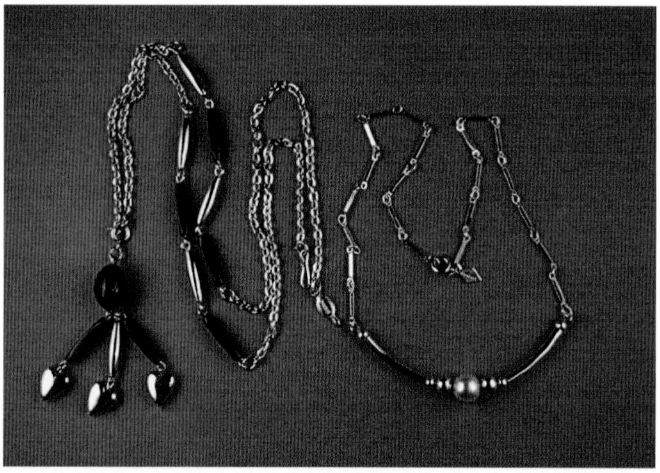

Limbo, 1979, 8592, $45, removable drop; *Samantha*, 1979, 8955, $25.

Dainty Dice, 1980, 8286, $30; *Butterfly Accent*, 1980, 8244, $40; *Skimmer*, 1980, 8370, $30; *Floral Locket*, 1980, 8256, $60; *Heiress*, 1980, 8355, $30; *Rendezvous*, 1979, 8176, $30; removable pendant.

Night Life, 1982, silver, 30-inch, 8192, $40; also silver, 16-inch, 8168, gold, 16-inch, 8166, and gold, 30-inch, 8167; *Motif*, 1977, 36-inch, 8563, $55; *Party Hearts*, 1977, 20-inch and 33-inch chains, 8634, $45; *New Seasons*, 1978, 24-inch, 8874, $40; *Indian Summer*, 1979, 35-inch, 8045, $40.

Bernie the Frog, 1975, 8200, $60; *Tiger Fish*, 1976, 8606, $65; *Hawaiian Fantasy*, 1971, 8450, $60.

Gracious Lady, 1979, 8906, $55; *Interlude*, 1977, 8836, $75; *Encounter*, 1975, 8128, $65; *Credo Cross*, 1975, 8277, $65.

On Time, 1978, 8693, $45; *Sweetheart Locket*, 1973, 8869, $75; *Contempo*, 1975, 8205, $65; *Happy Heart*, 1977, 8575, $60; *Bird of Paradise*, 1978, 8898, $60.

Fashion Zodiac, 1973, 8857–8863, $85; all zodiac signs available, two pieces of plastic put together which will cloud if the seal breaks, shown in 1973 *Woman's Day* magazine.

Original Design Zodiac, 1975, 8754-8765, $75; all zodiac signs available, shown are Libra and Sagittarius; *Turn-About*, 1975, 8110, $70; both sides shown.

Wire Wrap, 1979, 8877, $60; *Three Timer*, 1975, 8246, $55; *Tri-Fashion*, 1973, 8845, $70; pendant, pin, and bracelet. The bracelet section is a tassel drop and not shown.

Birthstone, 1967, T805-T816, $25; shown are May and December; *Secret Heart Birthstone*, 1980, 8221-8232, $30; shown is March, and the back has a heart cut-out in the gold frame; *Birthstone*, 1980, 8911-8922, $30; shown are January, February, May, July, and December, and there was a variety of stiffness to the chains.

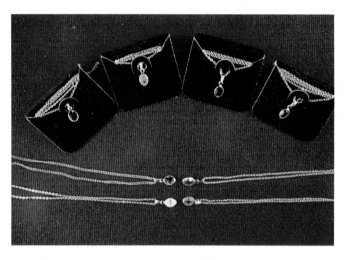

Miss Sarah Birthstone, 1974, 8911-8922, $30; shown are February, March, July, and September on cards, and April, May, November, and December in front.

Zodiac Pendant, 1970, 8300-8311, $30.

Forever Yours Birthstone, 1977, 8859 – 8870, $40; not shown is November.

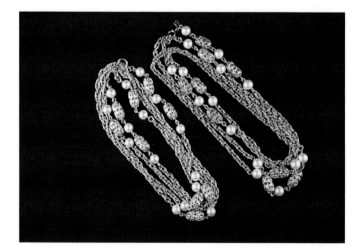

Filigree Lady, 1973, gold, 8847, $60; silver, 8846, $60.

Allure, 1976, silver, 8677, $25; gold, 8678, $25.

Cross Over, 1978, silver, 8894, $50; gold, 8895, $50; *Trinity*, 1972, silver, 8501, $30; gold, 8500, $30.

Tricia, 1971, gold, 8410, $35; silver, 8411, $35.

Instant Fashion, 1968, gold, 8204, $45; silver, 8205, $45.

Pirouette Lariat, 1980, gold, 8263, $40; silver, 8262, $20; *Sparkle Beauty*, 1980, gold, 8234, $40; silver, 8235, $40; *Faith*, 1966, gold, 8654, $25; silver, 8630, $25.

Top to Bottom: *Update*, 1984, 8940, $30; *Elizabeth*, 1978, unsigned, 8618, $55; *Liquid Fire*, 1977, unsigned, 8771, $35.

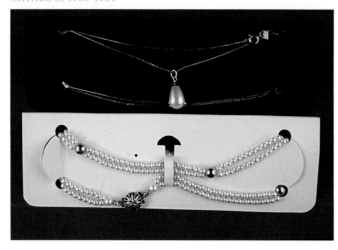

La Parisienne, 1980, 8361, $35; *Symphony*, 1981, 8237, $35.

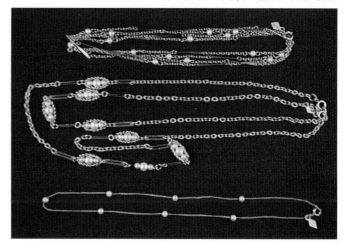

Top to Bottom: *First Love*, 1976, 54-inch chain, 8399, $50; *Promenade*, 1979, 17-inch and 26-inch chains, 8056, $50; *Classic Choice*, 1976, 8735, $35.

Contessa, 1966, 8595, $85.

Moon Beam, 1982, 2115, $40; also stick pin, 2216, pierced earrings, 2116, and ring, 2117-2119, sizes 5-7; *Solo*, 1967, T800, $30.

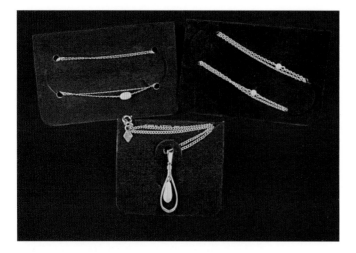

Flirtation, 1980, 8268, $25; *Baby's Breath*, 1980, 8358, $15; **Bottom:** *Snowdrop*, 1970, 8359, $25.

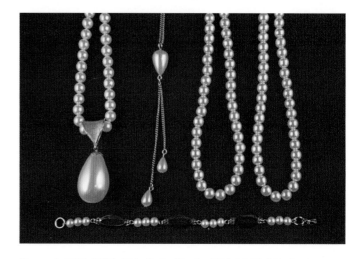

Pompeii, 1974, 8952, $50; *Satin Magic*, 1979, 8076, $40; *Luster Glo*, 1979, 36-inch, peach, 8104, $40; lavender, 8079, $40; **Bottom:** *Tempo Bracelet*, 1975, 9291, $30.

Inside to Outside: *High Society*, 1974, 8066, $40; *Tara*, 1981, 28-inch, 8471, $100; also 18-inch, 8470; released again in 1982 with new sizes and item numbers: 16-inch, 2098, 18-inch, 2097, 24-inch, 2096, 28-inch, 2095, and 7-inch, 2099.

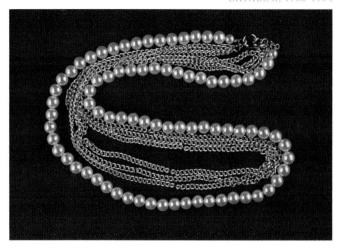

Curtain Call, 1973, 25-inch chains and 25-inch pearl chain, 8842, $50; also bracelet, 9842.

First Lady, 1969, 8218, $35.

Jet Streamer, 1979, 8854, $50; *Satin Beauty*, 1978, 8561, $50; *Duo-Heart*, 1976, 8702, $40; *Jet Elegance*, 1984, necklace, 8903, $40; also pierced earrings, 7903; *Encore*, 1977, 8639, $55.

Sophisticate, 1975, 20-inch and 30-inch chains, 8187, $120.

Fashion, 1970, 60-inch, 8298, $45; 90-inch, 8299, $60.

Collectibles, 1984, 8946, $35; bow charm holder with 3 tiny starfish, shell, and butterfly charms; *Tradewinds*, 1977, 8245, $50; *Nite-Owl*, 1974, 8871, $60; *Heirloom Locket*, 1972, 8471, $55; *Tiara*, 1978, 8451, $50.

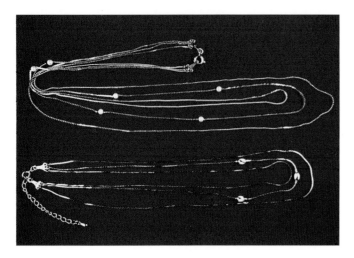

Top: *New Yorker*, 1981, 23-inch, 25-inch, and 27-inch chains, 8519, $50; **Bottom:** *Review*, 1984, 17-inch, 18-inch, and 19-inch chains, white bead, 8986, $30; also black bead 8984.

Cameo Fashions, 1976, 24-inch and 30-inch chains, 8195, $75; *Magic Moods*, 1973, 22-inch and 32-inch chains, 8562, $65; has removable pin and removable tassel.

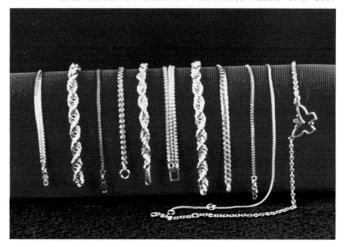

Bold Herringbone 7-inch Chain, 1983, 3609, $20; also 8-inch, 3608, 16-inch, 3607, 18-inch, 3606, 21-inch, 3605, 24-inch, 3901; *Twisted Rope*, 1980, 7-3/4-inch, 9259, $25; also 7-1/4-inch, 9258; *Serpentine 7-inch Chain*, 1980, 14 KT gold, 6208, $115; *Tender Touch*, 1978, 9526, $25; *French Rope*, 1982, 9716, $20; *Gentle Trio*, 1979, 9005, $40; *Twisted Rope*, 1980, 7-1/4-inch, 9260, $25; also 7-3/4-inch, 9261; *Classical Chain*, 1979, silver, 9224, $25; also gold, 9225; *Serpentine 7-inch Chain*, 1984, sterling silver, 3874, $15; *Zebra Ankle Bracelet*, 1981, silver, 9081, $20; also gold, 9082; *Butterfly Ankle Bracelet*, 1977, 9667, $20.

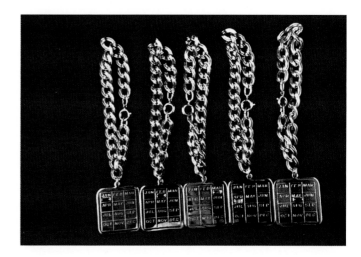

Birthstone Bracelet, 1968, 9784-9795, $30 each; January through May shown.

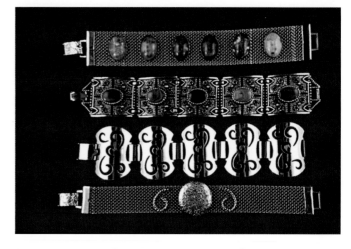

Sonnet, 1974, 9937, $75; *Granada*, 1972, 9495, $65; *Fashion Cuff*, 1966, 9593, $55; *Secret Love Locket*, 1975, 9186, $85.

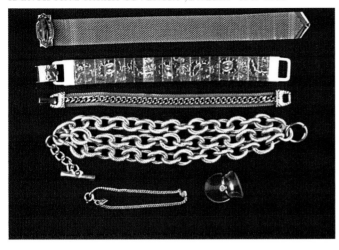

Vanessa, 1977, 9932, $50; *Mural*, 1976, 9727, $60; *Classic Elegance*, 1978, 9531, $50; *French Cuff*, 1971, 9426, $35; *Betsy*, 1979, bracelet, 9041, $20; ring, 5053, $15.

Miss Sarah Birthstone, 1974, 9013-9024, $30; March, September, October shown.

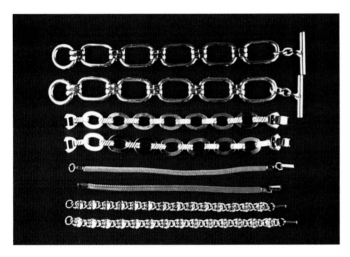

French Links, 1973, gold, 9778, $35; silver, 9777, $35; *Simplicity*, 1970, gold, 9321, $35; silver, 9322, $35; *Avenue*, 1978, silver, 9221, $25; gold, 9222, $25; *Echo Bracelet*, 1974, gold, 9046, $15; silver, 9045, $15.

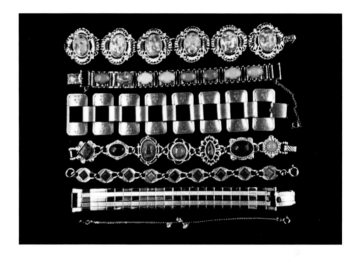

Partytime, 1974, 9880, $65; *Party Pastels*, 1966, 9594, $60; *Melody*, 1976, 9586, $45; *Frolic*, 1972, 9542, $45; *Harlequin*, 1967, unsigned, 9707, $40; reverses to a silver side with sea shell motif; *Roundabout*, 1976, 9102, $60; *Sentiment*, 1981, 9103, $35; also necklace, 8169, and pierced earrings, 7170.

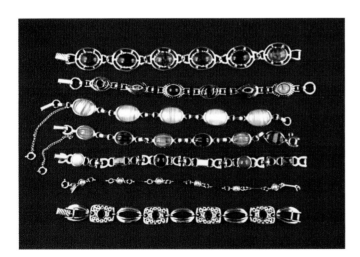

Festoon, 1974, 9929, $40; *Fascination*, 1976, 9057, $60; *Pink Shadows*, 1969, 9213, $25; *Earth-Tones*, 1975, 9131, $40; *Colorama*, 1979, 9003, $40; *M' Lady*, 1979, 9040, $30; *Butterscotch*, 1974, 9064, $40.

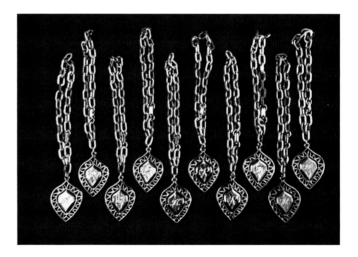

Golden Shield Initial, 1975, 9957-9982, $35; all initials available.

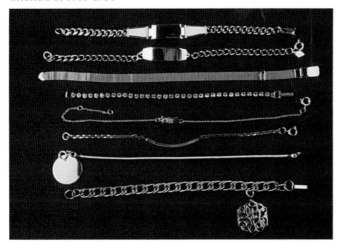

Friendship, 1974, 9025, $50; *ID Bracelet*, 1967, T901, $10; *Mesh Links*, 1980, 9043, $25; also necklace, 8043; *Stargazer*, 1976, 9361, $45; *Monogram Ankle Bracelet*, 1980, 9065, $30; *Paramount*, 1978, 9827, $45; *Tourister*, 1969, silver, 9214, $25; also gold, 9215; *Young Charmer*, 1967, 9681, $20.

Coffee and Cream, 1973, unsigned, ivory and amber, 9714, $40; ivory, 9713, $40; *Vibrations*. 1976, 9731, $35; *Star Bangle*, 1967, 9675, $35; *All Around*, 1978, 9121, $25; *Light 'N Lacey*, 1981, 9079, $30; *Double Twist*, 1979, gold, 9033, $20; also silver, 9034; *Star Attraction*, 1975, 9190, $55; *The Skimp*, 1975, unsigned, 9350, $15.

Petite, 1975, silver, 9363, $25; gold, 9362, $25; *Captive Heart*, 1977, 9841, $20; *Lucky Girl's*, 1971, 9346, $15; *Little Bugger*, 1977, 9558, $20; *Color Trio*, 1975, 9138, $20; has red, white, blue insets; *Bright 'n Beautiful*, 1980, silver, 9055, $35; gold, 9056, $35.

Heritage, 1966, unsigned, gold, 9628, $55; in 1967, silver, 9697, $55; *Cosmopolitan*, 1969, gold, 9257, $50; silver, 9258, $50; *Designer's Choice*, 1973, gold, 9574, $60; silver, 9575, $60.

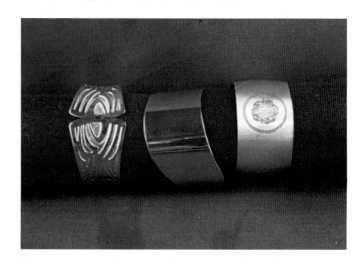

Congo, 1979, 9020, $55; *Empress*, 1977, 9539, $45; *Classic Cuff*, 1977, 9358, $35.

Twist-A-Part, 1967, unsigned, T900, $30; *Dolphin*, 1978, 9537, $40; *Highlight Hinged Cuff*, 1983, 2028, $50; *Suit-able*, 1976, 9730, $50; *Soft Swirl*, 1982, 2012, $80; *Lattice*, 1979, unsigned, 9002, $30; *Futura*, 1980, 9047, $30; *Tri-Twist*, 1977, 9570, $40; *Impressions*, 1979, 9007, $50; *Sweet Hearts*, 1979, 9223, $15.

133

Peeping Tom, 1977, 9772, $25.

Charm Bracelet, 1975, 9231, $25; *Spirit of '76 Charms*, 1975, Quill, 9232, Cannon, 9233, Flag, 9236, Coin, 9235; Drum, 9234, $25 each.

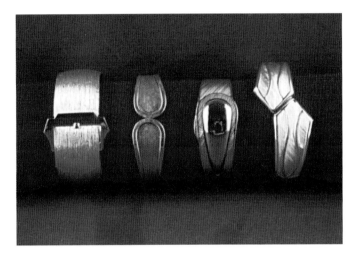

Buckle, 1973, 9853, $55; *Boulevard*, 1978, 9631, $35; *Golden Cuff*, 1967, 9729, $70; *Tailored Cuff*, 1970, 9289, $45.

Christmas Charm, 1975, 9643, $40; reversible, two shown; *Every Day Child Charms*, 1975, Sunday's Child, 9351; Monday's Child, 9352; Tuesday's Child, 9353; Wednesday's Child, 9354; Thursday's Child, 9355; Friday's Child, 9356; Saturday's Child, 9357; $25 each.

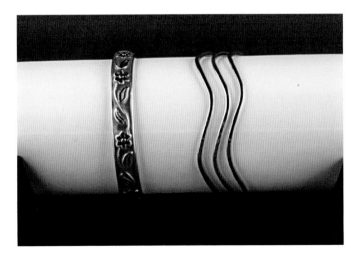

Garland, 1983, unsigned, 2283, $90; *Triple Bangle*, 1978, unsigned, 2 goldtone and 1 silvertone bangles, 9416, $40; both bracelets from the collection of Joy Robson.

Charm Links Bracelet, 1975, 9284, $25; *Sweetheart*, 1975, 9786, $25; *Graduation*, 1974, 9789, $25; *Stork*, 1975, 9784, $25; *Mother's Day*, 1975, 9787, $25; *All Occasion*, 1975, 9785, $25; *Birthday*, 1975, 9788, $25; *Coin*, 1974, 9171, $25; both sides are shown.

Charm Bracelet, 1980, 9050, $25; *Monogram Charms*, 1980, Boy, 9062, Girl, 9063, $20 each; *Charm Bracelet*, 1979, 9032, $20; *Endangered Species Charms*, 1979, Eagle, 9008; Panda Bear, 9009; Lion, 9010; Seal, 9011; Tortoise, 9026; $20 each.

Drops. **Top:** *Jug of Wisdom*, 1976, 8805, $20; *Flirtation*, 1982, 3833, $20; *Saturn*, 1976, 8426, $25; *Emeraude*, 1976, 8050, $20; **Bottom:** *New Image*, 1977, 8550, $20; *Italian Horn*, 1976, gold, 8725, $10; silver, 8724, $10; *Shark's Tooth*, 1976, 8722, $10; *Sea Shell*, 1982, 2025, $45; *In the Swim*, 1977, 8666, $15.

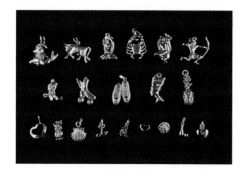

Drops, all unsigned: **Top:** *Zodiac*, 1980, 8754-8765, $25 each, all symbols available; **Middle:** *Western Boot*, 1982, 9682, $15; *Roller Skate*, 1981, 9684, $15; *Ballet Slippers*, 1982, 9683, $15; *Egyptian Profile*, 1980, 8251, $15; *Pineapple*, 1981, 9077, $20; **Bottom:** *Open Heart*, 1982, 9681, $15; *Owl*, 1980, 8375, $10; *Shell*, 1982, 9680, $20; *Initial with ½ point Diamond*, 1982, 3669-3694, $25; all initials available; *#1 Drop*, 1980, 8382, $10; *Flat Open Heart*, 1981, 10kt gold, 3277, $40; *Sand Dollar*, 1981, 9078, $10; *Up Your Alley*, 1982, 9688, $10; *Puffed Heart*, 1980, 8239, $15.

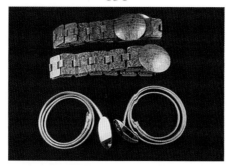

Camelot Belt, 1971, pewter, 8446, $95; antique bronze, 8447, $95; *Twist About Belt*, 1979, gold, 8016, $70; in 1980, silver, 8238, $70.

Mood Mate Belt, 1973, 8477, $45.

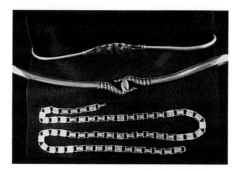

Rich Girl Belt, 1982, 29-32-inch, 2018, $100; also 24-28-inch, 2017; *Serpentine Belt*, 1973, 8568, $90; *Chain Belt*, 1967, T905, $40.

All unsigned. *Trio Belt*, 1974, white, brown, and black leather, 8034, $115; *Belts*, 1981, reversible blue/red and white/red leather, 8707, $30; *Cord Belt*, 1979, 8152, $55.

Tapestry Belt, unsigned, 1983, 2287, $65; from the collection of Joy Robson.

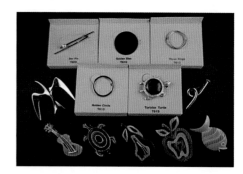

Top: *Bar Pin*, 1967, unsigned, T-609, $20; *Golden Disc*, 1967, T610, $15; *Three Rings*, 1967, unsigned, T612, $15; spelled *3 Rings* in the catalog; **Middle:** *Swedish Modern*, 1967, T611, $25; released again in 1974 as *Mr. Sea Gull*; *Golden Circle*, 1967, unsigned, T613, $15; *Tortoise Turtle*, 1967, T615, $35; *Bent Nail*, 1967, unsigned, T603, $15; **Bottom:** *Gee-tar*, 1967, T614, $30; *Myrtle*, 1967, T605, $30; *Fashion Pear*, 1967, T606, $30; *Big Apple*, 1967, T607, $30; *Gold Fish*, 1967, T608, $20.

Top: *Fire 'N Ice*, 1973, 6829, $30; *Hat*, 1981, unsigned, 6098, $35; *Jade Garden*, 1966, 6642, $25; **Middle:** *Accent*, 1968, 6200, $20; *Feather Bright*, 1973, 6642, $20; *Tracery*, 1974, 6955, $30; **Bottom:** *Golden Acorn*, 1973, 6639, $20; *Family Parade*, 1975, pin, 6161, $65; this came with a choice of 9 Dangles, and numbers for the Dangles are: Pearl Dangle, 6155; Boy Dangle, 6156; Girl Dangle, 6157; *Victoria*, 1972, 6528; $30.

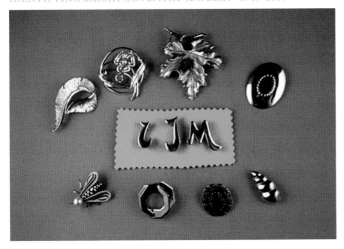

Top: *Feather-Brite*, 1968, 6735, $20; *Precious*, 1973, 6857, $20; *Bit O' Fantasy*, 1966, 6585, $55; *Roma*, 1981, 6087, $30; **Middle:** *Sincerely Yours Initial*, 1980, 6061-6086, $25; all initials available; **Bottom:** *Stinger*, 1967, T604, $25; *Octagon*, 1979, 6003, $25; *First Lady*, 1978, 6469, $20; *Conch Shell*, 1981, 6089, $30.

Pert, 1982, 6835, $15; *Swan*, 1980, 6042, $15; *Americana*, 1976, 5976, $30; *Kitten*, 1980, 6043, $15; *Chatelaine Apple Tac*, 1980, 6048, $30; *Stallion*, 1979, 6034, $15; *Timely Twist*, 1980, unsigned, 6044, $25.

Fleurette, 1974, silver, 6989, $25; gold, 6990, $25; *Saucy*, 1972, silver, 6510, $20; gold, 6511, $20; *Space Age*, 1970, gold pin, 6342, $35; gold ring, 5168, $35; in 1976, silver ring, 5718, $25; there was no silver pin; in 1977, gold ring re-issued with number 5758.

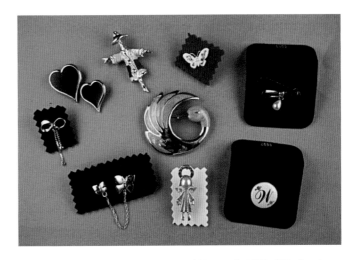

Top: *Black Magic*, 1976, large, 6419, $25; small, 6420, $20; *Patches*, 1969, 6278, $20; *Butterfly*, 1979, 6036, $20; *Minuet*, 1984, 6913, $20; **Middle:** *Morning Dove*, 1983, 2290, $80; **Bottom:** *Dainty Bow*, 1979, unsigned, 6039, $30; *Butterfly Duo*, 1979, unsigned, 6004, $25; *Sarah's Angel*, 1967, 6760, $25; *Porcelain Initial Tac*, 1981, unsigned, 6875-6900, $25; all initials available.

Top: *Peace*, 1971, 6408, $20; *Mr. Sea Gull*, 1974, 6908, $35; *Snow Blossom*, 1973, 6559, $35; **Middle:** *Bamboo*, 1981, 6088, $20; *Silvery Swirl*, 1972, 6460, $20; *Carousel*, 1978, 6532, $25; *Snowfall*, 1977, 6450, $25; **Bottom:** *Silent Spring*, 1970, 6341, $25; *Jubilee*, 1975, 6185, $15; *Silvery Nectar*, 1975, 6121, $25; *Key to My Heart Key Ring*, 1977, 5971, $15.

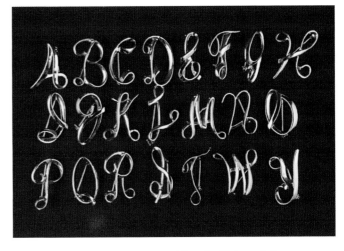

Multiple Choice, 1975, 6298-6323, $25; all initials available.

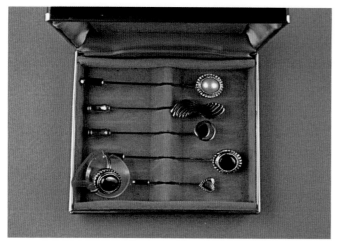

Elegance, 1979, 6677, $25; *Fashion Twist*, 1979, 6676, $20; *Fashion Mate*, 1979, unsigned, 6002, $20; *Moonmist*, 1976, stick pin, 6139, $30; ring, 5721, $30; *Dainty Heart*, 1979, 6032, $15.

Canary, 1980, 6050, $20; *Monogram*, 1980, 6052, $35; this came with 3 free initials, and many managers used SCM for Sarah Coventry Manager, which are the initials on this pin; *Panorama*, 1980, 6051, $20; **Middle:** *Antique Scroll*, 1979, 6005, $20; *Seabreeze*, 1982, 2120, $40; *Spring Time*, 1982, 2204, $25; *Vintage*, 1979, 6041, $55; **Bottom:** *Contour*, 1980, silver, 6046, $15; gold, 6045, $15; *Fan Bar*, 1980, silver, 6053, $40; gold, 6054, $40; *Bouquet*, 1980, 6060, $20; *Heart Delight*, 1980, 6049, $30.

Mother's Pin, 1969, 5044-5054, $155, 1-11 stones; *Sarah's Mother's Ring*, 1969, 5001-5009, $45-$50, 1-9 stones; *Family Bouquet Ring*, 1976, 5570 – 5582, $200, sizes 4-10.

Tic-Tac-Toe, 1967, 6706, $35.

Top: *Minnie*, 1979, 6037, $20; *Zebra*, 1969, 6229, $35; *Demi*, 1972, 6577, $55; **Middle:** *Gypsy*, 1977, 6329, $20; *Sabu*, 1972, 6512, $20; *Slow Poke*, 1968, 6780, $20; **Bottom:** *Sign of Spring*, 1974, 6038, $30; *Slick Chick*, 1975, 6283, $20; *Porcupine*, 1980, 6047, $25.

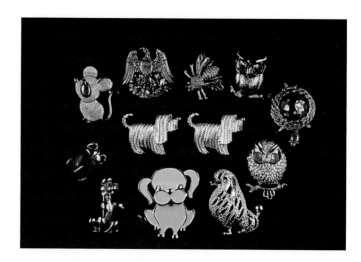

Top: *Squeaky*, 1976, 6701, $25; *Americana*, 1968, 6797, $20; *The Sting*, 1975, 6251, $30; *Professor*, 1975, 6192, $35; *Scented Traveler*, 1969, 6280, $50; **Middle:** *Bug-A-Boo*, 1966, 6611, $25; *Shaggy Dog*, 1970, gold, 6325, $20; silver, 6324, $20; *Hooter*, 1970, 6353, $25; **Bottom:** *Frenchie*, 1966, 6626, $20; *Puppy Love*, 1973, 6555, $30; *Suzette*, 1971, 6424, $20.

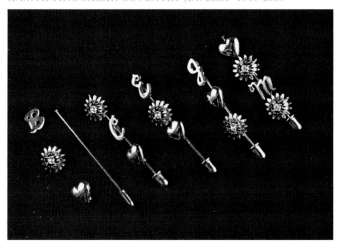

Changing Times, 1978, 6006-6031, $40. This came with 1 initial, 1 heart, and 1 flower, and you had to order 2 pins if you wanted more elements.

Top: *Mini-Fleur*, 1968, 6207, $20; *Floral Delight*, 1978, 6660, $60; **Bottom:** *Morning Frost*, 1982, 6833, $35; *Wings of Fashion*, 1974, 6033, $35.

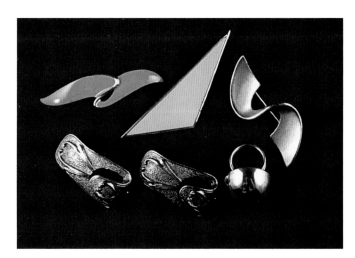

Top: *Special Effects Hair Comb*, 1983, 6845, $25; *Geometric Pin*, 1981, 6091, $35; *Sultry*, 1982, 2013, $40; **Bottom:** *Split Trick*, 1973, silver, 6835, $25; gold, 6836, $25; *Uptight Scarf Ring*, 1971, 8406, $40.

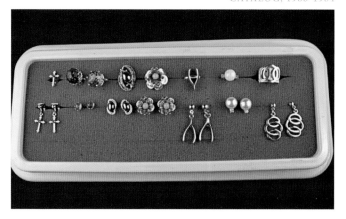

Charity, 1975, ring, 5565, $20; in 1976, clip earrings, 7679, $25; *Bermuda Blue*, 1970, ring, 5228, $45; pierced earrings, 7367, $40; *New Bermuda Blue*, 1970, ring, 5255, $35; *Ebb Tide*, 1971, ring, 5263, $30; in 1972, pierced earrings, 7504, $30; *Blue Buttercup*, 1971, ring, 5292, $35; in 1972, pierced earrings, 7469, $30; *Wishbone*, 1975, ring, 5526, $25; pierced earrings, 7365, $40; *Debutante*, 1973, ring, 5464, $35; pierced earrings, 7849, $35; *New Twist*, 1974, ring, 5519, $30; in 1975, pierced earrings, 7529, $30; *Ring and Earrings Display Box*, 1979, H119, $10.

Top: *Silvery Lace*, 1974, ring, 5483, $20; in 1975, pierced earrings, 7175, $35; *Golden Lace*, 1974, ring, 5484, $20; in 1975, pierced earrings, 7174, $35; **Bottom:** *Queen's Lace*, 1977, gold ring, 5735, $15; pierced earrings, 7564, $30; silver ring, 5736, $15; pierced earrings, 7565, $30.

Feather Brite, 1982, clip earrings, 2041, $40; also pierced earrings, 2040, ring, 2132-2134, $40, sizes 6-8; ring from the collection of Joy Robson.

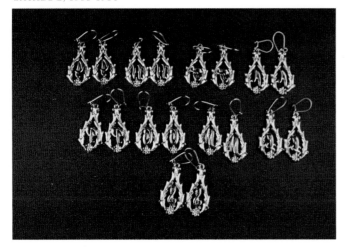

Personally Yours, 1974, pierced earrings, 7957-7982, $25; all initials were available.

Pierced Heart Hoop, 1978, pierced earrings, 7464, $20; *Harmony*, 1977, 7654, $55; *Basic Beauty*, 1979, gold, 7321, $15; also silver, 7322.

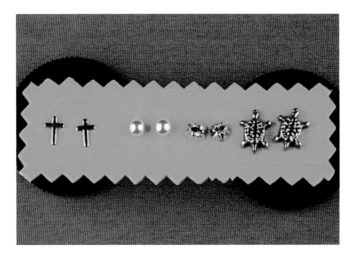

Pierced earrings: *Little Cross*, 1977, 7714, $15; *Miss Anne*, 1977, 7713, $15; *Starburst*, 1981, silver, 7127, $20; also gold, 7126; *Tiny Turtle*, 1975, 7181, $30.

Pierced earrings: *Hollywood Squares*, 1975, 7182, $40; from the collection of Fay Williquette; *Bluebell*, 1971, 7457, $35; *Button*, 1981, 7134, $15; **Bottom:** *Carousel*, 1983, 7767, $45; also necklace, 8767.

Pierced earrings. *Tiny Cross*, 1971, 7395, $30; *Festive*, 1974, 7925, $25; *One 'n Only*, 1974, 7062, $30; **Bottom:** *Fleur De Lis*, 1972, 7505, $30; *Dove of Peace*, 1976, 7366, $20.

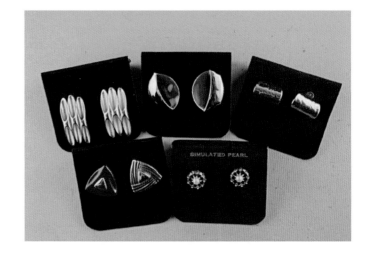

Pierced earrings. *Show Off*, 1984, 7921, $35; *Crescents*, 1984, turquoise, 7045, $20; also fuchsia, 7046; lavender, 7044; black, 7043; white, 7042; red, 7041; *Roll Call*, 1977, 7463, $20; **Bottom:** *Turn About*, 1984, 7951, $20; red jacket reverses to gold, both sides shown; *Petite*, 1973, 7839, $30.

Top: *Moon Drops*, 1974, gold, 7927, $25; also silver, 7926; *Starlite*, 1984, 7763, $35; Bottom: *Dew Drops*, 1967, pearl, 7678, $50; crystal, 7677, $50.

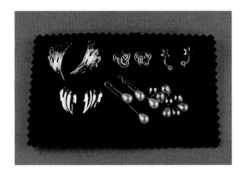

Pierced earrings: Top: *Fanfare*, 1980, silver, 7088, $20; also gold, 7987; *Blue Bell*, 1983, 7842, $35; *Shooting Star*, 1979, 7901, $25; Bottom: *Clean Sweep*, 1982, 7265, $25; also gold, 7276; from the collection of Connie Hoffman; *Satin Drops*, 1980, white, 7020, $50; with 12K gold-filled posts and chains, and you had to purchase the white if you wanted to wear the pink or gray drops; pink drops, 7106, $15; gray drops, 7105, $15.

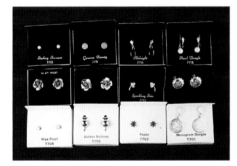

Pierced earrings: Top: *Sterling Treasure*, 1967, 7715, $40; *Genuine Beauty*, 1967, 7711, $55; *Midnight*, 1967, 7716, $35; *Pearl Dangle*, 1967, 7718, $40; Middle: *Golden Rose*, 1967, 7714, $40; *Silvery Rose*, 1968, 7816, $40; *Sparkling Trio*, 1967, 7712, $45; *Violet*, 1975, dangle only, 7135, $35; Bottom: *Miss Pearl*, 1967, T704, $30; *Golden Buttons*, 1967, clip earrings, T709, $15; *Poppy*, 1967, T703, $40; also spelled *Poppys*; *Monogram Dangle*, 1967, T701, $35.

Clip earrings: *New York*, 1970, 7361, $45; *Paris*, 1970, 7363, $65; *Holiday Ice*, 1967, 7758, $55.

Glamour Wardrobe, 1970, pierced earrings, 7328, $60.

Luster Glo, 1984, clip earrings, 7934, $60; also necklace, 8934; from the collection of Joy Robson; *Crimson Ice*, 1983, clip earrings, 2275, $70; also necklace, 2286; from the collection of Joy Robson; *LUV*, 1983, pierced earrings, 7812, $25; the top portion is worn at the front of the lobe while the dangle hangs from the back; Bottom: *Daisy*, 1984, pierced earrings, 7039, $25.

Chicken Clip, 1974, 7056, $20; *Illusion Clips*, 1976, 7056, $20; same set and number previously called *Chicken Clips*; *Ear Wires*, 1974, 7053, $20.

Saucy Swingers, 1968, clip earrings, silver, 7747, $30; gold, 7746, $30.

Clip earrings: *Pearl Showers*, 1973, gold, 7851, $40; silver, 7852, $40; *Senorita*, 1968, gold, 7204, $40; silver, 7205, $40.

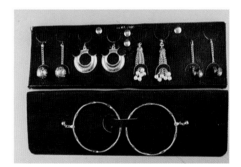

Pierced earrings: *Wardrobe*, 1968, 7796, $65; *La Grande Hoop*, 1975, pierced earrings, 7260, $30.

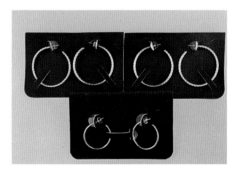

Pierced earrings: *Whirlwind*, 1979, gold, 7030, $20; silver, 7031, $20; Bottom: *Simplicity*, 1977, gold, 7319, $20; also silver, 7320.

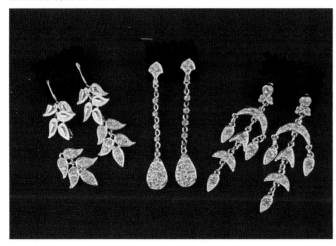

Clip earrings. *Night N'Day*, 1967, 7727, $55; has detachable rhinestone section; *Elegance*, 1967, 7757, $55; *Hong Kong*, 1970, 7362, $60.

Clip earrings: *Surfin'*, 1966, white, 7657, $35; pink, 7656, $35.

Clip earrings: *Carnival*, 1971, turquoise, 7392, yellow, 7390; pink/purple, 7393, red/white/blue, 7389, white, 7391, $35 each.

Top: *Fashion Find*, 1976, pierced earrings, gold, 7140, $30; silver, 7141, $30; *Cosmo*, 1976, pierced earrings, 7210, $30; **Bottom:** *Silvery Fern*, 1978, pierced earrings, 7338, $25; clip earrings, 7339, $25; *Sundance*, 1983, pierced earrings, 7799, $25.

Pierced earrings: *Zodiac Circle*, 1976, 7621, $40; *Gypsy*, 1972, 7496, $60.

Top: *Distinction*, 1978, pierced earrings, 7499, $25; *Sun Ray*, 1979, pierced earrings, 7024, $20; *Rosebud*, 1974, pierced earrings, 7877, $40; **Bottom:** *Polka Dots*, 1967, clip earrings, T705, $25; *Metric*, 1979, pierced earrings, 7925, $20; *Dragon Fly*, 1973, pierced earrings, 7417, $25.

Pierced earrings: *Flings*, 1984, 7002, $15; *Ceramic Symmetry*, 1984, 3960, $50; *Red Cap*, 1983, 7840, $30.

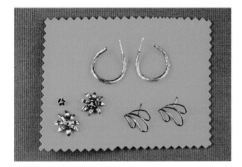

Pierced earrings: *Little Twinkler*, 1981, convertible 7125, $30; *Sahara*, 1980, 7038, $25; *Triple Tears*, 1984, 3696, $30.

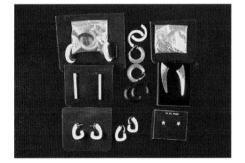

Top: *Variations*, 1977, pierced earrings, 7509, $40; clip earrings, 7508, $40; *Clipmates*, 1982, clip earrings, 7262, $20; **Middle:** *Light Line*, 1984, pierced earrings, 7952, $30; *Drama*, 1984, pierced earrings, 3962, $45; **Bottom:** *White Tempo*, 1980, pierced earrings, 7083, $20; clip earrings, 7082, $20; shown in June 1980 *Woman's Day*; *Micro-Mini*, 1968, pierced earrings, 7815, $30.

Pierced earrings: **Top:** *Windswept*, 1982, 2049, $25; *Wishful*, 1984, 7925, $40; *Senorita*, 1976, gold, 7623, $30; silver, 7624, $30; **Middle:** *Golden Swirl*, 1973, 7848, $40; *Simplicity*, 1982, large 3265, $65; also small, 3263, and medium, 3264; *Stylish*, 1982, 7823, $30; also silver, 7824; **Bottom:** *Chimes*, 1984, 7937, $40; *Endless Hoop*, 1982, medium 3261, $60; also small, 3260, and large, 3262.

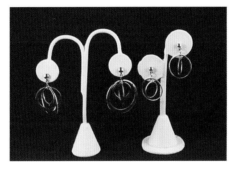

Pierced earrings. *Mobile*, 1975, 7133, $50; *Mobile*, 1978, 7825, $25.

Clip earrings. *Café Society*, 1966, gold, 7662, $30; silver, 7663, $30.

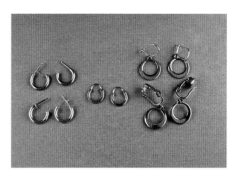

Young Spirit, 1979, gold, 7026, $15; silver, 7027, $15; *Circlet*, 1966, small 7608, $35; also regular, 7655; *Gypsy*, 1966, pierced earrings, 7665, $35; clip earrings, 7603, $20.

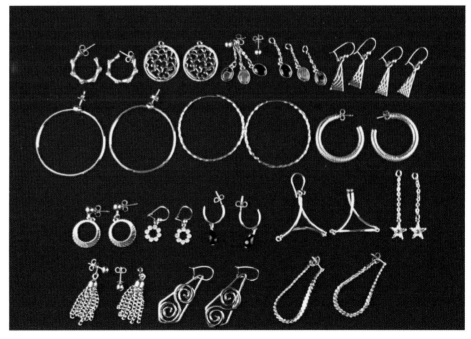

Pierced earrings. **Top:** *Bamboo Hoops*, 1977, 7552, $20; *Oriental Dangle*, 1974, 7996, $20; *Capers*, 1975, 7254, $45; *Flim Flam*, 1973, silver, 7662, $25; gold, 7661, $25; **Row 2:** *Hula Hoop*, 1975, 7177, $25; *Fashion Circle*, 1974, 7831, $30; also gold, 7052, name changed in April 1975 to *Twister* with same item numbers; *High Fashion Loop*, 1975, silver, 7942, $40; also gold, 7943; **Row 3:** *Combo*, 1973, 7838, $40; *Evening Star*, 1974, 7901, $25; *Silver Jet*, 1969, 7262, $35; *Flair*, 1976, 7622, $20; *Starburst*, 1979, 7037, $35; **Bottom:** *Classic Tassel*, 1975, removable tassel, silver, 7274, $40; also gold, 7273; *Sing Song*, 1973, 7623, $45; *New Edition*, 1979, silver, 7013, $40; also gold, 7012.

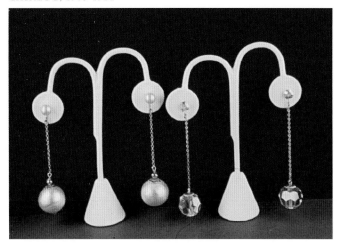

Clip earrings: *Hi-Swinger*, 1967, 7664, $25; also known as *High Swinger*; *Crystal Lights*, 1967, 7756, $35.

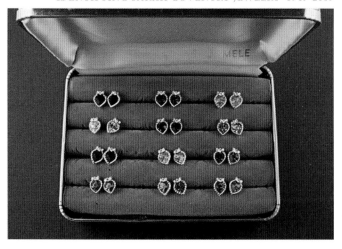

Pierced earrings. *Love Story*, 1974, 7881-7892, $35; January at top left and December at bottom right.

Pierced earrings. **Top:** *Montego*, 1981, 7129, $35; *Dusty*, 1984, 7797, $45; *Trilogy*, 1983, 2291, $45; *Great Shape*, 1984, silver, 7898, $20; gold, 7897, $20; **Middle:** *Intrigue*, 1976, silver, 7684, $25; gold, 7685, $25; *Sea Treasures*, 1982, 2107, $45; also clip earrings, 2108; *Patterned Drops*, 1984, 14KT gold-filled, 3698, $30; **Bottom:** *Impressions*, 1982, 7285, $25; *Cylinder*, 1978, 7002, $25; *Simply Elegant*, 1982, 7313, $30; *Tailored Classic*, 1976, silver, 7348, $30; gold, 7347, $30.

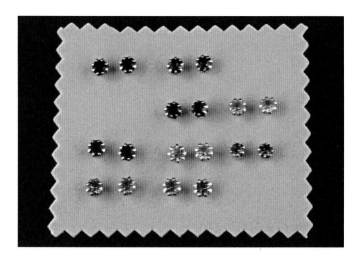

Pierced earrings. *Sarah's Birthstone*, 1978, 7070-7081, $20; January at top left and December at bottom right; March, April, and December not shown.

Pierced earrings. *Quick Change*, 1976, 7241, $40.

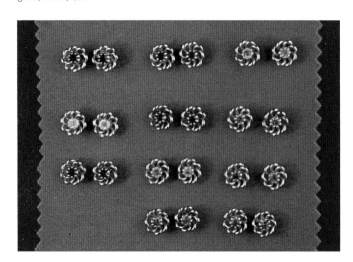

Pierced earrings. *Happy Talk*, 1974, 7142-7153, $30; January at top left and December at bottom right, October not shown.

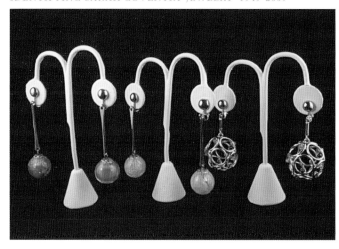

Clip earrings. *A-Go-Go*, 1966, blue, 7660, $35; yellow, 7661, $35; *Futurama*, 1967, 7759, $55.

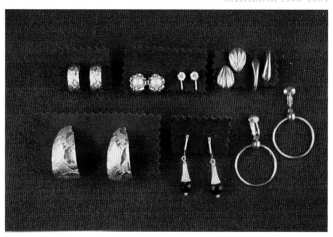

Clip earrings. **Top:** *Braids*, 1984, gold, 7918, $20; also silver, 7919; *Timeliness*, 1979, 7006, $25; *Cubic Zirconium*, 1982, 3888, $35; *Forecaster*, 1980, gold, 7048, $30; also silver, 7049; *Downtowner*, 1979, 7005, $20; **Bottom:** *Watusi*, 1973, 7585, $40; *Dancing Jet*, 1966, 7604, $20; also pierced earrings, 7666; *Golden Hoop*, 1970, 7369, $35.

Pierced earrings. **Top:** *Bouncy*, 1973 7854, $40; *Shadows*, 1977, 7572, $25; **Bottom:** *Tango*, 1974, 7063, $35; *Ultima*, 1977, gold, 7435, $35; also silver, 7436.

Clip earrings. **Top:** *Satin Buttons*, 1976, silver, 7998, $35; also gold, 7999; *Reflector*, 1979, silver, 7016, $20; also gold, 7017; **Bottom:** *Overcast*, 1978, 7903, $25; *Basic Hoop*, 1979, silver, 7022, $25; also gold, 7021; *Wedding Band*, 1968, 7751, $30.

Clip earrings. **Top:** *Fortune Cookie*, 1982, gold, 2219, $35; also silver, 2220; also pierced earrings, gold, 2217, silver, 2218; *Teardrop*, 1981, 7101, $30; *Sun Spots*, 1977, 7465, $20; **Middle:** *Gateway*, 1982, 2230, $35; also pierced earrings, 2231; *Feather Brite*, 1982, 2041, $40; also ring, 2132-2134, sizes 6-8; *Socialite*, 1979, 7014, $30; *Times Square*, 1978, 7408, $30; **Bottom:** *Daisy*, 1967, T700, $15; *Hullabaloo*, 1966, orange, 7658, $35; red, 7659, $35.

Clip earrings. **Top:** *Two-Timer*, 1972, convertible, silver, 7482, $35; gold, 7481, $35; *Impulse*, 1982, gold, 7725, $30; silver, 7727, $30; **Middle:** *Color Frame*, 1969, reversible, gold, 7283, $30, white reverses to orange; silver, 7282, $30, white reverses to black; *Textured Hoop*, 1975, gold, 7119, $45; silver, 7137, $45; **Bottom:** *Matchmaker*, 1976, silver, 7717, $30; gold, 7716, $30; *Easy Going*, 1978, silver, 7519, $20; gold, 7520, $20; *Flattery*, 1976, silver, 7615, $35; gold, 7616, $35.

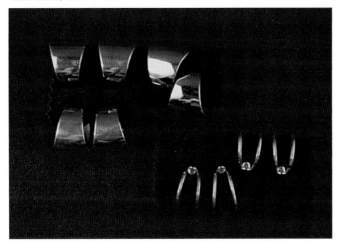

Showtime, 1976, gold clip earrings, 7421, $30; gold pierced earrings, 7422, $30; silver clip earrings, 7423, $30; also silver pierced earrings, 7424; *Show-Stopper*, 1979, clip earrings, gold, 7008, $30; silver, 7009, $30.

Wedding Band, 1975, pierced earrings, 7176, $25.

Clip earrings. *Button Pearl*, 1966, medium, 7588, $20; dainty, 7646, $15; in 1968, bold, 7755, $20.

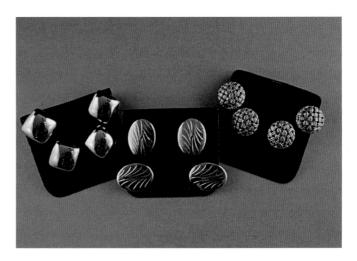

Flair, 1981, pierced earrings, 7722, $35; clip earrings, 7723, $35; *Wayside*, 1978, clip earrings, gold, 7442, $25; silver, 7441, $25; *Basket Weave*, 1981, pierced earrings, 7120, $30; clip earrings, 7119, $30.

Top: *Hoop-La*, 1972, pierced earrings, 7484, $35; *Loop-La-Loop*, 1976, clip earrings, 7584, $40; the rings can be removed for a variety of different combinations; **Bottom:** *Free Style*, 1978, pierced earrings, 7417, $25.

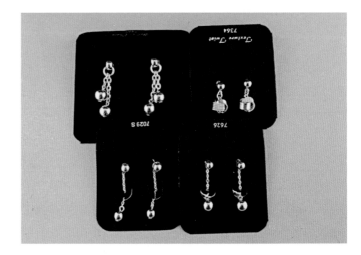

Pierced earrings. **Top:** *Ball and Chain*, 1972, 7467, $30; also gold, 7468; *Texture Twist*, 1975, 7634, $45; **Bottom:** *Twice As Nice*, 1979, silver, 7029, $25; also gold, 7028, removable dangle; *Swing Away*, 1976, silver, 7626, $30; also gold, 7625; removable dangle, larger ball and shorter chain than *Twice As Nice*.

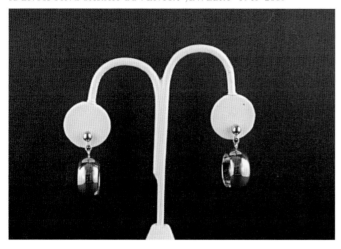

Wedding Ring, 1976, pierced earrings, 7627, $30.

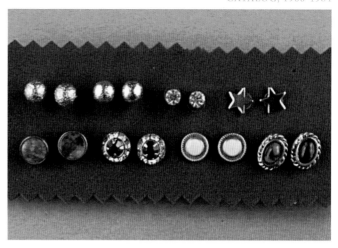

Pierced earrings. **Top:** *Textured Lady*, 1970, gold, 7371, $35; silver, 7372, $35; *Diamonice*, 1969, 7263, $30; *Twinkle*, 1977, 7777, $20; **Bottom:** *Jade Treasures*, 1966, 7607, $50; *After Five*, 1966, 7606, $35; *Pair Ups*, 1978, 7470, $15; *Royal Flush*, 1973, 7837, $35.

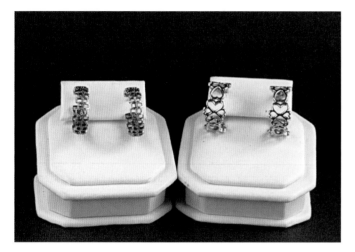

Pierced earrings. *Honeycomb*, 1977, 7323, $30; *Love Beat*, 1977, 7941, $30.

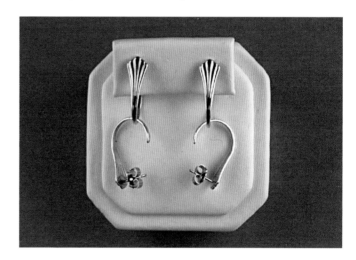

Pierced earrings. *Venetian*, 1980, gold, 7051, $25; silver, 7050, $25.

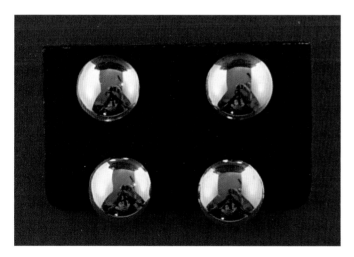

Clip earrings. *Classic Beauty*, 1975, gold, 7188, $40; silver, 7189, $40.

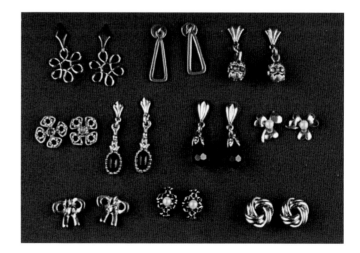

Pierced earrings. **Top:** *Snowflake*, 1968, 7810, $35; *Tango*, 1977, 7466, $20; *Party Lites*, 1974, 7938, $35; **Middle:** *Sweetness*, 1973, 7666, $35; *Tear Drops*, 1972, 7532, $30; *Ember-Time*, 1972, 7539, $30; *Clover*, 1968, 7814, $30; **Bottom:** *Beau-Knot*, 1973, 7667, $30; *Antique Pearl*, 1972, 7456, $30; *Love Knot*, 1983, 7793, $30.

Pierced earrings. *Coin Trio*, 1971, 7397, $35; *Aristocrat*, 1976, gold, 7457, $25; silver, 7458, $25; *Love Birds*, 1967, T707, $45; **Bottom:** *Tailored Rope*, 1974, dangle only 7059, $20.

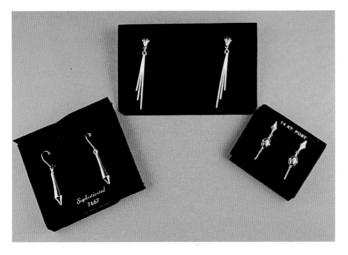

Sophisticated, 1966, pierced earrings, 7667, $35; also clip earrings, 7605; *Silvery Fringe*, 1971, pierced earrings, 7418, $30; *Icicle*, 1968, pierced earrings, 7809, $30.

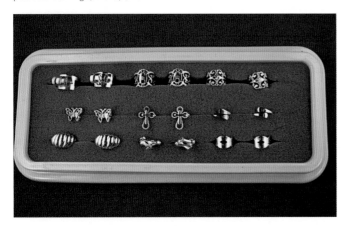

Top: *Cosmic Wrap-Around*, 1971, gold, 5259, $30; silver, 5260, $30; *Queen's Lace*, 1977, gold, 5735, $15; silver, 5736, $15; *Golden Lace*, 1974, 5484, $20; *Silvery Lace*, 1974, 5483, $20; **Middle:** *Madam Butterfly*, 1976, gold, 5658, $20; silver, 5659, $20; *Serenity Cross*, 1975, gold, 5612, $30; silver, 5611, $30; *Wrap-Up*, 1978, gold, 5786, $15; silver, 5787, $15; **Bottom:** *Shrimp Design*, 1969, gold, 5219, $30; silver, 5220, $30; *Bamboo*, 1973, gold, 5402, $20; silver, 5403, $20; *Fashion Braid*, 1976, gold, 5731, $20; silver, 5730, $20; *Ring and Earrings Display Box*, 1979, H119, $10.

Turn-About, 1971, 5293, $45; both sides shown.

Stardust, 1973, 5461, $25; *Symphony*, 1968, 5186, $35; *Regency*, 1970, 5167, $45; *Multi-Lites*, 1973, 5395, $35; *Neptune*, 1975, 5524, $50, sizes 4-6; also 5525, sizes 6.5-9.5.

Continental, 1977, 5765, $20; *Too Blue*, 1968, 5187, $30; *Elite*, 1977, 5747, $35; *Plumb Mist*, 1977, 5741, $40; *Mediterranean*, 1977, 5770, $30.

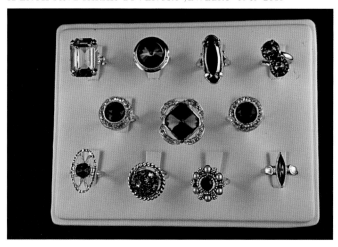

Top: *Lagoon*, 1974, 5496, $60; *Liquid Lights*, 1971, 5258, $35; *Misty*, 1976, 5653, $45; *Over the Rainbow*, 1971, 5265, $40; **Middle:** *Royal Velvet*, 1972, 5381, $40; *Majestic*, 1968, 5188, $30; *Irish Eyes*, 1972, 5374, $45; **Bottom:** *Mystique*, 1974, 5504, $30; *Northern Lights*, 1973, 5388, $40; *Viva*, 1974, 5498, $30; *Blue Night*, 1976, 5673, $25.

Starbright, 1976, 5661, $30; *Masquerade*, 1983, 5540-5542, $55, sizes 5, 7, 9; *Night Out*, 1975, 5634, $25.

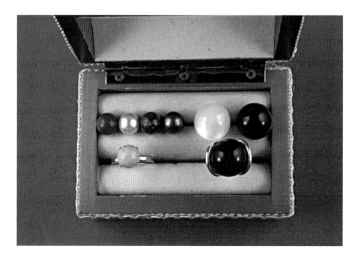

Genie, 1967, 5164, $35; *Can Can*, 1972, 5340, $30; both rings have interchangeable balls.

Silvery Bubbles, 1976, 5652, $35; *Fickle Heart*, 1975, 5596, $20; *Pebbles*, 1976, 5651, $35.

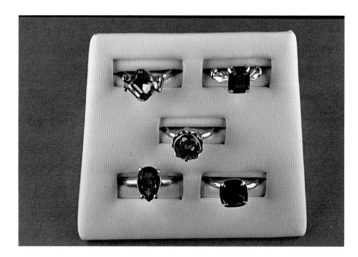

Twilight, 1971, 5173, $55; *Lavender Lites*, 1975, 5586, $65; *Evening Star*, 1976, 5719, $30; *Splendor*, 1975, 5531-5532, $35, sizes 4-6 and 6-9; *Deep Purple*, 1976, 5672, $30.

Top: *My Lady*, 1984, 5628-5630, $25, sizes 6-8; *Jet Navette*, 1972, 5378, $30; *Cotton Candy*, 1975, 5594, $20; **Bottom:** *Ultra*, 1977, 5743, $25; *Michelle*, 1977, 5744, $30; *Indigo*, 1974, 5509, $30.

Magic Ice, 1977, 5752, $50; this ring changes color from every angle.

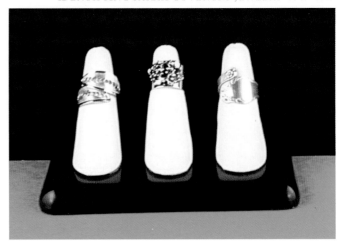

Caress, 1975, 5534, $15; *Coronet*, 1977, 5740, $30; *Personal Choice*, 1975, 5527, $30.

Wrap-Around Zodiac, 1975, 5618-5629, $45.

3rd Dimension, 1971, 5256, $55; fits on two fingers with interchangeable centers.

Nosegay, 1975, 5646, $25, sizes 4-6; also 5646, sizes 6.5-9; *My Bouquet*, 1976, 5669, $20; *Harmony*, 1981, 5427, $60; *Interweave*, 1978, 5779, $15; *New Design*, 1976, 5680, $20.

Top: *Capri*, 1974, 5505, $35; *Evening Sky*, 1975, 5631, $35; *Imperial*, 1974, 5503, $30; *Reflections*, 1973, 5466, $40; **Middle:** *Shalimar*, 1973, 5458, $30; *Sugarplum*, 1977, 5746, $20; *Priscilla*, 1979, 5860-5864, $25, sizes 5-9; **Bottom:** *Catherine*, 1973, 5387, $40; *Anniversary*, 1973, 5465, $30; *Gala*, 1967, 5157, $35; *Satin Elegance*, 1974, 5513, $40.

Navajo, 1973, 5399, $35; *Cleopatra,* 1972, 5329, $40; *Blue Sun*, 1971, 5264, $30.

Top: *Always*, 1978, 5772, $30; *Pacer*, 1976, 5722, $30; *Caged Pearl*, 1976, silver, 5654, $30, sizes 4-6; also silver, 5655, sizes 6-9, gold, 5656, sizes 4-6, and gold, 5657, sizes 6-9; **Bottom:** *Stardust*, 1978, 5793, $30; *Frosted Flower*, 1975, 5598, $30; *Everlasting*, 1982, 5461, $30.

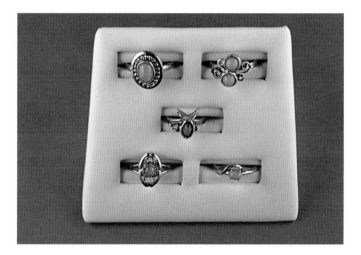

Suzette, 1978, 5774, $25; *Confection*, 1977, 5759, $30; *Angel Fish*, 1976, 5614, $25; *Finesse*, 1975, 5613, $25; *Harlequin*, 1980, 5345-5347, $60, sizes 5-7.

Top: *Birthstone Duet*, 1980, 5085, $40, sizes 4-6; also 5086, sizes 6-9; this could be any combination of birthstones; **Bottom:** *Personal Touch Birthstone*, 1979, 5002-5037, $25, sizes 6-8.

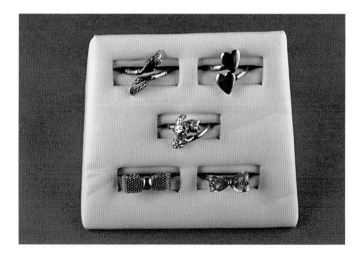

Leaf, 1981, gold, 5354, $20; also silver, 5355; *Affection*, 1975, 5638, $25; *Frenchie*, 1975, 5595, $30; *Bow Tie*, 1980, 5064, $35; *Desiree*, 1976, 5726, $30.

Golden Nugget, 1968, 5183, $30; *Golden Weave*, 1974, 5508, $25; *Cher*, 1975, 5642, $35, sizes 4-6; also 5648, sizes 6.5-9; *Shrimp*, 1981, 5348-5350, $20, sizes 6-8; *Vintage*, 1973, 5467, $35.

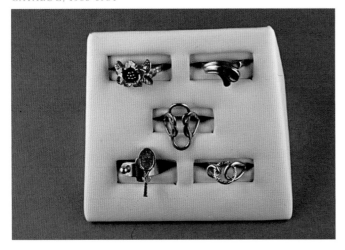

Strawflower, 1975, 5602, $30; *Tulip*, 1980, 5306, $20; *Crafted Knot*, 1980, 6244-6246, $35, sizes 4-6; *Sport*, 1975, 5515, $25, sizes 4-6; also 5616, sizes 6.5-9; *Swirl*, 1978, 5800, $30; in 1979, number changed to 5890-5894, sizes 5-9.

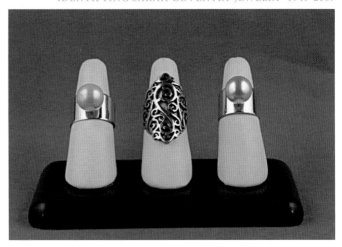

Space Age, 1970, gold, 5168, $35; in 1977 number changed to 5758; *Sterling Heirloom*, 1982, 3905-3909, $95, sizes 5-9; from the collection of Joy Robson; *Space Age*, 1976, silver, 5718, $25.

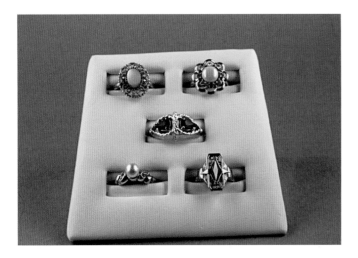

Satin Lace, 1978, 5784, $25; *New Luster*, 1975, 5607, $30; *Shadows*, 1975, 5592, $50, sizes 4-6; from the collection of Joy Robson; *Jacqueline*, 1980, 5325-5329, $20, size 5-9; *Regina*, 1979, 5858, $25.

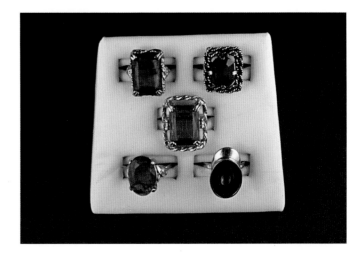

Twilight, 1973, 5457, $30; *Majorca*, 1969, 5189, $35; *Wild Honey*, 1970, 5166, $25; *Golden Embers*, 1967, 5161, $35; *Fire-Lite*, 1976, 5676, $55.

Angel, 1980, 5300-5302, $45, sizes 5-7; *Victoria Blue*, 1975, 5597, $30; *Aquarius*, 1970, 5170, $45; *Twin Jades*, 1967, 5160, $35; *Kari*, 1978, 5776, $25.

Crimson Lites, 1972, 5380, $40; *Marigold*, 1970, 5165, $35; *Jonquil*, 1968, 5184, $30; *Festive*, 1979, 5798, $35; *Coronation*, 1975, 5566, $30.

Top: *Blue Rose*, 1975, 5536, $30; *Flirt*, 1973, 5459, $35; *Evening Cluster*, 1978, 5785, $45; **Row 2:** *Rome*, 1975, 5564, $35; *Ebony*, 1978, 5794, $25; *Victorian Pinkie*, 1975, 5641, $25; *Polonaise*, 1975, 5666, $30; **Row 3:** *Sea Goddess*, 1967, 5156, $35; *Crimson*, 1981, 5322-5324, $45, sizes 6-8; *Hazy Dazy*, 1975, 5599, $30; **Bottom:** *Amber Light*, 1982, 5429-5433, $60, sizes 5-9; *Citation*, 1974, 5486, $25; *Tru-Love*, 1968, 5174-5180, $65, sizes 4-10; *Venetian Treasure*, 1976, 5640, $25.

Dazzler, 1971, unsigned, 5310, $50; *Queen's Choice*, 1970, 5171, $60; *Czarina*, 1971, 5261, $55.

Top: *Starlet*, 1973, 5396, $30; *Ember Beauty*, 1977, 5768, $30; *Volcano*, 1975, 5604, $30; **Bottom:** *Heart's Desire*, 1974, 5521, $30; *Pinkie*, 1973, 5383, $20; *Morning Star*, 1977, 5761, $25.

Fancy, 1975, 5589, $50; *My Valentine*, 1975, 5606, $30; *Deep Burgundy*, 1966, 5155, $30; *Coquette*, 1977, 5732, $20; *Dewdrops*, 1975, unsigned, 5590, $60, sizes 4-6; also 5591, sizes 6-9.

Top: *Blue Buttercup*, 1971, 5292, $35; *Moon Cloud*, 1974, 5492, $30; *Blue Moonlet*, 1972, 5330, $30; *Heritage*, 1976, 5727, $40; **Middle:** *Indian Princess*, 1977, 5737, $30; *Aztec Treasure*, 1977, 5762, $25; *Blue Feather*, 1976, 5664, $25; **Bottom:** *Blue Cloud*, 1977, 5753, $30; *Blue Lady*, 1973, 5393, $25; *Indian Maiden*, 1973, 5481, $25; *Zuni*, 1975, 5636, $30.

Marie, 1976, 5675, $30; *Cinnamon Flower*, 1974, 5494, $30; *Sparkling Burgundy*, 1973, 5397, $30; *Colleen*, 1975, 5584, $60; *Dawn*, 1982, 2147-2149, $55, size 6-8.

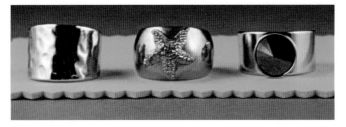

Scandia, 1977, 5764, $30; *Sea Star*, 1977, 5771, $35; *Jet Set*, 1976, 5723, $35.

South Seas, 1979, 5789, $25; *Moon Glo*, 1979, 5850, $25; *Golden Nest*, 1975, 5569, $25; *Double Play*, 1980, 5310-5311, $25, sizes 3-5 and sizes 5.5-7.5; *Ballerina*, 1967, 5159, $35.

Elegant, 1970, 5172, $70; *Dazzler*, 1974, 5520, $55; *Mystic Blue*, 1969, 5218, $35; *Pink Champagne*, 1974, 5516, $65; *Austrian Lites*, 1973, 5392, $40.

Sundown, 1975, 5600, $30; *Night Lights*, 1982, 2158-2160, $50, sizes 6-8; *Fire Fly*, 1973, 5460, $30; *Regency*, 1974, 5497, $35; *Royal Crown*, 1971, 5257, $35.

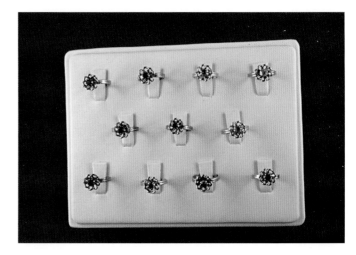

Happy Talk, 1973, 5405-5416, $25, sizes 3-6; June not shown.

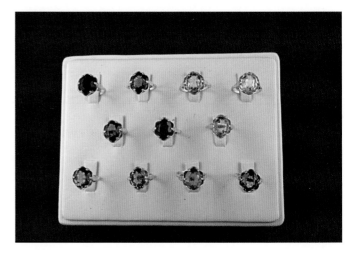

Sarah's Birthstone, 1972, sterling silver, 5316-5327, $65; June not shown.

Love Story, 1973, 5469-5480, $25.

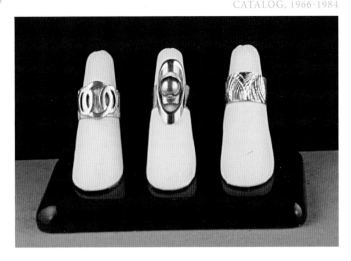

New Twist, 1974, 5519, $30; *Saturn*, 1971, 5296, $40; *Golden Swirls*, 1976, 5667, $25.

Comet, 1975, 5563, $30; *LaBelle*, 1976, 5716, $35; *Starlite*, 1979, 5799, $25; *Harbor Lights*, 1975, 5601, $30; *Starstruck*, 1983, 2188-2190, $40, sizes 6-8.

Midnight Magic, 1982, set of 3 stack rings, 2177-2179, $30, size 5-7.

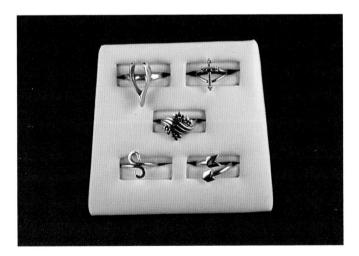

Wishbone, 1975, 5526, $25; *Charity*, 1975, 5565, $20; *Fieldflowers*, 1979, 5795, $20; *Scroll*, 1976, 5605, $20; *Curved Arrow*, 1976, 5681, $20.

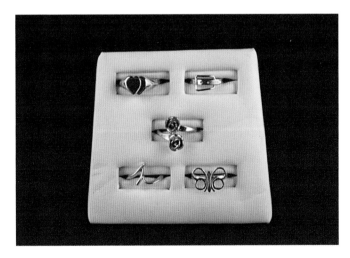

Heart to Heart, 1977, 5757, $20; *Buckle*, 1979, silver, 5062, $25, sizes 4-6; also silver, 5063, sizes 6-8, gold, 5054, sizes 4-6, and gold, 5055, sizes 6-8; *Antique Rose*, 1973, 5377, $25; *Sculptured*, 1980, 5303-5305, $25, sizes 4-6; *Papillon*, 1973, 5499, $25.

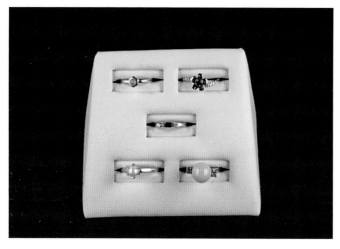

Betsy, 1980, 5053, $15; *Sara*, 1980, 5095-5097, $20, sizes 5-7; *Midnight Magic*, 1980, 5070-5072, $30, sizes 4, 6, 8; *Sterling Pearl*, 1971, 5301, $65; *Debutante*, 1973, 5464, $35.

Eric, 1976, 5682, $200; *Champion*, 1983, 5927-5932, $50, sizes 9-13; *Lucky Guy*, 1983, 5940, $80; **Bottom:** *Rally*, 1976, 5120, $20; *Centurion*, 1976, 5668, $25; *Jason*, 1977, 5749, $20.

Top: *Flattery*, 1974, 5506, $30; *Tutti-Frutti*, 1974, 5522, $35; *Hi-Note*, 1977, 5754, $25; *Folklore*, 1977, 5756, $35; **Middle:** *Ingrid*, 1976, 5725, $30; *Black Beauty*, 1972, 5376, $30; *Jet Set*, 1970, 5227, $30; **Bottom:** *Ebb Tide*, 1971, 5263, $30; *Vogue*, 1967, 5158, $35; *Nocturne*, 1974, 5485, $25; *Shangri-La*, 1972, 5372, $55.

Cleopatra Perfumed Ring, 1969, 5217, $50; came with a small tub of solid perfume.

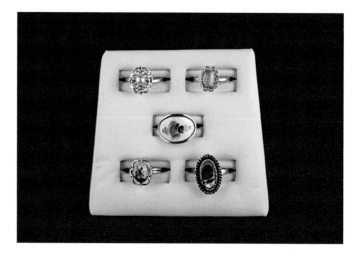

Dream Boat, 1974, 5512, $25; *Day Glow*, 1975, 5583, $30; *Melissa*, 1978, 5781, $40; *Katrina*, 1978, 5782, $30; *Sea Treasure*, 1977, 5733, $35.

Portrait, 1973, 5456, $35; *Angel Pink*, 1973, 5386, $30; *Whipped Crème*, 1974, 5493, $20; *Java*, 1974, 5511, $35; *Jet Elegance*, 1968, 5182, $35.

Blue Lace, 1973, 5382, $35; *Images*, 1973, 5468, $25; *Charmer*, 1971, 5338, $55.

Cameo Lady, 1973, 5462, $20; *Shadow Cameo*, 1972, 5373, $40; *Rose Cameo*, 1967, 5162, $40.

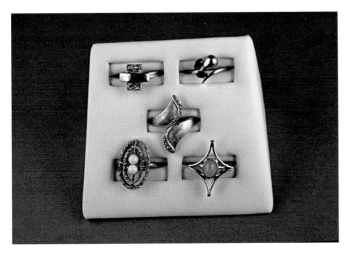

Debut, 1978, 5795, $25; *Satin Dove*, 1981, 5356, $30; *Starry Nights*, 1977, 5769, $45; *Soft Swirl*, 1973, 5390, $25; *Moon Beam*, 1977, 5748, $25.

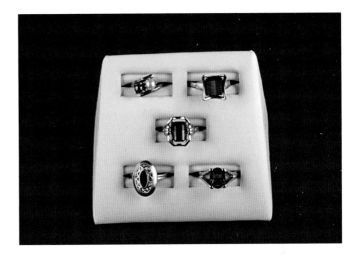

Ebony and Ivory, 1983, 5548-5552, $70, sizes 5-9; *Annette*, 1979, 5788, $30; *Twilight*, 1979, 5792, $30; *Jet Filigree*, 1979, 5855, $25; *Harvest*, 1976, 5662, $50, sizes 4-6; also 5663, sizes 6-9.

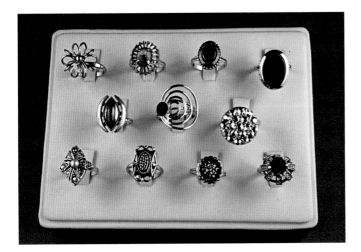

Top: *Love Knot*, 1974, 5501, $30; *Winsome*, 1974, 5491, $30; *Moonmist*, 1976, 5721, $30; **Middle:** *Locket*, 1974, 5510, $40; *Crescent*, 1974, 5482, $25; *Astrojet*, 1973, 5404, $35; *Sparkle Mountain*, 1974, 5489, $40; **Bottom:** *Illusive*, 1975, 5530, $65; *Odyssey*, 1979, 5038, $25; *Wildflower*, 1977, 5766, $20; *Enchantment*, 1974, 5502, $35.

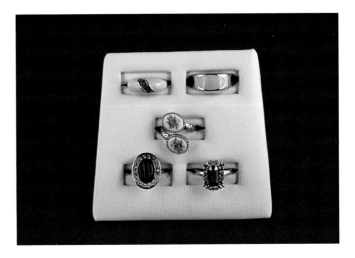

Sierra, 1979, 5859, $15; *Chiffon*, 1981, 5368-5370, $30, sizes 5-7; *Sweet Briar*, 1975, 5535, $20; *Exclusive*, 1978, 5783, $15; *Reflections*, 1977, 5767, $35.

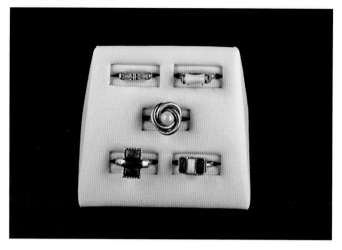

Coral Reef, 1983, 5563-5567, $80, sizes 5-9; *Spring Fever*, 1977, 5734, $25; *Lovers Knot*, 1969, 5221, $35; *Deco*, 1975, 5637, $30; *Three Cheers*, 1976, 5671, $20.

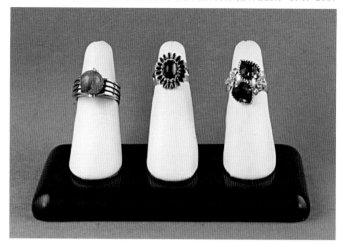

Egypt, 1973, 5385, $30; *Waltztime*, 1975, 5568, $25; *Love Story*, 1972, 5375, $25; the popularity of this ring started the Love Story birthstone series in 1973.

Sea Treasure, 1972, 5328, $45; *Taffy*, 1973, 5400, $35; *Cameo Portrait*, 1976, 5617, $35.

Interchange, 1979, 5856, $25; *Elegant Trio*, 1980, 5307-5309, sizes 5-7, $30; consists of one gold, one silver, and one rose gold band.

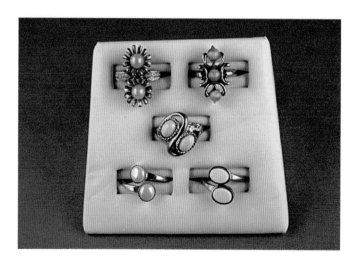

Morning Dew, 1973, 5398, $35; *Homestead*, 1978, 5790, $25; *Satin Sand*, 1974, 5490, $20; *Mellow*, 1975, 5630, $20; *Duo Fashion*, 1978, 5773, $30.

Directions, 1976, 5729, $30; *Sage*, 1978, 5775, $25; *Ceylon*, 1971, 5262, $45; *Wood Nymph*, 1972, 5339, $25; *Rosette*, 1972, 5341, $30.

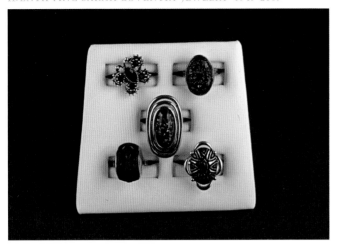

Butterfly, 1975, 5529, $30; *Light of the East*, 1969, 5216, $35; *Rainbow Cavern*, 1973, 5389, $40; *Ambrosia*, 1976, 5728, $40; *Tapestry*, 1973, 5391, $40.

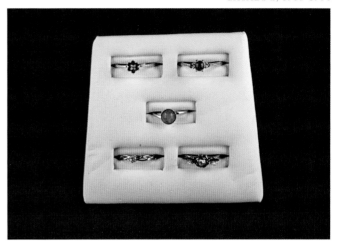

Starfire, 1982, 5494-5497, $40, sizes 5-8; *Dainty Combo*, 1979, 5056-5060, $75, sizes 5-9; *Date Mate*, 1967, T503, $15; *Delicate Braid*, 1979, 5885-5889, $35, sizes 5-9; *Rosalie*, 1975, 5632, $25.

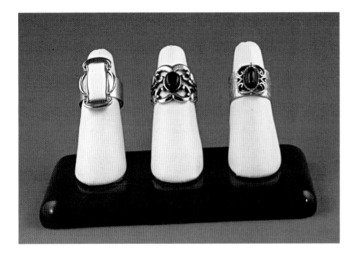

Summer Song, 1975, 5533, $30; *Courtnee*, 1979, 5796, $30; *Spanish Lites*, 1976, 5665, $30.

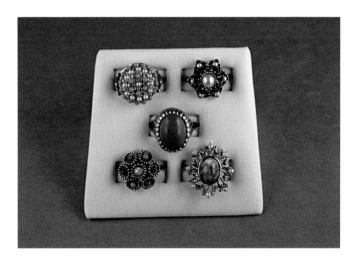

Ocean Star, 1968, 5181, $30; *Egyptian*, 1969, 5223, $35; *Prairie Princess*, 1982, 2238-2240, $55, size 5-9; *Antique Bouquet*, 1972, 5379, $30; *Azure Skies*, 1972, 5371, $35.

Camelot, 1969, 5224, $35; *Dawn*, 1974, 5515, $20; *Desire*, 1973, 5463, $35; *Dusk*, 1974, 5514, $20; *Princess*, 1975, 5488, $25.

Trio, 1971, unsigned, gold, 5294, $30; silver, 5295, $30; *Mixer*, 1975, gold, 5644, $25; silver, 5645, $25; *Beauty Glo*, 1966, gold, 5154, $30; in 1967, silver, 5163, $30.

Honey Berries, 1975, 5528, $35; *Jupiter*, 1974, 5523, $30; *Premier*, 1977, 5755, $40; *Burgundy Twist*, 1979, 5039, $35; *Yesterday*, 1973, 5394, $30.

Tri-Lites, 1972, 5315, $40.

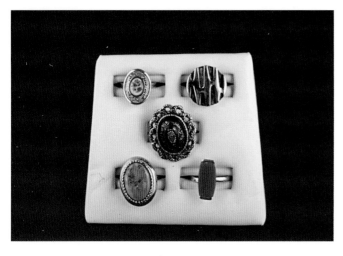

Victorian Bouquet, 1976, 5603, $30; *Danish Modern*, 1967, T501, $20; *Old Vienna*, 1975, 5567, $45; *Coraline*, 1974, 5495, $35; *Fashion First*, 1978, 5780, $25.

Pink Lady, 1974, 5500, $30; *Contessa*, 1975, 5608, $45; *Opalite*, 1966, 5185, $30.

Crystal Fire, 1982, 5454-5456, $60, sizes 5-9.

Bermuda Blue, 1970, 5228, $45; *Runway*, 1983, 5522-5524, $75, sizes 5, 7, 9; *New Bermuda Blue*, 1970, 5255, $35.

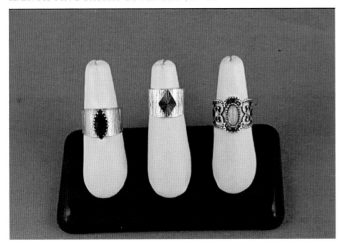

Ember Navette, 1973, 5401, $25; *Avante*, 1975, 5639, $30; *Lovely Lady*, 1976, 5650, $35.

Galaxy, 1977, 5750, $45.

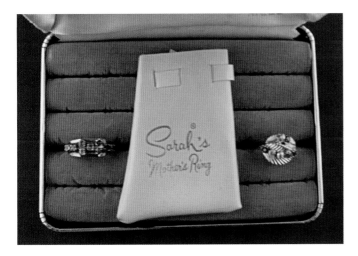

Sarah's Mother Ring, 1969, 5001-5009, $50; 1-9 stones, came in a blue leather pouch; *Family Bouquet*, 1976, 5570-5582, $200, sizes 4-10.

City Slicker, 1978, 5778, $25; *Autumn Haze*, 1974, unsigned, 5507, $65; *Jonquil*, 1974, 5518, $30.

Calypso, 1974, 5487, $30; *Desert Flower*, 1974, 5517, $30; *Hidden Rose*, 1976, 5679, $50; *Oriental Melody*, 1979, 5791, $30; *Seaswept*, 1976, 5717, $30.

Alexandria, 1975, 5643, $40; offered as a free gift in the January 1976 *Woman's Day* magazine if you became a Fashion Show Director and held your first Sarah show that January.

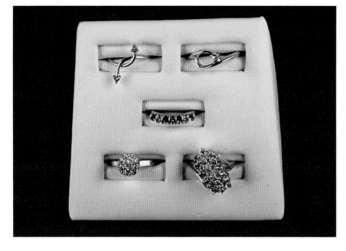

Top: *Caroline*, 1982, 5485-5487, $45, sizes 5, 7, 9; *Starbound*, 1980, 5080-5084, $50, sizes 5, 7, 9; **Middle:** *Encounter*, 1981, 5418-5422, $45, sizes 5-9; **Bottom:** *Hemisphere*, 1981, 5312-5316, $65, sizes 5-9; *Cascade*, 1984, 5503-5505, $75, sizes 5, 7, 9; all from the collection of Joy Robson.

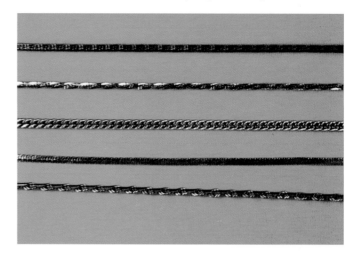

Top to Bottom: *Slicker 18-inch Chain*, 1979, gold, 8298, $35; also silver, 8299; *Coventry Square 20-inch Chain*, 1979, 8064, $35; *Gentry 20-inch Chain*, 1978, 8518, $25; *Herringbone 20-inch Chain*, 1980, 8462, $40; *Aaron 15-inch Chain*, 1978, 8121, $20.

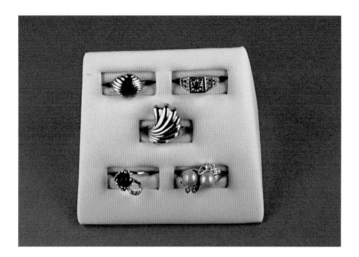

Top: *Shell*, 1981, 5377-5379, $25, sizes 5-7; *Garnet Antique*, 1984, 3675-3679, $75, sizes 6-8; **Middle:** *Feather Brite*, 1982, 2132-2134, $40, sizes 6-8; **Bottom:** *Spice*, 1982, 2141-2143, $55, sizes 5-7; *Snowflower*, 1982, 2194-2196, $55, sizes 5-7; all from the collection of Joy Robson.

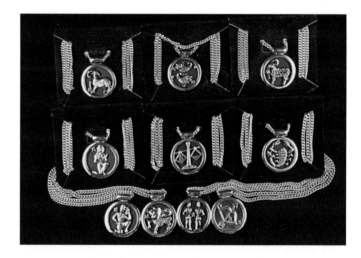

Astrology Pendant, 1978, 8082–8093, $50; all signs available.

Locket, 1967, T502, $35; in 1974, number changed to 5514; *Indigo*, 1980, 5333-5338, $55, sizes 4-9, from the collection of Joy Robson; *Missy*, 1981, 5358, $20.

Sun Signs Pendant, 1974, 8001-8012, $70; all signs available.

Aztec, 1979, 8029, $80; *Daytona*, 1976, 8433, $80.

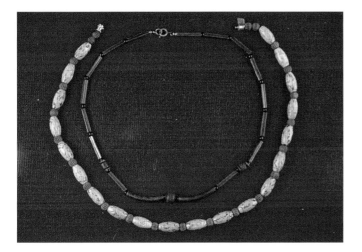

Inside to outside: *Gaucho*, 1977, 8555, $50; *Lumberjack*, 1977, 8556, $55.

His Cross, 1975, 8792, $50; *Superstar*, 1976, 8428, $50; *Devotion*, 1977, silver, 8574, $35; in 1978, gold, 8577, $40; Serenity Prayer on reverse of pendant; *Discovery*, 1978, 8504, $40; *Colonial*, 1980, gold, 8293, $35; silver, 8291, $35.

Apollo, 1979, 8899, $45; reversible, two are shown, one from the collection of June Wellisley and one from the collection of Joy Robson; *Ten-Four*, 1977, 8659, $45; *Anchors Away*, 1979, 8149, $40; *Golfer*, 1981, 8213, $25; *Bowler*, 1981, 8211, $25; *Runner*, 1981, 8209, $25; *Tennis*, 1981, 8210, $25; also *Skier*, 8212.

Indian Head, 1976, 8438, $70; *Arrowhead*, 1982, sterling silver, 3934, $95; *Danish Abstract*, 1979, 8072, $45; *Robbie Robot*, 1979, 8065, $25; *Phoenix*, 1978, 8694, $35; *Young Sailor*, 1980, 8233, $25; *Oxford*, 1980, 8254, $45; *Sarah's Dog Tag*, 1975, 8791, $45.

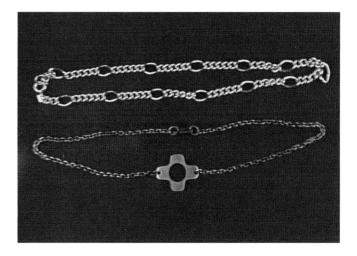

Duke, 1976, 8054, $40; *The Hustle*, 1977, 8776, $45.

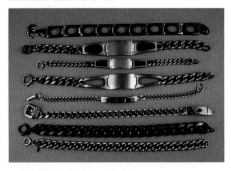

Top to Bottom: *Dare Devil*, 1974, 9995, $75; *Men's ID*, 1973, 5945, $70; *My ID*, 1975, 9376, $60; *New ID*, 1975, 9796, $60; *Monogram Bar*, 1980, 9068, $30; *Rogue*, 1980, 9054, $45; *Brute*, 1975, 9795, $55; *Cossack*, 1976, 9705, $30.

Modern Trio, 1979, 9031, $35; *Rally*, 1976, bracelet, 9104, $25; ring, 5120, $20; *Third Gear*, 1976, 9427, $40; *Spartan*, 1975, 9795, $60; *Explorer*, 1975, 9293, $40.

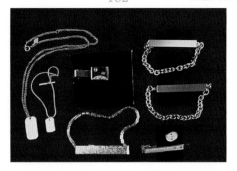

Top: *Men's Monogram Pendant*, 1980, 8323, $50; *Monogram Tie Chain*, 1981, 5987, $30; *Explorer Tie Bar*, 1970, 5876, $25; *President's Choice Tie Bar*, 1971, gold, 5926, $40; silver, 5925, $40. **Bottom:** *Sarah's Tie Bar*, 1976, 5969, $30; *Birthstone Tie Tac*, 1969, 5024-5033, $60 for one stone and, $20 for each additional stone; also known as *Father's Tie Tac*; *Birthstone Tie Bar*, 1969, 5034-5043, $75 for one stone and, $20 for each additional stone; also known as *Father's Tie Bar*.

Key Ringer Key Ring, 1973, 5940, $25; *Key Note Key Ring*, 1969, 5921, $20; *For Him Key Ring*, 1982, 5995, $35; *Key Largo Key Ring*, 1967, 5991, $25; *Special Express*, 1983, money clip, 5924, $45; tie bar, 5923, $35; also cuff links, 5921, tie tac, 5922, and key ring, 5925; *Money Saver*, 1973, 5947, $35; also money clip, 5996.

Venus, 1969, silver, 5918, $90; *Blue Surf*, 1970, 5061, $95.

Kentucky Derby, 1970, silver, 5062, $95; *Jupiter*, 1969, 5913, $70.

Anniversary Collection for Men, 1969, 5099, $200. This set commemorates the 20th anniversary of Sarah Coventry jewelry. You were able to pick six sets from a total of eight in the Out of This World series. **Top:** *Mars* 5914, *Saturn,* 5915; *Neptune*, 5916; **Bottom:** *Jupiter,* 5913; *Venus,* silver, 5918; *Mercury Dark,* silver, 5920. The two sets not shown are *Venus* gold, 5917, and *Mercury Light,* gold, 5919.

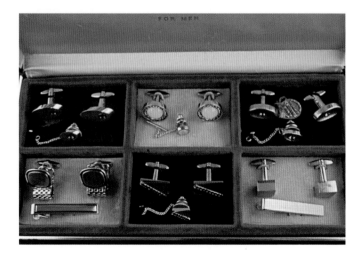

Jewelry Collection for Men, 1970, item number not known, $200. This set consists of six sets from a total of eight in the Man on the Go series. **Top:** *Blue Surf,* 5061; *Sun Valley,* 5057; *Riviera,* 5058; **Bottom:** *Kentucky Derby,* silver, 5062; with removable wrap-around mesh that is silver on one side and gold on the other side so it can be used on other cuff links; *Matador,* 5056; *Daytona 500,* gold, 5059. The two sets not shown are *Daytona 500,* silver, 5060, and *Kentucky Derby,* gold, 5082.

163

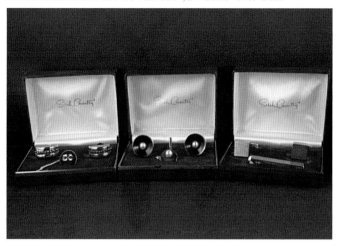

Mars, 1969, 5914, $90; *Saturn*, 1969, 5915, $90; *Daytona 500*; 1970, gold, 5059, $90.

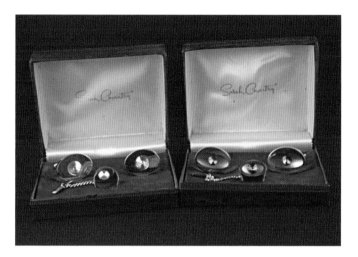

Neptune, 1969, 5916, $90; *Riviera*, 1970, 5058, $95.

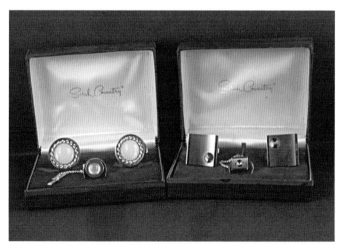

Sun Valley, 1970, 5057, $95; *Venus*, 1969, gold, 5917, $90.

Mercury Dark, 1970, silver, 5920, $95; *Mercury Light*, 1970, gold, 5919, $95.

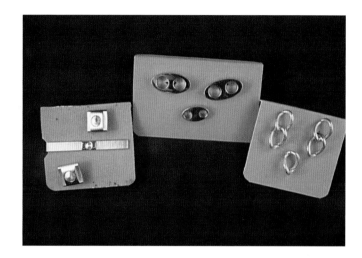

Paris, 1972, 5078, $95; *Switzerland*, 1972, 5076, $90; *Italy*, 1972, 5080, $70.

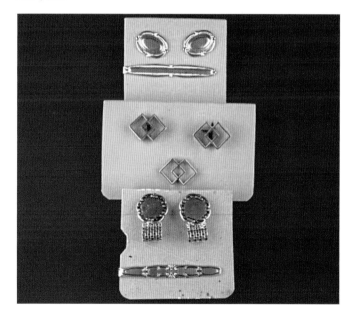

Top to Bottom: *Parliament*, 1973, 5083, $65; *Denmark*, 1972, 5079, $80; *England*, 1972, 5075, $90.

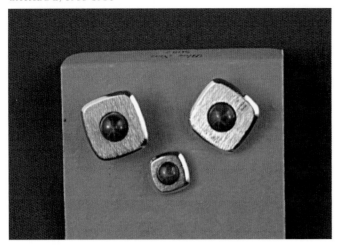

Blue Star, 1973, 5082, $75; also sold individually, cuff links, 5949, tie tac, 5950.

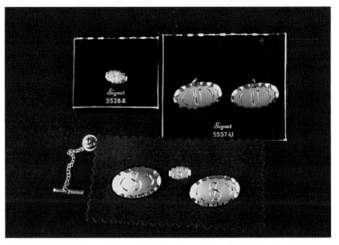

Signet, 1966, tie tac, 5511-5536, $20; cuff links, 5537-5562, $40; all initials available.

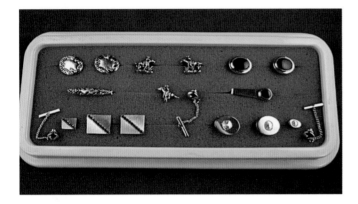

Top: *Antiqued Classic*, 1968, tie bar, 5750, $30; cuff links, 5771, $40; *Pony Express*, 1966, tie tac, 5992, $15; cuff links, 5993, $25; *Male Elegance*. 1967, tie bar, 5999, $25; cuff links, 5998, $40; **Bottom:** *Matador*, 1970, tie tac, 5860, $30; cuff links, 5861, $60; *Neptune*, 1969, tie tac, 5886, $35; cuff links, 5887, $55; *Ring and Earrings Display Box*, 1979, H119, $10.

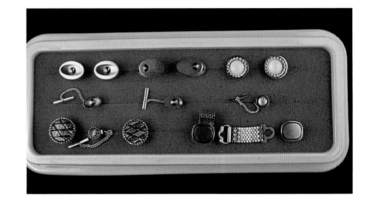

Top: *Riviera*, 1970, tie tac, 5864, $30; cuff links, 5865, $60; *Blue Surf*, 1970, tie tac, 5870, $35; cuff links, 5871, $55; *Sun Valley*, 1970, tie tac, 5862, $30; cuff links, 5863, $60; **Bottom:** *Mosaic*, 1972, tie tac, 5941, $25; cuff links, 5942, $70; also set, 5081; shown in October 1972 *Family Circle* magazine; *Kentucky Derby*, 1970, gold cuff links, 5875, $60 with removable wrap-around mesh that is silver on one side and gold on the other; also tie bar, 5874; *Ring and Earrings Display Box*, 1979, H119, $10.

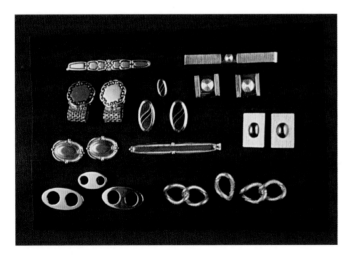

Top: *England*, 1972, tie bar, 5928, $20; cufflinks, 5929, $75, with removable wrap around mesh that is silver on one side and gold on the other side and can be used on other cuff links; *Regimental*, 1968, tie tac, 5908, $20; cuff links, 5909, $40; *Paris*, 1972, tie bar, 5935, $30; cuff links, 5934, $65; **Middle:** *Parliament*, 1973, tie bar, 5951, $25; cuff links, 5952, $40; *Germany*, 1972, cuff links, 5932, $50; also tie tac, 5933, and set, 5077; **Bottom:** *Switzerland*, 1972, tie tac, 5930, $30; cuff links, 5931, $60; *Italy*, 1972, tie tac, 5939, $25; cuff links, 5938, $45.

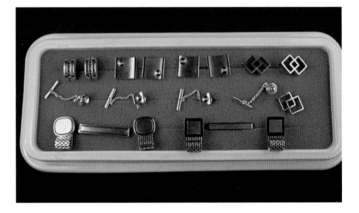

Top: *Mars*, 1969, tie tac, 5882, $30; cuff links, 5883, $60; *Venus*, 1969, gold tie tac, 5880, $35; cuff links, 5881, $55; silver tie tac, 5890, $35; cuff links, 5891, $55; *Denmark*, 1972, tie tac, 5937, $30; cuff links, 5936, $55; **Bottom:** *Mercury Dark*, 1969, silver tie bar, 5894, $30; cuff links, 5895, $60; *Kentucky Derby*, 1970, silver tie bar, 5872, $35; cuff links, 5873, $60, with removable wrap-around mesh that is silver on one side and gold on the other; *Ring and Earrings Display Box*, 1979, H119, $10.

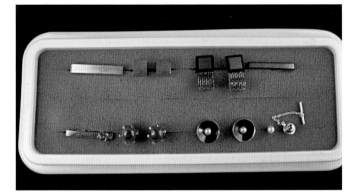

Top: Daytona 500; 1970, gold tie bar, 5866, $40; cuff links, 5867, $50; also silver tie bar, 5868, silver cuff links, 5889, silver set, 5060; *Mercury Light*, 1969, gold tie bar, 5892, $30; cuff links, 5893, $60; **Bottom:** *Jupiter*, 1969, tie bar, 5884, $30; cuff links, 5885, $60; *Saturn*, 1969, tie tac, 5888, $30; cuff links, 5889, $60 (We were unable to confirm which set of item numbers belonged to Jupiter and which set belonged to Saturn, and they could be switched); *Ring and Earrings Display Box*, 1979, H119, $10.

All tie tacs. **Top:** *Antique Auto,* 1980, 5973; *Big Red,* 1974, 5953; *Dune Buggy,* 1971, 5922; *Golden Setter,* 1968, 5907; **Middle:** *Birthstone,* 1975, 5957-5968, all birthstones available; *Flight,* 1971, gold 5924, silver 5923; *Varsity,* 1968, silver 5906, gold 5905; **Bottom:** *Skee-Do,* 1973, 5948 ; *Free Wheelin',* 1974, 5954; *Model T,* 1975, 5955 $20

Top: Eric, 1976, 5682-5694, $200, sizes 7-13; *Lucky Guy*, 1983, 5940, $200; *Champion*, 1983, 5927-5932, $85, sizes 9-13; **Bottom:** *Centurion*, 1976, 5668, $25; *Jason*, 1977, 5749, $20; *Rally*, 1976, 5120, $20; also bracelet, 9104.

Zodiac Drop, 1980, unsigned, 8754-8765, $50 each, all symbols available.

Limited Editions

Victorian, 1973, 8870, $60; *Florentine*, 1974, 8044, $55; *Peace*, 1975, 8130, $70; *18th Century*, 1976, 8649, $70; *Majestic*, 1977, 8439, $75.

Mythology, 1978, 8506, $65; *Celtic*, 1979, 8063, $65; *Renaissance*, 1980, 8260, $85; *Celebration*, 1981, 8218, $50; *Timeless*, 1977, no number given, designed by Charles Stuart.

Charms: *Cathedral*, 1972, 8555, $125; *Partridge In A Pear Tree*, 1974, 9154, $45; *Dove*, 1975, 9295, $35; *Madonna and Child*, 1976, 9649, $35; *Inspiration*, 1977, 9437, $35; *Three Wise Men*, 1978, 9506, $30; *Christmas Around the World*, 1979, 9042, $30; *Cherub*, 1980, 9058, $20; this series began in 1972, there was no Limited Edition charm for 1973, and the series ended in 1980.

Drops: *Christmas Heritage*, 1976, 8447, $50; *Gabrielle*, 1977, 8525, $45; *Holiday Dove*, 1978, 8015, $45; *Crystal Snowflake*, 1979, unsigned, 9044, $55; *Crystal Nativity*, 1980, unsigned, 9061, $55; this series began in 1976 and ended in 1980.

Lord and Lady Coventry

Amethyst Oval, 1972, bracelet, 9518, $140; pin, 6518, $135; clip earrings, 7518, $135; *Antiqued Amethyst*, 1973, necklace, 8693, $80; pierced earrings, 7693, $115; *Royal Purple*, 1974, necklace, 8068, $75; in 1975, pierced earrings, 7068, $90; the necklace in this set is identical to the *Antiqued Amethyst*.

Coral Angel Skin, 1970, necklace, 8334, $105; screw back earrings, 7334, $135; pierced earrings, 7335, $135; *Antique Moonstone*, 1972, necklace, 8520, $75; pierced earrings, 7520, $110; *Silvery Moonstone*, 1973, necklace, 8698, $60; pierced earrings, 7698, $95; *Silvery Moonstone*, 1974, necklace, 8069, $55; pierced earrings, 7069, $85; the necklace in this set is identical to the *Silvery Moonstone* of 1973.

Jade Goddess Set, 1967, necklace and screw back earrings, 5093, $170; *Jade Goddess*, 1967, necklace, 8601, $65; also screw back earrings, 7601; *Jade Oval*, 1969, necklace, 8242, $60; screw back earrings, 7242, $105; bracelet, 9242, $165; pierced earrings, 7243, $105; in 1970, pin, 6328, $175; the pieces in both sets are identical.

Onyx Tears, 1970, pendant, 8329, $70; bracelet, 9329, $215; pin, 6329, $175; screw back earrings, 7329, $80; pierced earrings, 7330, $80; shown in July 1970 *Redbook* magazine.

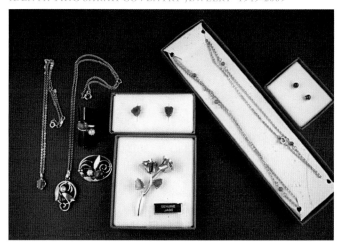

Genuine Jade, 1974, necklace, 8067, $85; also pierced earrings, 7067; *Jade 'n Pearl*, 1975, necklace, 8750, $105; pin, 6750, $105; ring, 5610, $105; *Jade Rose*, 1972, pin, 6517, $130; pierced earrings, 7517, $120; *Genuine Jade*, 1976, necklace, 8414, $120; pierced earrings, 7414, $50.

Saralite, 1973, pierced earrings, 7680, $125; ring, 5443-5455, $125, sizes 4-8 including half sizes; in 1974, necklace, 8680, $90.

Aqua Treasure, 1971, necklace, 8433, $90; pierced earrings, 7743, $110; ring, 5279-5291, $85, sizes 4-10 including half sizes; *Captive Opal*, 1970, necklace, 8332, $115; screw back earrings, 7332, $105; also pierced earrings, 7333; *Mother of Pearl Cameo*, 1969, necklace, 8244, $80; screw back earrings, 7244, $125; pierced earrings, 7245, $90; in 1970, ring, 5229-5241, $90, sizes 4-10 including half sizes; *Genuine Sodalite*, 1976, necklace, 8412, $85; pierced earrings, 7412, $45; ring, 5714, $50, sizes 4-6; also 5715, sizes 6-8.

Rejoice, 1978, necklace, 8454, $70; in 1979, ring, 5462, $55.

Carnelian Cameo, 1973, necklace, 8681, $80; ring, 5430-5442, $110, sizes 4-8 including half sizes; *Genuine Jade*, 1973, necklace, 8676, $90; ring, 5417-5429, $110, sizes 4-8 including half sizes; necklace from the collection of Louise Blood.

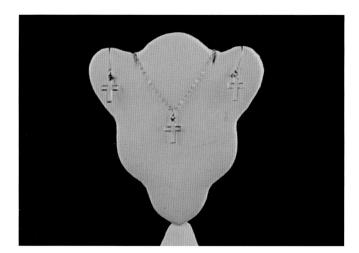

Sterling Silver Cross, 1976, pendant, 8844, $55; pierced earrings, 7844, $35.

Genuine Tiger Eye, 1976, necklace, 8843, $105; pierced earrings, 7843, $65; in 1978, ring, 5777, $75; *Tiger Eye*, 1973, necklace, 8694, $75; *Carved Tiger Eye*, clip earrings, 7694, $75; *Tiger Eye Butterfly*, 1975, pin, 6751, $70; *Genuine Tiger Eye*, 1978, pierced earrings, 7110, $50; *Precious Tiger Eye*, 1978, necklace, 8873, $70; *Tiger Eye Ring*, 1970, 5242-5254, $220, sizes 7-13 including half sizes.

Sterling Treasure Pin, 1972, 6521, $130; *Opal Treasure Bracelet*, 1973, 9696, $100; in 1974, name changed to *Antique Treasure Bracelet* with new item number 9096 and same value, both shown; *Filigree Onyx*, 1973, necklace, 8674, $55; bracelet, 9674, $80; in 1974, name changed to *Filigree Jet* with same item numbers and values.

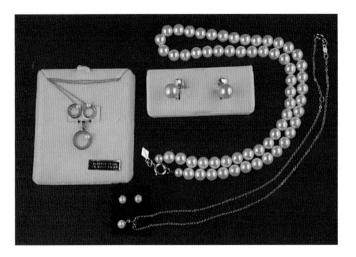

Top: *Cultured Pearl*, 1971, necklace, 8432, $85; pierced earrings, 7432, $90; *Lady Coventry Pearls*, 1966, clip earrings, 7551, $35; *Cultura 21-inch Pearls*, 1972, 8519, $160; **Bottom:** *Cultura Pearl*, 1976, necklace, 8655, $55; pierced earrings, 7655, $40.

Diamond Accent, 1975, 8173, $70; *Gala*, 1978, 8014, $105; *My Love*, 1975, 8675, $65; *Sterling Chai*, 1975, 8753, $75.

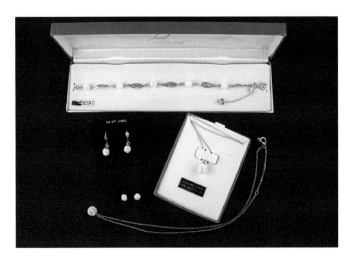

Filigree Ivory, 1970, necklace, 8331, $60; bracelet, 9240, $70; in 1969, pierced earrings, 7261, $35; *Genuine Ivory*, 1973, necklace, 8710, $60; pierced earrings, 7710, $45.

Birthstone Pendant, 1978, 8154-8165, $60; all birthstones available.

Sterling Locket, 1969, 8247, $100 (left); *Sterling Locket*, 1974, 8095, $90 (bottom); *Sterling Locket*, 1967, 8708, $70 (right).

Opal Treasure, 1967, 8709, $75; *Diamond Classic Set*, 1969, 5097, $215; *Lady Coventry 14K Gold Filled Chain*, 1980, 8751, $65.

Sterling Birth Chain, 1975, 22-inch, 8737-8748, $100; all birthstones available.

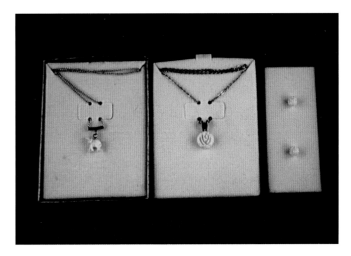

Genuine Ivory Elephant, 1976, 8415, $60; *Genuine Ivory Rose*, 1978, necklace, 8568, $40; *Genuine Ivory*, 1973, pierced earrings, 7710, $45.

Top: *Forget Me Knot*, 1979, 8876, $60; *Sterling Faith Cross*, 1973, 8695, $70; **Bottom:** *Genuine Crystal Heart*, 1979, 8096, $75; *Another Love*, 1978, 8768, $40.

Sterling Silver Bracelet, 1974, 9094, $60; *Sterling Birthstone Charm*, 1974, 9082-9083, $70.

Semi-Precious Turtle, 1969, 6248, $50; *Semi-Precious Pin*, 1973, 6712, $60; *Golden Scarab Bracelet* 1969, 9241, $165.

Lady Coventry Initial Earrings, 1979, pierced earrings, 7471-7496, $25; all initials available.

Flower of the Month, 1968, sterling silver pins, 6768-6779, $80 each; January–carnation, February–Violet, March–Daffodil, April–Daisy, May–Lily of the Valley, June–Rose, July–Lily, August–Gladiolus, September–Aster, October–Calendula, November–Chrysanthemum, December–Poinsettia.

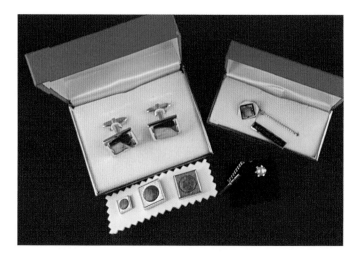

Lord Coventry. **Top:** *Tahitian Pearl*, 1969, tie tac, 5911, $45; cuff links, 5912, $75; **Bottom:** *Royal Jade Tie Tac and Cuff Links Set*, 1967, 5094, $100; *Cultured Pearl Tie Tac*, 1972, 5927, $45.

Togetherness Ring, 1972, women's, 5342-5354, $135, sizes 4-10 including half sizes; men's, 5355-5367, $160, sizes 7-13 including half sizes; *Wedding Band Ring*, 1976, 5695-5713, $85, sizes 4-13 including half sizes; also called "*Lord and Lady Ring;*" *Tiger Eye Ring*, 1970, 5242-5254, $220, sizes 7-13 including half sizes.

Top: *Carnelian Cameo*, 1973, 5430-5442, $110, sizes 4-8 including half sizes; *Golden Topaz*, 1969, 5190-5202, $85, sizes 4-10 including half sizes; *Genuine Jade*, 1979, 5865-5869, $40, sizes 5-9; *Genuine Jade*, 1973, 5417-5429, $110, sizes 4-8 including half sizes; **Middle:** *Rejoice*, 1979, 5462, $55; *Saralite*, 1973, 5443-5455, $125, sizes 4-8 including half sizes; *Genuine Tiger Eye*, 1976, 5777, $75; *Jade 'n Pearl*, 1975, 5610, $105; *Textured Sterling*, 1969, 5203-5315, $115, sizes 7-13 including half sizes; **Bottom:** *Aqua Treasure*, 1971, 5279-5291, $85, sizes 4-10 including half sizes; 5285, $25; *Genuine Sodalite*, 1976, 5714, $50, sizes 4-6; also 5715, sizes 6-8; *Mother of Pearl Cameo*, 1970, 5229-5241, $90, sizes 4-10 including half sizes; 5231, $20; *Genuine Opal*, 1979, 5880-5884, $80, sizes 5-9.

Stuart Collection, 1981, in a special program that ran from July 2 to July 16, 1981, designed as a salute to the entire corporation during Sarah Coventry's 32nd birthday celebration, was a collection of fashion jewelry available only to active Fashion Show Directors. There were a total of 29 items numbered 1600-1629. Shown are: Fairy Locket, 1629; Jade Penguin Pin, 1615; Butterfly Pendant,1626; Tiger-eye Heart, 1623; Cameo Necklace, 1625; Austrian Crystal Pave Necklace, 1619; Vase Necklace, 1624; Box Chain, 1622.

None of these pieces were for sale to the general public. They had to be earned through the point system, making all of them extremely rare.

Ultra Fashion Collection, 1969. **Clockwise from left:** Golden Ice Rose Pin Clip Earring Set, 6231, Golden Ice Leaf Pin, 6235; Golden Ice Starburst Pin, 6236, from the collection of Pam Eade; Golden Ice Hoop Clip Earrings, 7233; Golden Ice Dangle Clip Earrings, 7234; Golden Ice Bangle Bracelet, 9231; Golden Ice Ring, 5222; Golden Ice Sunburst Pin, 6237; Golden Ice Frog Pin, 6234; Peacock Frog Pin, 6232; Peacock Bangle Bracelet, 9232; Peacock Dangle Clip Earrings, 7232; Peacock Hoop Clip Earrings, 7231; Peacock Leaf Pin, 6233; Bahama Blue Leaf Pin, 6239; Bahama Blue Clip Hoop Earrings, 7235; Bahama Blue Wing Bracelet, 9329; Bahama Blue Wing Clip Earrings, 7236; Bahama Blue Sunburst Pin, 6238, from the collection of Pam Eade. The Golden Ice ring, 5222, was originally sold in the August 1969 catalog and is valued at, $30; but it is a match to the collection, and we chose to present it here.

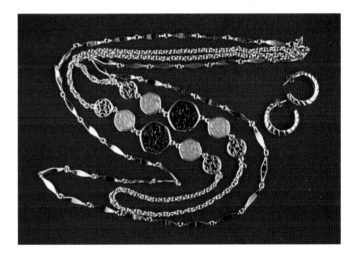

Silvery Taste of Honey, 1978, 37-inch and 40-inch chains, 0817; *Fashion Dash Earrings*, 1978, pierced, 0890; also clip, 0891.

Silvery Flutter Byes, 1978, 20-inch and 33-inch chains, 0828, pierced earrings, 0829.

Summer Seas, 1978, necklace, 0851, pierced earrings, 0983; *Three For The Road*, 1978, necklace, 0825; clip earrings, 0832; *Focus*, 1978, necklace, 0824, ring, 0831.

Bittersweet, 1971, pin and clip earrings, 5073; *Galaxy*, 1969, pin and clip earrings, 5015.

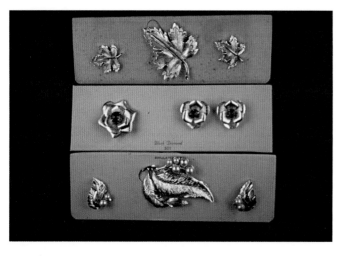

Nature's Choice, 1970, pin and clip earrings, 5068; *Black Diamond*, 1969, pin and clip earrings, 5011; *Silvery Splendor*, 1971 pin and clip earrings, 5074.

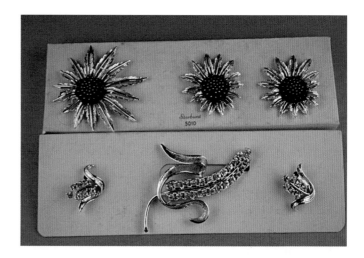

Starburst, 1969, pin and clip earrings, 5010; *Radiance*, 1970, pin and clip earrings, 5067.

Saucy, 1971, pin and clip earrings, 5072; *Kathleen*, 1969, pin and clip earrings, 5017.

Blue Lagoon, 1969, pin and clip earrings, 5012; *Bird of Paradise*, 1971, pin and clip earrings, 5071; *Fashion Flower*, 1971, pin and clip earrings, 5070.

Antique Garden, 1970, bracelet and clip earrings, 5064; *Cool Surrender*, 1969, necklace, 8000.

Midnight Magic, 1970, clip earrings, 5065; *Midnight Magic*, 1970, necklace, 5066; *Dancing Magic*, 1969, necklace and clip earrings, 5016.

Silvery Nile, 1971, necklace and clip earrings, 5069; *Sultana*, 1969, necklace and clip earrings, 5013.

Modern Classic, 1978, necklace, 0889; *Desert Sands Locket*, 1976, necklace, no number given in reference; *Coffee Break*, 1966, clip earrings, 0025.

Evening Glamour, 1980, necklace, 0807, bracelet, 0808; *Getabout 36-inch Chain*, 1978, silver necklace, 0859; *Silvery Goddess*, 1978, necklace, 0849.

Lavender Frost, 1980, 25-inch necklace, 0815; removable 8-inch bracelet.

Cool Surrender, 1969, bracelet and clip earrings, 5014; *Exclusive*, 1978, necklace, 0892; *Around the Corner*, 1978, silver pierced earrings, 0856; also gold, 0833; *Wings*, 1978, necklace, 0821.

Top: *Butterfly Duo*, 1980, pin, 5198; *Continental*, 1978, necklace, 0982, ring, 0981; *Gypsy*, 1978, pin, 0887; **Bottom:** *Seashore*, 1980, necklace, 5195.

Golden Avocado, 1969, necklace and clip earrings, 5018; *Golden Braids*, 1978, necklace, 0801.

Top: *Casual Classic Chain*, 1980, necklace, 5194; *Lady Links*, 1980, necklace, 0802; **Bottom:** *Isle of Capri*, 1980, necklace and bracelet, 5191.

School Days, 1978, necklace, 0860-0885; all initials available.

Fashion Heart, 1980, 5193; *Victoria*, 1978, necklace, 0809; also clip earrings, 0810; *Florentine Cross*, 1978, 0834.

Reflections, 1978, necklace, 0814.

Frosted Mint, 1980, necklace, 0816.

Top: *Trio Twist Bangles*, 1978, bracelet 0826; *Silverwood*, 1978, necklace, 0811, bracelet 0812; **Bottom:** *Tender Love*, 1978, necklace, 0857.

Getabout 36-inch Chain, 1978, gold, 0858; *Party Hearts*, 1978, 0853.

Amulet Pendant and Scallop Shell Drop, 1980, 5196; *Omega*, 1978, 0888; *Silvery Links*, 1978, 16-inch chain, 0822; *Dew Drop*, 1978, 0820.

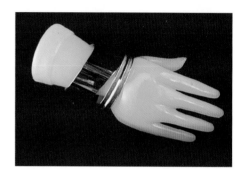

Silvery Empress, 1978, 0850; *Wrist-O-Crat*, 1978, 0818.

Autumn Mist, 1978, 0886; *Golden Duo Heart*, 1978, 0839; *Golden Pizzazz*, 1978, 0819.

Birthstone Heart, 1978, 0836-0847, all birthstones available.

Flower of the Month Charms, 1967, no numbers given in reference, **Top:** January–Snow Drop, February–Primrose, March–Jonquil, April–Daisy, May–Lily of the Valley; **Middle:** June–Honeysuckle, July–Water Lily, August–Poppy, September–Morning Glory; **Bottom:** October–Marigold, November–Chrysanthemum, December–Holly.

Top: *Helena*, 1978, 0950-0955, sizes 5-10; *Entwined*, 1978, 0835; *Victoria*, 1978, 5819-5824, sizes 5-10; **Row 2:** *Moon River*, 1978, 0985-0990, sizes 5-10; *Gleamer*, 1978, 0962-0967, sizes 5-10; **Row 3:** *Julia*, 1979, 5825-5830, sizes 5-10; *Tara*, 1978, 0852; *Laura*, 1979, 5178-5183, sizes 5-10; **Bottom:** *Maria*, 1978, 5807-5812, sizes 5-10; *Horizons*, 1978, 0956-0961, sizes 5-10.

Jan, 1978, 0893; *Roxanne*, 1979, 5118-5123, sizes 5-10; *Continental*, 1978, 0981; *Caress*, 1978, 0848;.

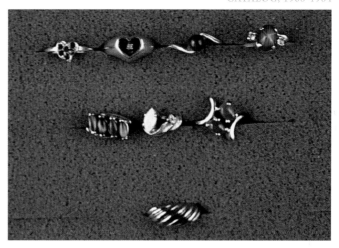

Top: *Tricia*, 1980, 5124-5128, sizes 5-10; *Wonder*, 1978, 0991-0996, sizes 5-10; *Lisa*, 1978, 5801-5806, sizes 5-10; *Cynthia*, 1980, 0111-0116, sizes 5-10; **Middle:** *Theresa*, 1979, 5837-5842, sizes 5-10; *Star Shine*, 1978, 0944-0949, sizes 5-10; *Elaine*, 1979, 5100-5105, sizes 5-10; **Bottom:** *Gina*, 1979, 5831-5836, sizes 5-10.

Northern Lights, 1978, 0827.

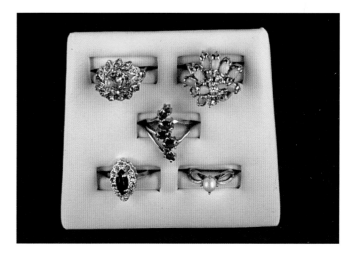

Top: *Camelot*, 1978, 0975-0980, sizes 5-10; *Romantic Cluster*, 1978, 0894-0899, sizes 5-10; **Middle:** *Mayfair*, 1980, 0437-0441, sizes 5-9, this ring was also available in Canada as a hostess item; **Bottom:** *Marcia*, 1979, 5112-5117, sizes 5-10; *Janell*, 1979, 5106-5111, sizes 5-10; the last four are from the collection of Joy Robson.

CHAPTER THREE

1985-2009

All of these items were from 1985-2009, when Sarah Coventry became a trademark of Licensing Unlimited. In 1985, R.N. Koch, Inc., which also sold under the name of New Dimensions Accessories, acquired use of the license and sold items in more than 6,500 drug, department, and grocery stores nationwide until 1994.

The Home Shopping Network years were 2002 through 2004.

The Sarah HPP group tried a revival of the home party plan in 2005 before going out of business in 2009.

Most items on the cards are unsigned.

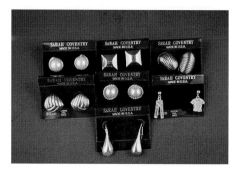

Lifestyle Brands, Ltd, 1988-1992. These earrings came on green cards with green velvet and had suggested retail prices. They were pierced and clips. If sold today, they would be priced about, $20.

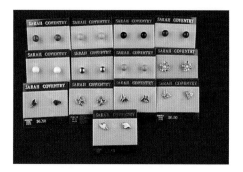

Lifestyle Brands, Ltd, 1985-1987. These pierced earrings came on gray cards with pink velvet and were pre-printed with suggested retail prices, which the stores were allowed to change. The backs of the cards include the information that Sarah Coventry is a trademark of Lifestyle Brands, Ltd, used under license by R.N. Koch, Inc. All carried a lifetime guarantee and could be returned to Sarah Coventry in Providence, Rhode Island, for repair or replacement. They came in a wide variety of colors, including gold and silver. If sold today, they would be priced about, $10.

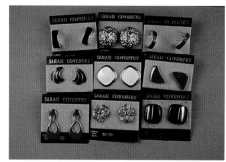

Lifestyle Brands, Ltd, 1985-1987. These pierced earrings came on gray cards with pink velvet in a wide variety of colors with suggested retain prices. If sold today, they would be priced about, $20.

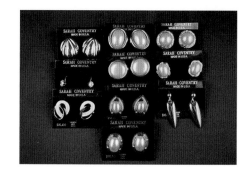

Lifestyle Brands, Ltd, 1988-1992. These earrings came on green cards with green velvet and had suggested retail prices. They were pierced and clips. If sold today, they would be priced about, $30.

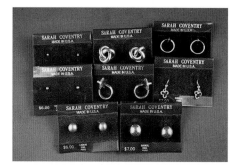

Lifestyle Brands, Ltd, 1988-1992. These items came on green cards with green velvet and had suggested retail prices. The backs of the cards include the information that Sarah Coventry is a trademark of Lifestyle Brands, Ltd, used under license by New Dimensions Accessories, Ltd. All carried a lifetime guarantee and could be returned to Sarah Coventry in Providence, Rhode Island, for repair or replacement. If sold today, they would be priced about, $10.

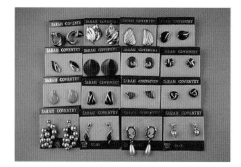

Lifestyle Brands, Ltd, 1985-1987. These pierced earrings came on gray cards with pink velvet in a wide variety of colors with suggested retain prices. If sold today, they would be priced about, $15.

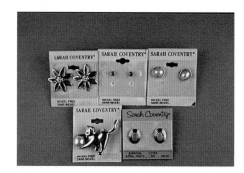

Lifestyle Brands, Ltd, 1993-1994. These unsigned items are on pink cards, but the backs are blank, indicating they could no longer be returned to the warehouse for repair or replacement. If sold today, they would be priced about, $10.

Lifestyle Brands, Ltd, 1985-1987. The charms are on black vinyl cards, and the tac pin is on a red card with pink velvet. The backs are blank. It is possible to find some red cards with R.N. Koch information and return instructions. If sold today, they would be priced about, $15.

Christmas Pins, circa 1981-1984. These were all sold after Lifestyle Brands acquired the Sarah Coventry trademark in 1981, and presumably, they were meant to replace the highly popular Limited Edition Christmas charms and drops that Sarah Coventry offered between 1972-1980. They came in black and white flip top boxes and are generally referred to as New Sarah Coventry. All are marked Sarah Cov, except the Candle, which is not marked. Item numbers are: Santa, 6624; Holly Bell, 6625; Christmas Tree, 6623. We do not know the item numbers for the Angel and the Candle. There are Angel pins in existence with red skirts and blue skirts, which are not Sarah Coventry.

Lifestyle Brands, Ltd, 1985-1987. Unsigned, necklace, $35; pierced earrings, $25.

Pearl Necklace Set. This is the only set we have from 1988-1992.

Scarves, 1988-1994. All the scarves were multi-colored beauties. They came in two sizes that we know about, 30-inches square and an oblong of 10-inches by 52-inches. All bore the Sarah Coventry logo, either sewn into the design or with a cloth nametag sewn to one edge. They were all made in Italy and distributed by New Dimensions Ltd.

Cologne, Bottom of bottles on left: "1 fl oz Cologne Spray Mist, Distributed by Speidel, Div Textron Inc, Prov. R.I. 02903 Made in U.S.A." Label of bottle on right: "Sarah Coventry Debut Cologne, 2 fl oz, Dist by Sarah Coventry Inc, Newark, NY 14513 Made in U.S.A."

Perfumed Body Powder, 2-ounces. The white puff has the familiar "SC" logo stitched into the center. Bottom is marked "Sarah Coventry Perfumed Body Powder. Dist. By Speidel, Div Textron Inc. Prov. R.I. 02903 Made in U.S.A."

New Seasons, 2002 HSN, necklace, 260713, $160; bracelet, 260701, $120; pierced earrings, 260714, $70; earrings are stamped on the plastic ring of the ear nuts.

Peace Cross, 2002, HSN, $50; *Cameo Ring*, 2002, HSN, $40; *Giving*, 2003, HSN, $40.

Miscellaneous Items. 2005-2009. The *Salamander* is articulated and signed on the head. The *Bead* necklace is signed on the chain. The *Train* is signed on the locomotive. The *Ring* and *Butterfly* are signed on the backs. The *Cat* is unsigned, but it came in a hard jewelry case with Sarah Coventry and the butterfly logo inside the lid.

Jeweled Butterfly, 2005, $100; Limited Edition, no item number.

All of these items were never offered for sale to the general public. They were earned through sales achievement or recruiting or they could be purchased by the Fashion Show Director to give to the party hostess.

Pins, about 1964. We've heard several stories on the *Lion*, *Scarecrow*, and *Tin Man* pins, and nobody is certain of their history, their true name, or how long they remained available, but everyone is in agreement that they were available only to the Managers. The story passed along in our family is that they were in honor of the 25th Anniversary release of the *Wizard of Oz* movie, which dates them to about 1964. Each one was separate, and we suspect they were award presentations at one of the conventions. They came packaged in the earliest version of the black and white boxes where the white top folds down over the black bottom.

Pins. **Top:** *Red Crown* sales award; *Blue Crown* sales award; *Hand Mirror* logo; **Middle:** *Direction 80* pin for the 1971 Manager's Award for 7 Recruits; *1965 Covered Wagon* award; *SCM Sarah Coventry Manager* pin; **Bottom:** *Sarah Coventry Name Tag*.

Pins. **Top:** *Gold Rose with Marine Insignia; Tomahawk; Lady Slipper;* **Middle:** *Gold Rose, Cannon; Roadrunner;* **Bottom:** *Rabbit; Bee; 1981 Shovel Gold Digger Award for Top Seller; Gold Miner; Top Hat and Cane; Rhinestone Slipper*.

Pins. **Top:** *Bicycle for Two; Gold Key, Manager's Award Statue; 1967 Million Dollar Weeks* calendar; **Middle:** *Pink Rose; Bell Ringers Zone A; Direction 80* tac; *SC* tie tac; *Palm Tree; Star Achiever* tac; **Bottom:** *1964 Million Dollar Weeks* tac; *Silver Key* tac; *1964 SC Zone E Million Dollar Weeks Lantern* tac; *Blue Urn Director's Award* tac; *Roadrunner*.

Sales Charms, unsigned, circa 1961-1981, designed for the Sales Leaders. The *$2500 Sales Charm* came with the silver bracelet, and all the other sales charms could be added to it. All Sales Charms were mailed automatically. From left:, $2000, $2500, $5000, $10,000 parchment, $15,000 money bag, $20,000 bar with attached nugget, $25,000 safe, $30,000 bank notes, $35,000 piggy bank, $50,000 bullion pile, $75,000; and, $100,000 (only charm that was in gold). The, $5000 sales charm is the only one signed.

Recruiting Charms. These were honor awards for recruiting 5, 10, 15, 20, and 25 "Personal Qualified Recruits." A Personal Qualified Recruit was a new recruit who had, $500 in Personal Net Sales within the first 5 consecutive bookings. You were allowed to select either a charm or a tie tac. The 5-Recruit Charm came with a bracelet. These charms were mailed upon request from your Manager. *Service Keys* were awarded for continuous years of service. Each time you qualified, your Key would be exchanged for a new Key of greater value. The Key had four locations for placing gemstones. For 1 year, there were no stones. For 5 years, it had 1 ruby. For 10 years, it had 1 ruby and 1 diamond. For 15 years, it had 1 ruby and 2 diamonds. For 20 years, it had 1 ruby and 3 diamonds. For 25 years, it was 4 diamonds. These were mailed upon request and presented by your Region Manager. *Activity Pins* were presented for 10 consecutive weeks of Sales of, $50 or more each week. Only Region Managers could send claim forms for Sarah's *Activity Pins*. For 10 weeks, the pin was goldentone and silvertone. For 20 weeks, it was silvertone. For 30 weeks, it was goldentone.

Charms. **Top:** *1971 Stock Certificate, Green Plaque, 1968 Fall Recruiting Red Apple, Blue Coat of Arms, Zone A* tie tac, *$1000 Club* tie tac; **Middle:** *Around the World; 1958 Champion's Cup, 1963 Court of Flags, 1st Place Blue Ribbon, We're No. 1;* **Bottom:** *1962 Manager's Award; 1959 Storybook of Sarah's Progress; 1962 Del Coronado Manager's Award; 1961 Million Dollar Weeks Award; Unidentified Manager's Award; Service Charms* for 1 year and 5 years.

Promotional Crest Charm, 1960. This Swarovski crystal is a highly faceted solid ball, see-through charm. Set inside is the Sarah crest, which can only be seen from the bottom, as shown.

25th Anniversary Charm Bracelet, 1974, charms are in recognition of special events.

Charm bracelets. **Top:** *Spirit of '76 Flag, Drum, Quill and Pen, Coin,* and *Cannon* from 1975 are the gold version of the silver charms sold in the catalog. We have the *Flag* in the original box, and it is the same drum box that was used for the silver charms, and we believe all the gold charms also came in this same packaging. We present them here because they do exist, but we have no further information on them. **Middle:** *Fashion Show Director* award from the 1970s spelling SARAH, used for several years; **Middle:** *Lamp Post Million Dollar Weeks* award from 1964; **Bottom:** The, *$1,000,000* gold charm bracelet award used for several years.

Charm bracelets. *Fashion Show Director* award with a telephone theme from 1964; *Fashion Show Director* award with a nature theme from 1966; *Fashion Show Director* award with an amusement park theme from 1965.

Bracelets and key ring. *Sarah World; Million Dollar Weeks of Nov 6-18, 1967; Sailing Vessel; Court of Flags Key Chain.*

Necklaces. *Court of Flags Headquarters; Decathlon Award,* inscribed on the back "Sarah Coventry's Decathlon 1984"; *Manager's Wheel Award; $30,000 Award; Gold Rhinestone Dollar Sign Necklace and Ring Awards.* The *Decathlon Award* necklace is the award version of the *Viva* necklace of 1984 and possibly the last award presented.

Charm awards. **Top:** *1959 Fashion Show Director, 1953 Fashion Academy Award, 1962 Wishing Mill, 1965 Partners in Adventure, 1960 Camelback, 1966 Silver Door;* **Middle:** *1960 100 recruits award, 1961 Sundial, 1970 Star, 1969 Break the Record Week, 1960 Champion, Treasure Island;* **Bottom:** *1965 Sarah International Sales Conference, Zone L 100 recruits award, Pace Setter, Gold Coat of Arms, Top Branch Manager Region, Alarm Clock, Cash Register, Fashion Show Direction* silver bell, *Fashion Show Director* gold bell.

Rose Set, Fashion Show Director Award from 1959 came with bracelet, clip earrings, key chain.

Manager's Ring, this ring dates to the mid-1960s, and we believe it was available for several years; *Bell Ringer Award* for top sales in 1970 and probably used for several years. It came in a gold special presentation box.

Parade of Champions Recruiting Award National Winner, 1963.

Bookend, mid-1960s, is the Manager's statue encased in Plexiglas.

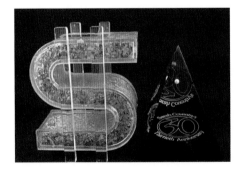

Top Fashion Show Director Award: 1977, plastic dollar sign filled with shredded American currency awarded for Million Dollar Weeks for Personal Net Sales; *Sarah Coventry 30th Anniversary Pyramid*.

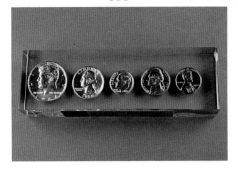

Branch Achievement Award: 1975, encased set of coins awarded to the Branch Manager with the average Sales of, $1000 per file count during Multi-Million Dollar Weeks of Oct 27-Nov 15.

Promotional items. **Top:** *Playing Cards*; **Bottom:** *Key Case H114, Pocket Mirror*.

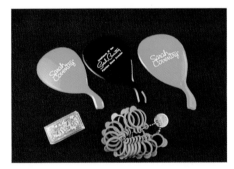

Promotional items. *Hand Mirror,* H111; *The Bank of Sarah Coventry* paperweight; *Ring Sizer,s* H115.

Gift Items, 1976.

Hand Lotion Pillows and *Sewing Kit*, H105 and H113, were used as free gifts to the party hostess. There are 5 pillows containing Balm Argenta in each hand lotion booklet. The sewing kit has one needle, several colors of thread, and 10 mini emery boards.

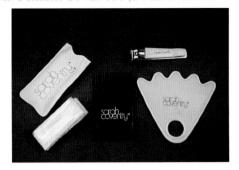

Gift items, 1976. At left is the purse-sized rain bonnet, H148, with the bonnet removed and lying next to the sleeve. Most commercial rain bonnets were plain see-through plastic, but Sarah's had a nice flower design. The middle is a hair lift, H154. At right is the fingernail palette, H147, for applying nail polish. You stuck your thumb through the hole, draped your fingers across the points, and painted away! There is no item number for the nail nipper.

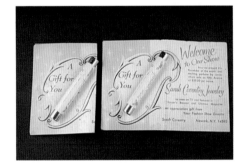

Gift items, 1975. The Perfume Appreciation Gift is a twist tube of the exotic and exciting perfume by Lanier, which sold on Fifth Avenue at, $50.00 per ounce. You pulled open one of the end caps, removed the plastic vial, snapped off both nips at the ends while holding the vial horizontal, and then you touched the nip slightly to your skin until the perfume flowed.

Academy Awards statues. *1979 Top Fashion Show Director; 1975 Recruiting Excellence; 1975 Top Branch Manager.*

25ᵗʰ Anniversary Mug, 1974.

Glass trinket tray, 1975, promotional trinket tray for small items in honor of the opening of the Sarah Coventry International Headquarters.

Pierced earrings holders. These are the only pierced earrings holders that we have, and there may be others. The wallet is satin lined, and it can accommodate 32 pairs of stud earrings. The tree, H146, only came in the dark smoke color. Each branch holds 11 pairs, and there are 4 branches. It is stamped Sarah Coventry on one of the branches, and it comes apart for flat storage.

Lincoln Memorial Coins, 1975, awarded for the Top Zone Sales during Multi-Million Dollar Weeks. It states "the Lincoln Memorial Cent was issued in 1909 as a monument to the man who rose from a humble log cabin to the Presidency of the United States. The profile of Abraham Lincoln was commissioned by Theodore Roosevelt and was designed by Victor D. Brenner from a Civil War photograph. The reverse is the Lincoln Memorial in Washington D.C. created from an engraving by Frank Gasparro. Mint marks (Denver-D; San Francisco-S.) are located just under the date; coins issued by the Philadelphia Mint bear no mark."

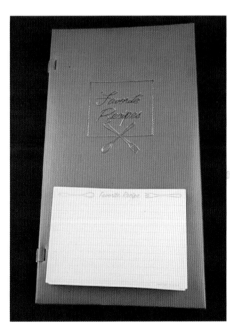

Recipe book and cards. Sarah Coventry had all sorts of items available to the managers as incentives for the various promotions for sales volume and recruiting. This recipe book came with two packets of 60 cards imprinted on the back "Favorite Recipe Cards for Sarah Coventry Cookbook."

Jewelry Chain Case, 1975. This was an award item, and the mailing box is dated Aug 1975. It ends chain tangle and helps prevent tarnishing. The storage area is 10-inches by 14-inches with top and bottom slots. The idea is to place the chains around the top and bottom tabs, and then push the tabs through the leather to the outside. There is a snap pocket on one end that is 6-inches by 3-inches for other jewelry. The case folds together and snaps shut. When closed, it measures 14-inches by 4-inches by ½-inch.

Lady Coventry Travel Case, 1975, leatherette travel case 6-inches by 12-inches. It is shown on the *Blue Display Cloth* used by the Sales Representatives when showing the jewelry.

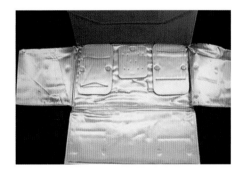

Lady Coventry Travel Case, 1975, open. The inside flats snapped out, and the satin side flaps then folded over to protect the jewelry.

Blue Display Cloth, this is a deep blue nylon cloth measuring about 7-feet by 4-feet and was used by the Sales Representatives to display the jewelry during the home parties.

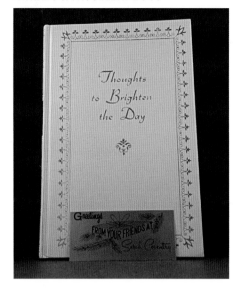

Thoughts to Brighten the Day, 1969. This book was an award choice in 1969. It is filled with 224 pages of selections from many sources providing reading for casual enjoyment, thoughts for patient perusal, and unusual poetry and prose to stimulate the imagination.

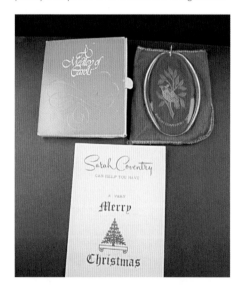

Christmas items. **Top:** Christmas ornament, *A Partridge in a Pear Tree,* from 1976. Inside the cover of the box, it states that it was the custom for lovers to exchange gifts on all 12 days of Christmas, which, during medieval times until about 1800; was celebrated from Christmas Eve to the Epiphany on January 6. Many Christmas presents came in sets of 12: spoons, goblets, or a zoo of tiny animals carved from ivory or sandalwood. Marie Antoinette once gave a miniature tree of silver hung with apples of solid gold to her husband, Louis XVI. According to the Christmas carol, the first day of Christmas was a partridge in a pear tree. Sarah's Christmas ornament is dated 1976. It is not known if there were 11 other ornaments to complete the Twelve Days of Christmas. The ones that do exist came in the felt pouch inside the storybook called A Medley of Carols. There are no carols in the box, just the ornament. **Bottom:** The Merry Christmas flyer is dated 1967, and it was used for recruiting during the holidays with promises of earning "that needed extra income for Christmas.".

Care Cloths, H103. This soft, re-usable jeweler's polishing cloth was given to all Sales Representatives to use before showing the jewelry, stating that the jewelry was to be "dust free and clean of fingerprints to look its loveliest." The one in the purple covering is from 1976 and could be used as a party hostess gift.

Recruiting and name tags. The one on the left is from 1967 and was used to notify headquarters of potential recruits. The one on the right is from 1976 and was used at the parties.

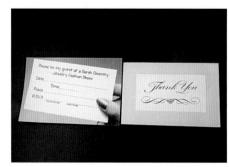

Postcards. The one on the left, item #45; is from 1978 and was used to invite guests to the party. The one on the right, item #36, is from 1977 and was used to thank guests for attending.

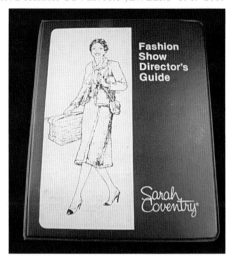

Fashion Show Director's Guide. This was given to all new sales recruits. It has 9 chapters: Introduction, You The Fashion Show Director, Your Product, Consumer Services, The Show, Booking and Recruiting, Aids, Opportunity, and Help Us Help You.

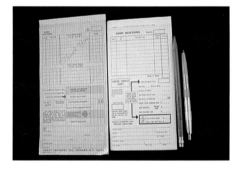

Order blanks, Pencil, Pen. The order blank on the left is from 1977. The one on the right is from previous years. The pencil, H102, and pen, H101, are each marked Sarah Coventry, Fine Fashion Jewelry, Newark, New York.

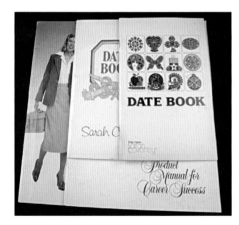

Sales books. This grouping of books for the sales representative dates from 1978 to 1982. The bottom is You're Invited To from 1978, and is Order Form 215. It discusses Sarah Coventry as a company. The *Product Manual for Career Success* is from 1982, and it explains the metals, stones, and processes used to make the jewelry. The *Date Books*, H117, are from 1978 on the left and 1982 on the right, and they are calendars for scheduling parties.

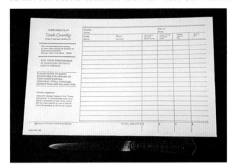

Deposit envelope and opener. Each Hostess was instructed to keep copies of the "Guest Selections" in the deposit envelope, Order Form 84, until the jewelry shipment arrived and could be distributed to the proper guests. The brass opener is dated 25th Anniversary 1974.

Bank bag, 1960, used for making deposits or carrying orders, from the collection of Pam Eade.

Individual ring boxes, 1978-1984, used with some of the Hostess rings; the three on the bottom are satin and the two on the top are velveteen.

Lord and Lady Coventry boxes. We show these because they exist, although they are not in good condition. The large cardboard box on the bottom is for both Lord and Lady Coventry, and it has 10 small wells and one large well, all in green velveteen. The small metal green box on the top is for Lady Coventry, and we believe it was one foam layer covered in green velveteen for pearls and similar pieces.

Miscellaneous *Ring Boxes*, H107, various types used over the years. All are slotted to hold 16 rings, and all have a satin insert with "Sarah Coventry Fine Fashion Jewelry" inside the lid. The harlequin box is metal and the bottom box is for the Bicentennial Ring Collection.

Earring Boxes, H108. These came in packages of 12 and were available over the years with different outer markings. They all have 12 wells for holding earrings or other small items. Inside the lid is a satin lining with "Sarah Coventry Fine Fashion Jewelry." The white cardboard boxes have purple wells, and the blue box has white wells.

Miscellaneous Jewelry Boxes. **Top:** *Ring Case*, HB002, $10; **Bottom:** *Pierced Earring Case*, HB003, $15. These are by Mele and are metal on the outside with a flocked inside. They could only be obtained as a hostess gift through the point system.

Cloth Covered Jewelry Box, HB0800. This was available as a hostess gift through the point system. It had small wells for rings, large wells for bangles, one long well for necklaces, and various slots for earrings.

Drum boxes, 1976. These were used for the Spirit of '76 silver charms sold in the catalogs to the general public and also for the gold version of the charms available only to the sales consultants.

Rulers & 1980 LPGA golf badges.

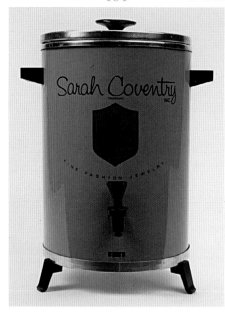

Coffee pot, 1975. This 30-cup coffee maker was an award item for top sales. It is extremely rare.

Wall cabinet, 1973. This matte gold, gilded wall cabinet was designed to fit in place of the typical bathroom medicine cabinet, or it could be hung on any wall. When the bathroom medicine cabinet was removed, this would slide into the vacancy, and the gilt framing would then be flush with the wall. When opened, it revealed a large mirror and two burgundy velveteen shelves with wells beneath the mirror for holding general medicine cabinet items. The doors were burgundy velveteen with gold hooks, several velveteen pockets, and ring slots for jewelry.

Bibliography

Baker, Lillian. *50 Years of Collectible Fashion Jewelry, 1925 – 1975*. Paducah, KY: Collector Books, 1995.

Brown, Marcia "Sparkles". *Signed Beauties of Costume Jewelry, Identification & Values*. Paducah, KY: Collector Books, 2002.

Brown, Marcia "Sparkles". *Signed Beauties of Costume Jewelry, Volume II, Identification & Values*. Paducah, KY: Collector Books, 2004.

DeLizza, Frank R. *Memoirs of a Fashion Jewelry Manufacturer*, New York: DeLizza Publishing, 2007.

Dippo, Cathryn S. and Janet L. *Emmons Fashion Magic Jewelry*, Atglen, PA: Schiffer Publishing Ltd., 2005.

Ettinger, Roseann. *Popular Jewelry of the 60s, 70s & 80s*. Atglen, PA: Schiffer Publishing Ltd., 1997.

Lindenberger, Jan & Jean Rosenthal. *Collecting Plastic Jewelry, A Handbook & Price Guide*. Atglen, PA: Schiffer Publishing Ltd., 1996.

Miller, Judith. *Costume Jewelry, The Complete Visual Reference and Price Guide*. New York: DK Publishing, Inc, 2003.

Oshel, Kay. *Jewelry from Sarah Coventry and Emmons*. Atglen, PA: Schiffer Publishing Ltd., 2005.

Rezazadeh, Fred. *Costume Jewelry, A Practical Handbook & Value Guide*. Paducah, KY: Collector Books, 1998.

Schiffer, Nancy. *The Best of Costume Jewelry*. Atglen, PA: Schiffer Publishing Ltd., 1996.

Simonds, Cherri. *Collectible Costume Jewelry, Identification & Values*. Paducah, KY: Collector Books, 1997.

Sturdivant, Sandra. *Identifying Avon Jewelry*, Atglen, PA: Schiffer Publishing Ltd., 2008

Index